CIVILIZATIONAL DIALOGUE

Asian Inter-connections and Cross-cultural Exchanges

Edited by

ANJANA SHARMA

Foreword by

KARAN SINGH

asean india
PROGRESS & PROSPERITY

ICCR

Nālandā
UNIVERSITY

MANOHAR
2013

First published, 2013

ISBN 978-93-5098-006-4

Published by
Indian Council for Cultural Relations
Azad Bhavan, I.P. Estate
New Delhi 110 002
website: www.iccrindia.net

and

Manohar Publishers & Distributors
4753/23 Ansari Road, Daryaganj
New Delhi 110 002

Typeset at
Digigrafics
New Delhi 110 049

Printed at
Salasar Imaging Systems
Delhi 110 035

Contents

Dr. Karan Singh

सत्यमेव जयते
MEMBER OF PARLIAMENT
RAJYA SABHA
(UPPER HOUSE OF PARLIAMENT)

PRESIDENT
INDIAN COUNCIL FOR
CULTURAL RELATIONS
(ICCR)

Foreword

The 10-nation ASEAN community enshrines the traditions of Temasek, Champa, Funan, Kataaha, Mataram and all the other lost kingdoms of the Sriwijaya and Majapahit empires that ancient Indians knew collectively as *Suvarnabhūmi* (Land of Gold). Indian scriptures and epics, dance, music and sculpture, the Sanskrit language and many other elements of India's civilization have had significant influence on the culture and existence of ASEAN societies for the past two thousand years.

The spread of ancient Indian Vedic/Hindu and Buddhist culture and philosophy from India into Myanmar, Thailand, Indonesia, Malaya, Laos and Cambodia forms a defining characteristic of the historical and cultural links within the ASEAN region. The important feedback, in art and architecture, in dress and cuisine and literature, that we in India received is less well documented, and deserves more serious attention, as does the continued study of Indian influence on South-east Asia.

A Civilizational Dialogue between India and ASEAN, such as the one organised in Patna this year, the proceedings of which are collected together in this volume, is an important tool in the on-going effort to create a pan-Asian identity which is assuming greater significance in the context of today's geo-politics. This book, which encapsulates the thoughts of important scholars, intellectuals and public figures on the subject, is a creative re-articulation of that Asian identity. The Patna Dialogue encouraged and defined the bilateral and multilateral bonds in the emerging geo-political architecture of the global society, and I hope this book will give permanence to those thoughts and emotions, and be a valuable reference source to those interested in creating a new and dynamic Asia that will take its due place as a leading contributor to world civilization.

Karan Singh

(KARAN SINGH)

Indian Council for Cultural Relations, Azad Bhavan, Indraprastha Estate, New Delhi-110002

Tel. : 23378616, 23370698, Fax : 23370702, Email : karansingh@karansingh.com / president@iccrindia.net

सत्यमेव जयते
SPECIAL SECRETARY
MINISTRY OF EXTERNAL AFFAIRS

Dr. Suresh K Goel

DIRECTOR GENERAL
INDIAN COUNCIL FOR
CULTURAL RELATIONS
(ICCR)

MESSAGE

The year 2013 marks a decade since the launch of the *Year of Dialogue among Civilizations*. In July 2012, the Indian Council for Cultural Relations organized a *Civilizational Dialogue between India and ASEAN* in Patna to explore this dialogue from an ASEAN perspective with the aim of relocating the influence and exchange of cultures amongst India and the ASEAN countries in the context of the current geo-political situation.

For India and Southeast Asia, culture played the role of building the dialogue without conflict. Ranging from tribal culture to sophisticated civilizations that created architectural wonders of Angkor Wat, Bagan, Borobudur, even the most important literary works of ancient India, the *Rāmāyaṇa*, has had a profound impact on art and culture of Southeast Asia.

The relationship between India and Southeast Asia has thrived on the idea of a balance of power. The empires in Southeast Asia were built largely through spread of cultural, economic and social influences. *Civilizational Dialogue between India and ASEAN* is therefore an initiative to explore not only the history and historical dimensions linking India and Southeast Asian countries but also the role these links will play in future world, where the youthful energy and creativity of India and Southeast Asia can become the nucleus of global prosperity.

Buddhism travelled from India to Sri Lanka and Myanmar in the third century BCE, and from there to Thailand, Laos, Cambodia, South Vietnam and Indonesia. Brāhmaṇical-Hinduism along with Buddhism have contributed to the religious beliefs, culture, tradition, identity, pride, language, ideology, life style, and architecture of the ASEAN region. The seminar clearly established that like their past, the people of India and the ASEAN have a shared future as well.

In the backdrop of the Summit in December, 2012 in New Delhi and the launch of *Civilizational Dialogue: Asian Inter-connections and Cross-cultural Exchanges*, proceedings of the seminar, I anticipate some wonderful opportunities for all of us to unite and move ahead in today's globalized world. The volume and the Summit are superb occasions to bring together ideas from all our neighbouring countries and deliberate upon the shared history of the Indo-ASEAN region.

(SURESH K. GOEL)

AZAD BHAVAN, INDRAPRASTHA ESTATE, NEW DELHI-110002
Telephone : 91-11-23370471, 23378103 Fax : 91-11-23378647
E-mail : dgiccr@vsnl.net, dgiccr@iccrindia.net, Website : www.iccrindia.net

Nalanda University 1st Floor, Indian Buildings Congress, Sector VI, R K Puram, New Delhi - 110 022 T +91 11 2617 8351 F +91 11 2618 1941

Nālandā UNIVERSITY

MESSAGE

Nalanda University is happy to partner ICCR in bringing out this volume of essays which are the result of a collaborative conference titled "Civilizational Dialogue between India and ASEAN" held in July 2012. It is befitting that Nalanda University's first conference in India brings together concerns that are local, regional and Asian in their character. The location of this conference in Patna, Bihar and the presence of so many Asian scholars revived the memory in small part of old Nalanda – a university that was the pivotal centre of learning which nurtured the diverse traditions of the East Asian Region and beyond and became a crucible for a learning model that went beyond boundaries.

The current volume entitled *Civilizational Dialogue: Asian Inter-connections and Cross-cultural Exchanges*, underscores the strong linkages that exist between India and her neighbours: linkages that have embraced the cultural diversity of the region and have their underpinning in the rich heritage and traditions of Asia. This volume is a welcome addition to the scholarship on both Southeast Asian studies and the wider and related field of Asian studies in general.

I would like to place on record our thanks to Dr. Anjana Sharma, Dean, Academic Planning at Nalanda University for bringing intellectual coherence to the conference that had participation from academia, diplomacy and other specialists. Dr. Sharma, in addition, had the onerous task of transforming these multiple views in multiple voices into one scholarly volume that advances both regional understanding and scholarship on the ASEAN.

I wish to thank all the contributors for sending in their papers more or less in time. I also wish to thank Deepti Bhardwaj and Disha Pokhriyal for their assistance in bringing out this volume.

Gopa Sabharwal
Vice Chancellor

RAJGIR OFFICE
Nalanda University, Rajgir, District Nalanda, Pin 803 116, Bihar, India, T +91 611 2255 330
www.nalandauniv.edu.in

Introduction

ANJANA SHARMA

Even before the announcement of Indian independence and the concomitant realization of the shocking split of India's Partition, at a time that undivided India was governed by an Interim Government lead by Pandit Nehru, the first ever Asian Relations Conference took place in Delhi from 23 March to 2 April 1947. It was a conscious effort by Asian countries to come together and forge partnerships and foster friendships uninflected by the colonial encounter that had erased – in a matter of centuries – millennia long histories of transmissions effected by trade, religion, and culture. The Conference was organized by the Indian Council of World Affairs, a non political body, which had been created by Congress leaders when they were in prison to counter Britain's active misrepresentation of Indian opinion in international fora. In such desperate times Sir Tej Bahadur Sapru and other leaders decided to establish an organization that would allow their point of view to be heard and understood. In fact, the decision to hold this Asian Relations Conference was taken in 1946, almost a year before when the interim National Government was not even in place.

Newspaper reports of the time indicate the scope and breadth of the Asian Relations Conference: approximately two hundred and fifty delegates from some thirty-two countries were present. Held in the open air, under a *pandal* (canopy) at the historic Purana Qila (Old Fort) in Delhi, the Conference began with the Chinese delegations' homage to an absent Gandhi and had the visual politics of Madam Chiang Kai-Shek dressed in a sari! In her opening remarks, India's Nightingale, the "poetess President," Sarojini Naidu, described the occasion as a "renaissance of the spirit of Asia." Thunderous applause from over ten thousand spectators, delegates and observers greeted Pandit Nehru's hopeful observations that as "the old imperialism is fading away – as the domination goes, the walls that surround us fall down" and that this experience "may well stand out as a landmark which divides the past of Asia from the future."[1]

Mahatma Gandhi, who was not in Delhi through much of the duration of the Conference, and who had earlier declined the invitation to attend, since he was busy with his village touring in Eastern India, was suddenly requested to come to Delhi for a meeting with the new Viceroy Mountbatten, and dropped in to the meeting on the afternoon of 1 April and attended the closing session of the conference on 2 April and addressed the audience. Espousing his dharma of peaceful transformation and non-violence he cautioned the delegates to not "wage a war against Europe, against America, or against non-Asians," but, rather, create a new world order based on mutual trust and respect for differences: "It will be a sorry thing if we go away from this conference without a fixed determination that Asia shall live as free as every other Western nation." His hope was that "all the representatives who have come here from the different Asian countries will strive their level best to have only one world."[2]

Nehru's and Gandhi's dream had also been earlier voiced by another luminous contemporary: Rabindranath Tagore, who had passed away in 1941. In the same vein as Gandhi, Tagore too had a healthy distrust of the Western model of nationalism as being narrow and divisive and unable to build bridges between peoples, ideas, politics and culture. But, Tagore's historically tenable critique is refracted by what distinguished Sinologist and historian, Prasenjit Duara sees as Tagore's deep understanding of "the hierarchical and static elements"[3] of Eastern or, more specifically, Indian culture. This nuanced understanding for Duara comes from the fact that "Tagore's cosmopolitanism was genuine but not rootless." Tagore's rootedness came from his travels across the length of the West and the East, thus making him for Duara "perhaps among the most well-travelled Indian public figure of his time".[4] Possibly it is this experiential self that even now finds resonance in Asian hearts. Three essays in this volume, the first by well-known historian, Sugata Bose, another by the Singaporean diplomat, K. Kesavapany and the third by a scholar of Philosophy at Seoul National University, Sung doo AHN find Tagore being recalled as a living presence both in terms of his Asian travel and the shared memory of his verse: both transcending regional and historical specificity.

Tagore's views live on in the twenty-first century in the thought of one of the most celebrated students of Tagore's historic Santiniketan, it being none other than the Harvard don, Nobel Laureate, Bharat Ratna and Chancellor of Nalanda University, Amartya Sen. His leadership of the project to revive Nalanda University as the first Asian University, fiercely resists regional parochialism and draws upon the fundamental belief that one cannot comprehend the West fully without knowing the contributions of the East and vice versa. The core of the Keynote Address he delivered at the 'Civilizational Dialogue' Conference in Patna, India in July 2012, which has resulted in this book, was his absolute conviction that "Asia" is not one monolith with a singular, distinctive civilization, but, instead, a global civilization with criss-crossing and interactive paths that have been well trod over millenia.[5]

Hence, almost sixty-five years later, with many conferences about Asian inter connections, having taken place, or in the process of being framed around the new-old questions of reviving shared histories, picking up the threads of interrupted conversations, and building bridges that span the abyss of cultural, political, economic and ethnographic divides, our ultimate bourne remains unchanged. At the heart of the ICCR-Nalanda University Conference on 'Civilizational Dialogue between India and the ASEAN' lies, what the former Foreign Minister and present Governing Board member of the Nalanda University, George Yeo, evocatively describes in his opening remarks to the Conference as the encounter not between "new friends but . . .old friends and relatives."[6] For, to quote from him again, when writing of the revival of the ancient Nalanda University elsewhere, he reminds us that: "Beneath the trade winds, there have evolved… [Asian] cultures that enable diverse ethnic and religious groups to co-habitate. This softness has its roots in Hinduism and Buddhism, which came to our shores more than 2,000 years ago."[7]

The "Civilization Dialogue" that this volume reflects took place over the span of three days from the 20-22 July 2012 in Patna, Bihar: a site that aptly knits together the glory of ancient India with a rich, multi religious tradition and a newly awakened desire to now participate in and benefit from the comingling of post modern aspirations in an increasingly interconnected world. The conference, in a happy departure from many purely "scholarly" conferences, was inspired by a spirit of inclusivity where diplomats, historians, linguists, archaeologists, literary persons, musicians, young researchers, and those committed to their own personal vision of India's long history of varied interactions with its near and far neigbours, shared their views. Fifteen countries, or what an alternate vocabulary can describe as fifteen member states, came together for a period that was at times characterized by emotional, at times by sharp intellectual or ideological difference, but all held together by a palpable excitement that old ties were being revived and new networks being nurtured.

PART 1: CIVILIZATIONAL DIALOGUE BETWEEN INDIA AND THE ASEAN

The opening essay by Sugata Bose in manifold ways knits together the themes that are later developed, explored and contested through the volume: the meshing of the idea of a socio-political-economic-cultural meta narrative with the micro narrative woven around individual experience and its capacity to alter the habits of the heart. In this case the individual is himself a repository of both the universal and the particular and fittingly the best representative of a multi regional dialogue that spans Asia: Gurudeva Rabindranth Tagore.

Bose's evocatively entitled essay, 'Modern Memories of Ancient Bonds: The Cultural Connections between South and Southeast Asia,' seamlessly weaves together the strands of personal experience, historical scholarship, and a literary sensibility to reflect upon Tagore's view of an interconnected and mutually transformed Asia, a view anchored in Tagore's personal encounters with Asian cultures and Asian peoples and Asian responses to the conundrum of life.

Tagore's experience though is given to us partially through the lens of Tagore's travel companion, Suniti Kumat Chattopadhyay, who in an account that Bose tells us is part memoir, part social commentary and part travelogue gives a vivid picture of Tagore at home in the world. Thus, we have a twin response: Tagore's happy sense of the syncreticism of Asian culture which leads to the poet's silence on the warlike and violent aspects of this cultural encounter. Eventually though, what Bose highlights is that Tagore's model of culture is non hegemonic and non competitive and should be the benchmark through which we should continue an inter-cultural dialogue.

This view, however, does not find favour in the next essay by Indian diplomat, Sudhir Devare where he comments on the multilayered structures of regionalism that comprise the ASEAN and India. Devare dwells on the fact that "regionalism" in Southeast Asia has evolved over several decades. Though, historically, it may have been conceived with the idea of creating a politically cohesive grouping, today, it is comprehensive in terms of its scope involving strategic, economic and socio-cultural cooperation. Moreover, as he points out, '*muafakat*' (consensus) and '*musyawarah*' (consultation) are two key words in the ASEAN vision.

He also voices a view long held by Indian scholars and diplomats working in the region that the "Indianization" of Southeast Asia, which took place for several centuries, has left a very lasting imprint and created a number of common bonds across the region. It is an idea that is now contested and increasingly problematised with many questions being raised (even in the conference) of the idea of a one way transmission: India as the culture that gave but itself remained essentially unchanged.

This long cherished belief about India's cultural supremacy and hegemonic status was at the center of a rich debate in the ASEAN region, particularly in the Southeast Asia, and has now a rich intellectual history with names such as Bosch and Coedes, Mus, Mabbett and de Casparis from an earlier time onto the commentaries of Kulke and Pollock in the present.[8] In this volume limited and limiting view of an outmoded Indianization theory is most clearly contested by Bose, Kesavapany and Vicziany. Kesavapany's 'Civilizational Dialogue between India and the ASEAN,' examines interaction in the early 1920s and tells us that history is replete with examples of interaction that were two way between India and ASEAN countries in ancient times. Countering the views of scholars of the Greater India School who felt that the civilizational influences were one-way, from India to Southeast Asia, Kesavapany turns to the example of recent work undertaken by researchers at the Nalanda-Sriwijaya Centre, located in the Institute of Southeast Asian Studies, Singapore and points out evidence that suggests otherwise. Moreover, he anchors his resistance in the new knowledge that shapes recent archaeological discoveries in Southeast Asia and South Asia which have revealed the interactions between these two regions extending back to a time before the so-called Indianization of Southeast Asia began.

Kesavapany examines the evidence that emerges in the early part of the twentieth century – the period that led to the modernisation of the region and subsequently, to the liberation of many countries from the shackles of colonialism and imperialism – and finds some interesting examples whose influence still lives on viz., the role of diasporic Indian women in societal change and their enduring Southeast Asian connections.

It is a question posed a bit differently by Razali Ismail in his essay: 'Normativity of Southeast Asia: Constraints and Options of Adapting to Global Change.' Mapping the gap between maritime Southeast Asia and a continental Southeast Asia he poses a fundamental query: does a region buy into the need to be ideologically and intellectually consistent with the world – in order to impress the West – or does it do what it can to transform itself based on the wisdom developed from ancient times in the East?

The final paper in the first part brings in, what I can only describe as the artist's view of the world! Alisjahbana's, 'India–ASEAN Strategic Partnership' is not an accurate description of an essay that begins with a delicate meshing of the poetic and the political with a one line epigraph: "Indonesia may trade with China but it sings and dances with India." The love for India, the need for India, the value of India to counter other supremacist, neo-colonial powers is a *leit motif.* Turning to the early twentieth century she wonders: if Gandhi and Nehru or Indonesia's Founding Fathers, Hatta and Syahrir were still alive today, they would undoubtedly be of the opinion that India and Indonesia have a moral duty to create a vision of a democratic Asia. In a moving example taken from history she shares that in the early twentieth century, when India experienced famine Indonesian nationalist forces collected rice to send to India; nationalist posters at the time cried out, "Help Mother India."

PART 2: TRADITION AND SHARED REGIONAL CONSCIOUSNESS

This part begins with a highly erudite essay on 'Funan within the Buddhist Network of Asia: The Story of Mandra' by Wang Bangwei. In this the historian-Sanskritist, Wang Bangwei, tells the story of many monks of the region and covers the period from the beginning of the sixth century CE to the middle of the seventh century CE. One example of these countries is Funan, or ancient Cambodia, which was the largest country in Indo-China from the first to seventh century. Possibly, as he mentions, the territory of Funan was larger than today's Cambodia, thus bringing into question the firmness of old and new borders and how they shape the way we read the borderland narrative. The connection between Funan and China had commenced quite early, in the time of the Three Kingdoms, that is, around the middle of the third century CE. During the Northern and Southern Dynasties a number of Buddhist monks arrived in China from Funan and Mandra and Sanghapāla were two of them. Their influence is the subject of this paper.

The Buddhist connection is further explored in terms of philosophy in the essay by Sung Doo AHN: 'Reception and Assimilation of the 'Buddha-nature' Idea in East Asian Buddhism.' She begins with the truism that the cultural influence of Indian Buddhism contributed to expanding the new horizon of human experiences of the East Asian people. Philosophically examining the transcreation of some key Buddhist ideas she focuses on the concept of "the Buddha-nature" (*tathāgatagarbha),* which played a minor role in Indian *Mahāyāna*-Buddhism. However, when the idea was imported to East Asian Countries, it soon dominated Buddhist views on reality and was regarded as the highest Teaching of the Buddha among the followers in East Asian countries.

From monks, and philosophy we move on to Buddhist terminology with Satya Vrat Shastri. For Shastri, as for many others, the key ingredient which for the longest time shaped the view of the India's transmission of her culture was the successful adoption and adaptation of the master language, Sanskrit. 'Indian and Southeast Asia – The Sanskrit Linkage' begins with the confident assertions that Sanskrit is a "loved" language, especially in Southeast Asia, but most particularly in Thailand. Moreover, while most countries in the region have Sanskrit as a root language it is only in the case of languages like Thai that the adoption is an ongoing process.

The last essay in this part, 'The Depiction of the Avalokiteśvara in Vietnamese Buddhism' by Nguyen Ngoc Quynh, has an interesting take on how Buddhism takes on a gendered character when it reaches Vietnam: its most noticeable characteristic is the existence of Goddesses. Curiously, the rationale for this departure (especially since we live in a world transformed by feminism's impact from the mid-twentieth century) is not ideologically driven, rather, its roots lie in the land itself. Vietnam is located in Southeast Asia. From early times, it had its own cultures of wet-rice cultivation. The culture of wet-rice pays more attention to fecundity and women are representatives of that value, and consequently, the worship of Goddesses is understandable. This also melds with the most ancient beliefs in Vietnam characterized by the worship of goddesses generally.

Regardless of Goddesses though there is also the further complication of the over thousand years of domination by China that followed. Hence, it is not India alone but China too which has left its signature on Vietnamese religions. According to the author, the most striking feature of Buddhism in Vietnam is the integration of Buddhist, Taoist and Confucian traditions. This being the case, however, the key manifestation of the Buddha that most appeals to the Vietnamese is the figure of the Avalokiteśvara. Possibly because the mercifulness of Avalokiteśvara corresponds with the religious spirit of Vietnamese people particularly Vietnamese women. In this manner India, Buddhism and China all coalesce to make one rich, multifaceted whole.

PART 3: TRAVELLING TEXTS, HISTORIES, CULTURE

If Buddhism was the religion/philosophy that captured the soul of many Asian countries then the *Ramayana* and the *Mahabharta* won the imagination and hearts of India's neighbours in possibly even more tangible ways. Understood as guidebooks on right living and thinking, or, works on governance and statecraft, their texture, colour, action and emotional graph underwent startling alterations depending on which country and which people read, performed, or simply watched performances of these two epics.

We make an oblique entry into this thesis through Vo Van Sen's comments on the textual and religious links in 'The Significance of Vietnam – India Cultural Exchanges for India – ASEAN Development.' According to Sen, Indian values did not spread by means of war at all. In fact, they were not characterized by any direct political control over the place. Instead, Sen holds a view, now increasingly contested, that in the case of India there was no clash of civilizations as it was a non aggressive transmission of Indian core values. Rather, India's influence always proved to be gentle with the peaceful and moderate nature of Buddhism in Southeast Asia stemming from this inherent gentleness.

Looking forward towards an action plan he advocates fostering closer academic linkages and educational opportunities and also an enhanced cultural cooperation. Furthermore, he suggests that in order to build up friendships between young people from the region and globally, and the India-ASEAN Cooperation Project should include setting up a cultural hub between India and ASEAN countries.

Culture and its transformative capacity is what Joefe B. Santarita dwells on in 'Capitalising on Cultural Connections: Indian Influences in the Philippines.' The essay begins with the understanding that culture is a resource and has the capacity to aspire. Santarita mixes history and personal history to evaluate how to make the long lost connections between India and a resurgent Philippines, especially given the historical interruption where earlier Indian influences are overlaid by the more recent advent of Spanish colonialism that has effectively displaced the memory of the earlier contact. The task for Santarita is to try and recover the vestiges of the Indian influences in the country particularly related to the *Ramayana*, Sanskrit vocabulary and the presence of some Hindu-Buddhist artefacts.

In terms of textual history, however, it is the *Ramayana* which is seen as the mother text that is integrated, altered, and rewritten regionally. These cultural links reveal the presence of the *Ramayana* in multiple variants. In the Philippines, the Rama story is popularly known as *Maharadia Lawana* which Dr. Juan Francisco discovered in 1968 as a Maranaw narrative. Its performative structure, though altered, has survived the Spanish Christian history of Filipino domination.

Travelling texts and travelling religions also become the centerpiece of Chirapat Prapandvidya's 'Buddhism and the *Ramayana*: Their Strong and Lasting Impact on the Minds of the People of Southeast Asia with Special Reference to Thailand.' Both archeological and epigraphic evidence show ancient books percolating into ancient Thai culture. It is a commentary that documents, via illustrations, the claim made in the essay title.

In the account of Thailand's efforts by M.R. Chakrarot Chitrabongs: 'Experiences in ASEAN Cultural Relation Activities,' we get a sense of the ongoing efforts at the level of the Thai government to keep this relationship ever present rather than letting it lapse and be forgotten as in the case of the Philippines. The essay briefly lists the history of ASEAN cultural activities, how they evolved, and helped create a sense of being one region. The author's own personal involvement has been in two distinct fields: *Ramayana* presentations and in the study of ancient Tribhumi Cosmology. Moreover, he also tells us how valued ancient Indian epics are even now in Thai culture and that the Thais' delight in using the *Ramayana* as a vehicle to exhibit their sense of honour in their sovereign king.

PART 4: TOWARDS CULTURAL SYNCRETISM: TEXTS, PERFORMANCE, HISTORY

If the epics have variously impacted and transformed the region and its culture what of a little text embedded in the larger discourse of the *Mahabharata*? The first essay in the part comes home to India and sets up a dialogue with a text that is possibly better known in the Western world than in the ASEAN region: the *Bhagvad Gita*. For Indians, more than the *Mahabharata* of which it is a significant part, from the late nineteenth century it is the philosophic commentary that is imbedded in the *Gita* that has become the locus of both personal salvation and nation building to name just a few of its influences.

Meghnad Desai's 'The *Bhagvad Gita*: Outlines of a Secular Critique,' is a revisionist view of this culture-text. Desai begins with the query: why has the *Bhagvad Gita* permeated both individual and national conscious to the degree that it has? His answer lies in its unique characteristic; it has divine authorship, or at least purportedly is a "real" account of Lord Krishna's words to the beleaguered and deeply conflicted warrior, Arjun.

The interesting nugget of information in this essay is that unlike the epic to which it purportedly belongs, the *Gita* was first revived in the eighteenth century as part of the oriental resurgence in Europe and from there travelled back to India where it assumed many avatars, gaining special status during the Indian nationalist struggle. But, at the same time as it became a kind of mother text for revolutionary action the *Gita* was also being questioned in the newly emergent Dalit discourse. But the key question that underpins the whole argument is Desai's contention that far from being a monologic, monolithic, single author text it is a dialogic, polyglot, multi author text. The changes, emendations, and variants, furthermore, are not accidents of history but reflect the changing power relationships between Buddhism and Brahmanism.

If the *Gita* is the primary text for India and the West then, it is the aforementioned *Ramayana* that is the cultural repository for many countries in the ASEAN region as shown in the account of its Javanese history in Vinod Khanna's 'The Old Javanese *Ramayana*'. He begins by looking at culture through the lens of foreign relations and diplomacy and from that vantage point agrees with scholars who now interrogate the Indianization theory. He also suggests – based on his own experience as a diplomat in Java – that the precise nature of the cultural encounter between India with Indonesia in ancient times has often been misunderstood. Thus, while Indonesia accepted such of Indian cultural elements as appealed to it, it simultaneously and creatively transformed them into integral parts of its own very rich culture. The *Ramayana* is now a very important partner in this amazingly productive civilizational phenomenon.

Consequently, in the course of history, Indonesia – like India – saw the birth of many *Ramayanas*. The work with the greatest claim to be Indonesia's *Adikavya* is the *Ramayana* written in Central Java some thousand years ago. This work belongs to the genre of Old Javanese poetry known as *kakawin* written in various metres largely borrowed from classical Sanskrit literature and it is a lively work, full of drama and colour.

If the dialogue between India and the region is textual, as I mentioned earlier, it is also religious. More specifically, it is about the deep influence exerted by Buddhism in neighbouring cultures, long after it went underground in India. Khin Maung Nyunt's, 'Civilizational Dialogue between India and Myanmar,' examines this in the context of both India and China. Interactions brought on by its political geography (a coastal country comprising one geographic entity), Myanmar has both land and sea routes by which her interactions with the big neighbours have been effected.

Thus, Chinese versions of Buddhism coexist with the Mandala system of Hindu Buddhist cosmography which is faithfully followed. Additionally, planet-worship still persists, with Hindu priests being revered and respected as Gurus by the society from monarchy to the grass roots. Indian Buddhism, though, is not forgotten as later Myanmar history and literature have accounts of Myanmar Buddhist monks spending long years of their life in pursuit of Tipitakas, writing commentaries and sub-commentaries at the Nalanda

University and other Buddhist centers at Varanasi, Rajasthan, Kusinagara, etc.

Performance, nevertheless, is the heart of the cultural encounter and, once again, it is the *Ramayana* that has an undiminished cultural currency. Malini Saran's 'The Changing Faces of *Ramayana* in the Performing Arts of Java and Bali' takes over in part the dialogue between this text and Javanese cultural history. Underlining the claim made by Vinod Khanna, Saran concurs that one of the prominent feature in the transmission of India's knowledge systems to Southeast Asia, particularly on the islands of Java and Bali in Indonesia, was the hold of Hindu and Buddhist narrative traditions on the popular imagination.

However, in a very interesting cultural interpolation, her essay looks at how the Hindu epics survived a change of masters and altered religious codes brought in by Islam. Hence, instead of being banished as being Hindu, when the courts of Java adopted Islam in the sixteenth century, the pace of change in *Ramayana* was accelerated by the requirements of the new religion. Thus, the *Ramayana* was consciously tailored to suit Islamic norms in newly written texts in several languages, skilfully and peacefully transforming sacred Hindu gods into the cultural heroes of Java. While, in Bali, which resisted the tide of Islam, it preserved the sanctity of its *Ramayana* culture in an unbroken tradition, clinging to it's uniquely Hinduised way of life tied to rituals and rice growing. Even today, the Old Javanese *Ramayana kakawin* lives on in Bali through arts that are considered sacred and organically integrated with daily life yet have acquired a modern character.

PART 5: ANCIENT MATERIAL CULTURE AND SHARED HISTORIES

With Marika Vicziany's essay '"Indianization" and the Religious Sites of Southeast Asia' we circle back to the questions about Indianization and it's now dubious provenance. Vicziany's essay is in two parts. The first part looks back to the influence of the scholar Paul Mus' work and reflects on its contemporary relevance. In the second half of this essay, Vicziany considers new work on the religious sites of Southeast Asia, specifically the chapters in a new publication by the Monash Asia Institute in 2012 titled: *Old Myths and New Approaches: Interpreting Ancient Religious Sites in Southeast Asia* edited by Alexandra Haendel. This work is sympathetic to Mus' insights from the early twentieth century while being simultaneously impacted upon by the nature of the changed historical, socio cultural, and political transformations between India and Southeast Asia.

The essay also looks at the complex religio-cultural and ecological history of the iconic temple Angkor Vat and ascribes new reasons for its destruction. In fact, citing the influence of new methods of scholarship, what we now have is an altered grid of questions about Angkor's collapse. Through the use of a multidisciplinary analysis what emerges is excitingly new: there were ecological and environmental reasons for the collapse of Angkor lead on by wrong agricultural practices that stripped the environs of their natural resources, thus, making it impossible for the community around the vast temple complex to sustain itself. This altered consciousness brought on by newer forms of research forces us to re-think cultural and civilizational clashes and sets up new paradigms for the way we will now dialogue in the region.

Citing the work of Fletcher and Evans', she suggests that their conclusions on the reasons for the destruction of Angkor for instance have a tremendous significance for the long-term peace and stability of mainland Southeast Asia today. It also reminds us that at all times we live in a fragile, interconnected eco system and one collapse can trigger off another and then another. If Angkor collapsed under its own cultural-cum-environmental weight, then neighbouring peoples and states, particularly Thailand, were not to blame.

If Vicziany's scholarship is about integrating science, technology with the contours of archeology and history then with K.T.S. Sarao we return to a view of temple architecture that is descriptive and illustrative in his 'Banteay Srei, the Cambodian Citadel of Women: A look at the scenes from the Ancient Epics and the *Puranas*.' He tells us that the temple's modern name, BanteaySrei "citadel of women" or "citadel of beauty" is most probably related to the intricate bas-relief carvings that can be found on the walls as well as the tiny dimensions of the structures themselves.

This illustrative and descriptive path is echoed by Nirmala Sharma in 'Meditational Symbolism of the Borobudur.' Sharma avers that contemplation needs a visual symbol and for her the Borobudur accomplishes this purpose structurally by being, as if, built, to follow and support structures of meditation. It is thus, like most sacred spaces, both real and symbolic.

PART 6: INDIAN HERITAGE AND CULTURAL REPRESENTATION

The overwhelming presence of Hinduism and Buddhism seems to suggest that only these two religio-philosophical systems shaped the way Indian heritage travelled and lived on in a transformed yet enduring manner. This doubling and privileging by most writers – even within the covers of the present volume – begs the question of the role of Islam in the socio-cultural life of Southeast Asia and beyond.

This dominant yet absent trope is the locus of essay 'India and the ASEAN: The Islamic Linkages of the Past' by B.A. Hussainmiya. In the essay, Hussainmiya comments how, as mentioned earlier, for several decades the terms Indianization, Brahmanization and Sanskritization had been dominant themes in academic scholarship in explaining the characteristics of early contacts.

This, he thinks, is because for many stated and unstated reasons it was assumed that the Indian cultural influences were only a one way transmission. However, if this was the case, and moreover, if Hindu texts and Buddhist discourse were the only markers of this encounter then who was responsible for the introduction Islam in Southeast Asia?

Opinions differ on this issue and various theories have been forwarded citing Arabia, Bengal and Gujarat in India, China and last but not the least South India as the possible sources of Islamization of Southeast Asia.This essay, however, seeks to focus on the role of South Indian Muslims, from the Ma'bar and Malabar regions as important source of the introduction of Islam in Southeast Asia, especially in the Malay world. Why are Ma'bar and Malabar important for our study of this region? Because, both these regions were connected to the port cities in Southeast Asia in many ways. As a result, through commerce and resultant cultural exchanges the South Indian Islamic communities interacted continuously with other Islamic communities from an early time period.

However, even in recent, more inclusive scholarship, the mode has been to highlight the contribution of Gujarati Muslims and Bengali Muslims. This bias, according to Hussainmiya, tends to ignore the importance of the strategic locations of the Ma'bar community in the transmission of Islamic religion in Southeast Asia. The essay is suggestive and forward looking and creates a new scholarly space for a more inflected and nuanced reading of the region and its conversations with each other.

Hussainmiya's intervention is apposite when we look at the historian and her/his methodology and ideology, not only in their interpretation of the public sphere but how that larger world is imaged through the individual curve of experience of every single commentator/writer of history or the historical narrative. It is an idea that is sharply brought forth by the distinguished historian, South Asianist, Sinologist and public intellectual, Wang Gungwu, in a book length interview on, among other topics, as to his reasons for choosing the historian's vocation over his first preference of literature.

In his eightieth year, casting a long look back at his life and career, Gungwu states the reasons why he chose to study and research Chinese history; his awareness of his own parents' decision to move out of China, his being raised and educated in Malaysia and subsequently moving to a country which has only now started seeing itself as possibly Asian: Australia. He states:

> These memories and my subsequent choices of research topics leads me to believe that historians are influenced by personal experience, although not all of them as directly as my own. Therefore, I tend to assume . . . that my students are not that different than me in this respect and that future generations in Asia will ask quite different questions from those I had asked over the years. They will reflect their own experiences of an even more globalized world, their greater hopes from an "Asian renaissance" and the self confidence

and dignity that preceding generations did not have. I have no doubt these will shape the ways they think about the past and guide them to re-interpret that past in the history they will eventually write.[9]

The individual experience is also echoed in Geetesh Sharma's personalized narrative in the 'Impact of Indian Culture in Vietnam.' It is a voice of a generation that sees the steady erosion – despite the recent concerted and regulated efforts – of the easy and seemingly natural modes of past cultural transmission and he argues that the time has come to revive these ancient links. In an omission, that he finds strange, he wonders why despite the remarkable similarity between Sanskrit and Champa language the connections have escaped the attention of Indian historians and linguists. Furthermore, though India has shared warm and cordial relations with Vietnam in the past, nevertheless, in the last sixty five years there has not been a serious effort to further explore the new findings and discoveries.

If remembrance of times past and their secret and sometimes hidden manifestations is the theme that runs through the volume then we close with an essay that mourns the almost absolute loss of the memory of India in the Philippines. Jose J. Valenciano's, 'A Review of Indian Cultural Representation in the Philippine Urban Setting: Reconnecting and Realigning with an Earlier Value System,' strikes an elegiac note; his country has erased its Indian past connection from its composite cultural memory. To prove his contention he looks at his own personal encounter with Indian culture and details his own journey of becoming a student of Indian classical music and the sitar in particular. This desire made him come to India where he further developed his need to educate himself in Indian religious and cultural mores and immersed himself in Indian culture by becoming a *shishya* of his Indian guru.

This personal journey notwithstanding, what Valenciao mulls over is the strange conundrum – that in an age of instant information transfers, or, to put it other words, in what we can name as the Age of Google – there is no felt need on the part of his Filipino compatriots to know more about the cultures that at one time embraced it. Having posed the question though, he provides the answer too: with Philippines (and one can even say much of Asia) looking to the West is the way to find the *raison d'être* for its aspirational dreams and, hence, it is no surprise that the Indian connection is tenuous and obscured.

This volume then serves as a signpost – to borrow a phrase from the novelist, E.M. Forster, a writer who wrestled with the relationship between civilizations, cultures, and peoples – we must through this conference, this volume and these critical reflections strive to "only connect." And if we continually do so, then the dream set out by Jawaharlal Nehru and the Asian Relations Conference will ultimately bridge the gap of both the burden of colonialism and the existential crisis of post colonialism to create a brave, new, borderless, porous world where "an Asian Community becomes a reality" based on the acknowledgement and celebration of a shared past. A palimpsest of multiple realities that are at once multi voiced, multifaceted, and multi layered.[10]

NOTES

1. All references from Anjana Sharma and Gopa Sabharwal, *India 1947: Lives Lived*, Penguin India, forthcoming.
2. From Anjana Sharma and Gopa Sabharwal, *From Noakhali to New Delhi: Gandhi, 1947-48*, Penguin India, forthcoming.
3. Prasenjit Duara. 'Community, Nation and Sustainability: The Contemporary Relevance of Tagore', in Tan Chung et al., eds. *Tagore and China,* New Delhi: Sage 2011: 337.
4. Ibid.
5. Amartya Sen. 'Keynote address and ADRI Foundation Lecture', at the ICCR-Nalanda University Conference 'Civilizational Dialogue between India and ASEAN', Patna, 20-22 July 2012.
6. George Yeo. Opening Remarks at the ICCR-Nalanda University Conference 'Civilizational Dialogue between India and ASEAN', Patna, 20-22 July 2012.
7. George Yeo. 'Nalanda re-awakening: An Asian Renaissance in the Making', *QS Showcaes Asia.* QS Asia Singapore: Quacquarelli Symonds Pvt Ltd., 2011.
8. Pierre-Yves Manguin. 'Introduction', *Early Interactions between South and Southeast Asia: Reflections in Cross-Cultural Exchange*, in Pierre-Yves Manguin, A. Mani and Geoff Wade, eds., New Delhi/Singapore, Manohar/Institute of South East Asian Studies, 2011: xiv.
9. Asad-ul Iqbal Latif. *Wang Gungwu Junzi: Scholar-Gentleman.* Singapore: ISEAS, 2010: 163.
10. Lakhan Lal Mehrotra. 'India's Look East Policy: An Overview'. Nalinikant Jha and Subhash Shukla, eds., *India's Foreign Policy: Emerging Challenges*. New Delhi: Pentagon Press, 2012.

PART 1

Civilizational Dialogue between India and the ASEAN

1

Modern Memories of Ancient Bonds: The Cultural Connections between South and Southeast Asia

SUGATA BOSE

When I was an undergraduate at Presidency College, Kolkata, the very first historical excursion I undertook with my classmates was to Nalanda, Rajgir and Bodhgaya. Any visit to the triangle that formed the meeting-point of South and Southeast Asian learning in ancient times is bound to leave a lasting impression. It engendered in me a desire to break out of the shackles of the history curriculum that was a legacy of colonial times in its over-emphasis on the relationships between Europe and India to explore the connections that tied India together with its neighboring regions. I am delighted that there is today interest across the whole of Asia in revitalizing the spirit of Nalanda.

Commentaries on history and culture during the last two decades have tended to oscillate between global civilizational discourses on the one hand and local communitarian or fragmentalist discourses on the other. Any new effort to recover the cultural connections between South and Southeast Asia would do well to steer clear of both. Navigating one's way out of this universality-alterity dichotomy is, however, no easy challenge. Universalist claims in the modern age have rarely managed to avoid the taint of imperialism which in turn has led local cultures under siege to assert their difference. Yet, a more discerning historical investigation makes clear that universalism was hardly a quest on which European modernity had any kind of monopoly. Local, regional and national cultures in different parts of the globe were not just jealous guardians of their own distinctiveness, but also wished to participate in and contribute to larger arenas of cultural exchange. This was a process that spawned competing and multiple universalisms – the European assortments rivalled by varieties of Asian, Buddhistic, Islamic, Chinese, Indian and other universalisms. Studies of the interaction between South and Southeast Asia need to be informed by this basic premise.

"It is necessary above all", K.N. Chaudhuri admonishes us, "to banish the term 'Indian colonisation' from the vocabulary of social analysis." For the peoples of Southeast Asia the 'interweaving' of Indian, Buddhistic, and Islamic cultural patterns with pre-existing local ones was, a more complex process than the simple transfer of social and cultural forms by people who [we]re already part of these structures'.[1] Chaudhuri's admonition and similar warnings by many historians of Southeast Asia must be read in the context of a significant corpus of early twentieth-century European colonial anthropology and the scholarship of a strain of colonized, nationalist intellectuals in India that narrated – with an arrogant whiff of (sub) imperialism – the story of the subcontinent's civilizational gifts to Southeast Asia. Yet the frontiers of colonies and nation states as well as the boundaries of area-studies in the Western academy in the era of the Cold War may have obstructed the study of the process of 'interweaving', a topic that could legitimately provide the subject matter for an insightful comparative and connective history. The complexity and the multi-directionality of the process did not go wholly unrecognized by the more perceptive minds deeply involved in the quest for some kind of a 'greater India'. In other words, there is a need to distinguish the loftier aspiration of universalism from the haughtier expression of cultural imperialism, even though the line between the two occasionally gets blurred. The universalist current was more creative and generous in its delineation of cultural commonalities and differences. Riding this current, Buddhist missionaries, Sufi mystics, anti-colonial visionaries and humanist scholars have traversed the Indian Ocean from South to Southeast Asia over the centuries. Today I would like to evoke modern memories of ancient bonds by taking such a voyage with the poet, Rabindranath Tagore, in 1927.

IN SEARCH OF 'GREATER INDIA'

> India's learning had once spread outside India. But the people outside accepted it... We have embarked on this *tirthajatra* (pilgrimage) to see the signs of the history of India's entry into the universal.[2]

It was as an intellectual pilgrim that in July 1927 the poet travelled east from Madras on the French ship *Amboise*. His primary motive in making this journey in response to an invitation from archaeologists in Java was 'to collect source materials there for the history of India and to establish a permanent arrangement for research in this field'.[3] On the eve of his voyage to Java, Tagore's Bengali followers quickly established a Greater India Society in Calcutta, and a small but formidable team of intellectuals and artists accompanied him, including Suniti Kumar Chattopadhyay, Surendra Nath Kar and Dhirendra Krishna Brahma.

One of Tagore's companions, the famous linguist Suniti Kumar Chattopadhyay has left a vivid, detailed and learned travelogue-cum-historical thesis concerning the journey and the idea of 'greater India'.[4] 'The foreign land to which we are travelling', Chattopadhyay wrote on 16 July 1927, 'does not seem especially foreign to us. We are going with a conception that this *bidesh* (alien land) we are moving towards is part of our *desh* (homeland) – a conception born out of historical sense.'[5] The destination of the *Amboise* was Haiphong in French Indo-China. The five hundred odd passengers came from a variety of national and religious backgrounds. There were a good number of French citizens. Among the Indians there were Tamils from Pondicherry as well as other Tamil Hindus, Tamil Muslims, and Tamil Christians; Mappilla Muslims from Malabar; a few Telegus; and, of course, the Bengali Hindus who made up Tagore's party. Among the 'Annamese' there were two types: the 'northerners' from Tonkin who 'had painted all their teeth black' and the 'southerners' from Cochin-China 'whose teeth were natural white'. Some sixty or seventy Arabs from Algeria and Aden worked in the machine room of the ship. In addition, there were Creoles from Madagascar and Mauritius, a few Africans ('Kafri' was the term Chattopadhyay used without seeming to be concerned about its possible pejorative connotations) who served in the canteen and a handful of Chinese.[6]

At one end of the deck a Mappilla Muslim prepared a sheep roast as a group of French and 'Annamese' soldiers looked on. Nearby, Lakshminarayan was using a huge pestle from Madras to grind chillies, turmeric, ginger, cumin and pepper into paste as Suniti-babu chatted with him in Hindustani and with the French soldiers in French. Not far away a Tamil Muslim chef diced a large quantity of potatoes, while another made huge piles of onion and garlic. The Tamil Hindus, he discovered, were mostly engaged in *tejarati* (moneylending), while the Tamil Muslims tended to be small retailers in Hanoi, Hue, Saigon and Phnom Penh. Suniti-babu made friends with one Abdul Saheb who informed him in 'Annami' that he had been running a cloth trade in Saigon for thirty years. The Hindu 'Chettis' (Chattopadhyay's term for the Chettiars) and the Tamil Muslim traders mixed quite easily, displaying no evidence of the well-known Hindu upper-caste notions of 'untouchability'. The ship, Suniti-babu concluded, was 'the great leveller'.[7]

The *Amboise* arrived at Singapore on 20 July 1927. All the arrangements for Tagore's tour of the Malay peninsula had been made by Ariam Williams (Aryanayakam), a Tamil Christian scholar of divinity who originally hailed from the Jaffna peninsula of Ceylon. The poet's stopover in the Malay peninsula afforded an opportunity for a rapturous welcome by Indian and Ceylon Tamils as well as Gujarati Khojas and Banias. The reception given to the poet by the Indian Association in Singapore attracted a large number of ordinary Indians – small traders, motor-car drivers, security guards from a variety of communities including Sikhs, Pathan and Punjabi Muslims, Tamil Hindus and Muslims, and Gujarati Bhatias, Khojas and Bohras. Tagore's gracious host in Singapore was an Iranian businessman, Mohammed Ali Namazi, who had come to Southeast Asia via Madras. Suniti Chattopadhyay was struck by the admiration in which this Shia Muslim family held 'Hindu civilization' and found himself arbitrating in intra-family debates on the precise nature and direction of the 'Aryan' link between Iranians and 'the Brahman and Kshatriya castes' of India.[8]

Tagore's moment in the Malay peninsula gave him a chance to have a conversation with the Chinese literati. The Chinese had named the Indian poet Chu Chen-tan (Thunder and Sunlight of India) based on the following equations: Rabi = Tan = Morning Sun, Indra = Chen = Thunder, India = Thien-chu = Heavenly Kingdom (an ancient Chinese name for India). Among the Malayan Chinese Tagore met was the barrister Song Ong Siang, who had authored a book titled *One Hundred Years' History of the Chinese in Singapore, 1819-1919* in 1923. Another was Dr Lim Boon Keng, who along with Song had run the *Straits Chinese Magazine* from 1897 to 1907. In 1911 Lim had gone to Europe to take part in the Universal Races Congress in London. He was by now the head of Amoy University funded by the Singapore Chinese tycoon Tan Kah Kee, but as a product of the famous Raffles School retained close ties with the city founded by Raffles. Lim Boon Keng had recently completed an English translation of *The Li-Siao: An elegy on encountering sorrows* by the fourth century BCE. Chinese poet Qu-yuan. Tagore was much enchanted by the life, work and death of Qu, who had in the end drowned himself in the Mi-Lo River in Hunan. Once Lim sent him a copy of his manuscript, Tagore wrote a foreword for the book in Penang.[9]

A trip to the Malay peninsula was unthinkable without including a visit to Malacca. Tagore made the journey from Singapore to Malacca by sea. From Malacca the sea presented a serene spectacle. The ocean beach was spread out in front of the poet in the shape of a half moon. The hue of the shallow waters made the sea look as if it was clad in the earth's saffron end of a *sari*. On the left were coconut trees leaning on one another for support.[10] A group of Punjabi Hindu, Muslim and Sikh men came to pay their homage to the poet in Malacca. According to the Muslim, Tagore was not only a poet of the highest calibre but by the grace of Khudatallah had also attained *tassawuf*, the enlightenment of a Sufi mystic. But the idyll was soon to be rudely disturbed. Subbaya Naidu came to Malacca to tell Tagore about the dismal condition of Indian labourers on the rubber plantations – of whom 80 per cent were Tamils, 9 per cent Telugus, 4 per cent Malayalam-speaking Mappilla Muslims and the remainder Hindustanis and Punjabis. Some of the British rubber barons seemed unhappy with the Indian poet's 'triumphal progress' through the Malay Peninsula. On 2 August 1927 the *Malay Tribune* published an editorial on 'Dr Tagore's Politics' that was a blistering attack on the poet for something he had purportedly written in the *Shanghai Times*. Tagore was quoted as having said: "Asia prepares her weapons in her armouries for a target which is bound to be the heart of Europe". The poet had not actually written or said anything to the Chinese paper. During a visit to China in 1924, he had been greatly disturbed to see the brutal use of Sikh armed police against the Chinese in

Shanghai, and had written an article in Bengali protesting against the British practice of using Indian troops overseas. An English translation of the article was published in the *Modern Review* in early 1927, and this piece was then recycled in garbled form in the *Shanghai Times* and the *Malaya Tribune*. An energetic young Tamil scholar in Malaya noticed the distortions and the Indian paper *Malayan Daily Express* published a strong rejoinder under the title 'Anti-Tagore Bubble Pricked: An Object Lesson in Dishonest Journalism'. Tagore himself was as worried by the new aggressive forms of nationalism as he was about British imperialism. Before leaving Malaya the poet issued a stern warning to anti-colonial activists in a lecture on 15 August 1927 at Penang, saying they should not imitate the monstrous features of European nationalism.[11]

On 16 August, Tagore set off from Penang on board the *Kuala* for Singapore on his way to the Dutch East Indies. He had always been less enthused by Indian military conquests in Southeast Asia than by the processes of cultural interaction facilitated by 'Hindu Brahmanas' and 'Buddhist Shramanas'. On board the *Plancius*, which he took from Singapore across the straits of Malacca to Batavia, Tagore wrote his poem 'Srivijayalakshmi', celebrating the renewal of a bond after a thousand-year separation.[12] The Sriwijaya empire had given patronage to the Buddhist university at Nalanda and enjoyed friendly ties with the Pala kingdom of Bengal; both had suffered military defeat at the hands of the Cholas of south India in the 1020s.

A leading Javanese poet Doetadilaga (Timboel) composed a long and classical response to Tagore's poem whose fourth and fifth stanzas went:

Angengeti doeking dangoe,
tan njana kapisah ing sih,
dene anggoeng goegoeloengan,
goemolong woes noenggal boedi,
sasat sadjiwa saraga,
lir moring kawoela goesti.

(Remember how we never could believe in days past that our love would know separation; perfect was our harmony, one our thought, one our soul and one our body, – the unity of God and creature nigh.)

Marma panganggeping oeloen,
kadi kadang toewa jekti,
mring padoeka kang soesatya,
nenoentoen reh silastoeti,
sastra basa parikrama,
kagoenan preloening oerip.

(Verily I saw in you my elder brother guiding me in the ways of the world, teaching me scripture, tongue and behaviour, and all that we need to exist.)[13]

The *Plancius* carried a varied contingent of Malays and Chinese as well as Indian Tamils, Gujaratis and Pathans. A venerable Baghdadi Jewish merchant, who had migrated to Surabaya via Bombay and Singapore, had read Tagore's books and was delighted to have a private meeting with the poet. In Batavia some forty or fifty Indians, many of them Sindhi merchants, came to greet Tagore at his hotel, but a full exploration of Java had to wait until after a pilgrimage to Bali, the island where Dutch scholars claimed to have discovered a living museum of early Indian religion and customs.[14] Tagore was soon to discover that 'Hindu' religious sentiment and ritual pervaded life in Bali, but in very distinctive form.

During a silent drive with the ruler of Karangasem a gap in the surrounding forest revealed the blue ocean. The king at once uttered the Sanskritic word '*samudra*' (ocean). Seeing that Tagore was astonished and thrilled, he gave further synonyms for ocean – "*sagara, abdhi, jaladhya.*" He then recited: "*saptasamudra* (the seven seas), *saptaparbata* (the seven mountains), *saptavana* (the seven forests), *sapta-akash* (the seven skies)". Having given a rather obscure Sanskrit word *adri* for mountain, he then rattled off "Sumeru, Himalaya, Vindhya, Malaya, Hrishyamuka" – all names of Indian mountains. At one place a small river was flowing below the mountain. The king muttered "Ganga, Jamuna, Narmada, Godavari, Kaveri, Saraswati" – names of key rivers in north and south India. Tagore reflected: "In our history Bharatvarsha (India) had realized its geographical unity in a special way." That mode of imagining the unity of natural and sacred space had crossed the great eastern ocean to reach distant islands. At the same time, Tagore noted that the Indus was missing in Balinese vocabulary, and the same was true of the five rivers of the Punjab and the Brahmaputra flowing through Assam. He concluded that these regions were not culturally part of the ancient India that had spread its influence across the Bay of Bengal at a particular moment in history.[15]

Upon arriving at the palace, Tagore and his companions found four Brahman priests worshipping Buddha, Shiva, Brahma and Vishnu.[16] The next day some Brahman *pandits* arrived with a set of coconut-leaf manuscripts – one of them the 'Bhishmaparva' (chapter on Bhishma) of the *Mahabharata*. Arjuna was their ideal man. But there were subtle variations. Shikhandi, the half-man and half-woman, who rode on Arjuna's chariot to undermine Bhishma's ability to fight, had turned in the Balinese version into Srikanti, Arjuna's wife. The differences in the Southeast Asian versions of the great epics *Ramayana* and *Mahabharata* enabled Tagore through comparative study to advance some very insightful interpretations of plains-forest tension as well as issues of race and gender that animate these stories. If Malay literature had recreated the Indian epics as their own, Balinese dance depicted tales related in the Indian *Puranas*. But the 'Hindu' ethos of the island was no bar to Arab Muslims, Gujarati Khoja Muslims and Chinese merchants conducting trade.[17] After his departure from the island Rabindranath wrote one of his most beautiful poems,

'Bali', which was later renamed more generically 'Sagarika' (Sea Maiden) of which the opening verse read:

Sagara jale sinan kori sajala elo chule
bashiachhile upala-upakule.
Shithila peetabash
matir pare kutilarekha lutilo charipash.
Nirabaran bakshe taba, nirabharan dehe
chikan sona-likhan usha ankia dilo snehe.
Makarachura mukutkhani pori lalatpare
dhanukbaan dhori dakhin kare
danranu raj-beshi
Kahinu "ami eshechhi pardeshi".

(Having bathed in the sea with your wet tresses
you sat on the rocky beach.
Your loose yellow robe
drew a forbidding line around you on the earth.
On your uncovered breasts and unadorned body
the morning sun painted a gentle golden hue.
With a *makara*-crested crown on my forehead
bow and arrow in hand
I appeared royally adorned
And said, "I have come from another land".)

Tagore's pleasure in discovering India in Bali was disturbed only by news of the appearance of Katherine Mayo's best-selling pot-boiler *Mother India.* Sitting on a hilltop at Munduk, Tagore wrote an angry denunciation of the book that was published in *The Manchester Guardian* and later reprinted in the American Rev. J.T. Sunderland's book *India in Bondage*. From Bali Tagore travelled to Surabaya on the predominantly Muslim island of Java. It was sugar from here, he wrote in one of his letters, that now went into the *sandesh* (Bengali sweet) made by the famous confectioner, Bhim Chandra Nag, of the Bowbazaar area in Calcutta. Hosted by the family of the seventh *monkonegoro* of Suryakarta, he was amazed by the extent to which stories of the *Ramayana* and *Mahabharata* suffused the dance and drama of the Muslim Javanese. The islands known as the Dutch Indies could be more appropriately named, according to Tagore, as 'Vyas Indies'. One evening the theme of the dance would be the fight between Indrajit, the educated demon-prince of Lanka, and Hanuman, the monkey; on another the sultan's brother would himself play the role of Ghatotkacha, a *Mahabharata* character, who had undergone considerable creative transformation in the Javanese variant of the epic. The verandah of the raja's home was decorated with beautiful silk scrolls on which events of the *Ramayana* were painted. The poet inaugurated a new road in Suryakarta, called Tagaro Straat. The temple ruins at Prambanan reminded him of Bhubaneswar in Orissa. In Yogyakarta Tagore was a guest of the *paku-*

alam. The Sultan' daughters danced and the entire family got together to perform the story of the killing of the great bird Jatayu in the *Ramayana*. Tagore lamented the lack of more comparative studies of the epic. "One day some German scholar will do this work," he wrote. "After that by protesting against or substantiating that thesis we will earn Ph.D.'s in the university."[18]

A visit to the great Saiva-Buddhist temple complex of Borobodur proved to be something of an anti-climax. Tagore found it to be big in scale but not in majesty,[19] but he was rather more generous in his assessment in his poem 'Borobodur'. On the ship *Maier* travelling from Java to Singapore Tagore wrote what was to become one of his most popular songs:

Sakaruna benu bajaye ke jai, bideshi naye
tahari ragini lagilo gaye.[20]

(Who goes playing that plaintive flute on a foreign boat
I can feel the touch of that melody.)

But it had been a hectic trip. Recalling Coleridge's lines about water everywhere in the ocean but not a drop to drink, Tagore felt he was drifting in the ocean of time and yet could not snatch even an iota of it.[21]

He pursued the Buddhist connection further in Siam on the way back. In Bangkok Tagore met the prince of Chantabun who had published multiple volumes of the Pali *tripitaka* in Thai script. His poem 'Siam' composed on 11 October 1927 gave a final expression to Tagore's search for a greater India:

Aji ami tare dekhi labo
Bharater je mahima
Tyag kori ashiachhe apon anganseema
arghya dibo tare
Bharat bahire taba dware.[22]

(Today I will bear witness
to India's glory
that transcended its own boundaries
I will pay it homage
outside India at your door.)

CONCLUSION

Despite Tagore's obvious pride in "India's entry into the universal", three features of his perspective on Southeast Asia deserve attention. First, Tagore makes a rather self-conscious attempt to downplay the episodes of military aggression in an attempt to highlight the theme of cultural exchange. This form of strategic essentializing gives a partial view of the historical relations between the two regions, but seems clearly designed as a prescription for models that ought to be eschewed or followed in the present and the future. Second, Tagore does not treat India as a monolith in discussing the ways in which cultural influences radiated out of the subcontinent to reach the shores of Southeast Asia. By contrast, there is a story of regional differentiation within India that is told along with an attempt at periodizing the spread of such influence. The thousand-year old tie with Sriwijaya was clearly one fostered by the Palas of eastern India. The attempt to date the forging of particular links across the eastern Indian Ocean is based on a study of the regionally differentiated literatures, cultural practices and histories of India. Third, the Southeast Asian negotiations with Indian cultural forms and products are regarded throughout by Tagore as a creative process conducted by active historical agents. There is no sense of hierarchy, for example, in analyzing the many versions of the *Ramayana* and *Mahabharata*. "India's true history reflected in the many stories of the *Ramayana* and *Mahabharata* will be seen more clearly", he writes, "when we are able to compare with the texts that are to be found here [in Southeast Asia]".[23] Once 'colonization' in its pernicious forms has been banished from our scholarly vocabulary, Tagore's discovery of Southeast Asia gives hope that there is a subject out there awaiting comparative, historical inquiry.

As we consider establishing an international Asian university at Nalanda, it would be wise to adopt a Tagorean perspective on inter-cultural relations and also learn a few lessons from his attempts to create a modern Nalanda in Santiniketan during the early twentieth century. Nalanda's location in Bihar will necessitate striking a fine balance between the regional, national and international levels of decision-making, funding and management. Patna, New Delhi, Beijing, Tokyo and Singapore all need to be involved in a process of dialogue and reciprocity. It may be pertinent in this context to recall that ancient Asian polities propounded an idea of unity that was at sharp variance with what another Bengali sage, Aurobindo Ghose, described as "a mechanical western rule" that had "crushed out all the still existing communal or regional autonomies and substituted the dead unity of a machine". Indian history did, of course, afford an instance of expansion or conquest that spread "the Buddhistic idea" and its associated thought and culture to the lands abutting the eastern Indian Ocean. "The ships that set out from both the eastern and western coast were not," as Aurobindo correctly pointed out, "fleets of invaders missioned to annex those outlying countries to an Indian empire." But he slipped inadvertently into the language of cultural imperialism when he described this as a movement of "exiles or adventurers carrying with them to yet uncultured peoples Indian religion, architecture, art, poetry, thought, life, manners". But this slippage did not vitiate the main point that he wished to make about the ideal of unity. "The idea of empire and even of world-empire was not absent from the Indian mind," Aurobindo argued, "but its world was the Indian world and the object the founding of the imperial unity of its peoples." It was this idea that animated efforts at unity through the ages of the Vedas, the Epics, the Mauryas, the Guptas, the Mughals and the Marathas until came a final failure after which the British imposed "a uniform subjection in place of the free unity of a free people". Aurobindo then touched upon "the secret of the difficulty in the problem of unifying ancient India". It was that "the easy method of a centralized empire could not truly succeed in India". The rishis from the Vedic age onwards, therefore, propounded "the ideal of the Chakravarti, a uniting imperial rule, uniting without destroying the autonomy of India's many kingdoms and peoples, from sea to sea".[24] New Delhi and Patna will, I hope, be able to adjust the claims of unity and autonomy in crafting the Nalanda project for the benefit of the whole of Asia.

Finally, there is another kind of autonomy that will also have to be nurtured – that of scholars vis-à-vis the Asian states that will doubtless have to play a key role in bringing the Nalanda project to fruition. Xuan Zhang (Hiuen Tsang) and the eleven Chinese and Korean travelers who followed him to Nalanda within thirty years of his departure were scholars in the main. In concentrating on Nalanda, let us not ignore Bodhgaya which had a significant Chinese and Burmese scholarly presence. Let us also try to avoid the pitfalls of a modern Buddhist revival in Asia that seeks to invent an ancient 'pure' Buddhist past. Places like Nalanda, Bodhgaya and also Paharpur had multiple religious and historical strands that deserve scholarly recognition. As for the mutual recognition between South and Southeast Asia, we cannot go astray if we follow Tagore's footsteps in making new rediscoveries of old relationships.

NOTES

1. K.N. Chaudhuri. *Asia Before Europe: Economy and Civilisation in the Indian Ocean from the Rise of Islam to 1750.* Cambridge: Cambridge University Press, 1990, p. 58.
2. Rabindranath Tagore to Nirmalkumari Mahalanobis, 1st Sraban, Bengali 1334, 15 July 1927, in Rabindranath Tagore, *Java Jatrir Patra* (Letters of a Traveller to Java) in *Rabindra Rachanabali*, vol. 19 (Calcutta, 1957).
3. Rabindranath Tagore to Ramananda Chattopadhyay, 28 May, 1927, cited in Prabhat Kumar Mukhopadhyay, *Rabindrajibani*, vol. 3, (3rd Edition, Calcutta, 1991), p. 312.
4. Suniti Kumar Chattopadhyay. *Rabindra-Sangame Dweepmaya Bharat O Shyama-desh (With Rabindranath in Island India and the Country of Siam).* Calcutta, 1940, 1964.
5. Ibid., p. 4.
6. Ibid., p. 21.
7. Ibid., pp. 22, 41, 44-5.
8. Chattopadhyay, *Dweepmaya Bharat*, pp. 61-9. Susan Bayly has recently pointed out the connections between British ideas about caste and ethnological race science in the later nineteenth century. See her *Caste, Society and Politics in India from the Eighteenth Century to the Modern Age* (Cambridge, 2000). It is not yet fully appreciated the extent to which Indian and Iranian intellectuals, Hindu and Muslim alike, imbibed and internalized nineteenth-century European theories about the Aryan race. Ayesha Jalal shows how the great Urdu poet Muhammad Iqbal described Indian Muslims as having combined 'the sterling qualities of their Semitic father and the softness of their

Aryan mother'. See idem., *Self and Sovereignty: the Muslim Individual and the Community of Islam in South Asia since c. 1850* (London: Routledge, 2001). The Aryan issue is discussed further in chapter 7 of Sugata Bose, *The Indian Ocean Rim: An Inter-Regional Arena in the Age of Global Empire* (forthcoming).

9. Chattopadhyay, *Dweepmaya Bharat*, pp. 83-6, 124-6, 235-8.
10. Rabindranath Tagore to Nirmalkumari Mahalanabis, 28 July 1927, in Tagore, *Java Jatrir Patra*, p. 467.
11. Chattopadhyay, *Dweepmaya Bharat*, pp. 198-9, 203-7, 237.
12. See Mukhopadhyay, *Rabindrajibani*, vol. 3, pp. 314, 323.
13. Chattopadhyay, *Dweepmaya Bharat*, pp. 690-4.
14. Ibid., pp. 259-61, 272. On the Dutch invention of Balinese tradition see Adrian Vickers, *Bali: A Paradise Created* (Rigwood, 1989) and Henk Schulte Nordholt, 'The Making of Traditional Bali: Colonial Ethnography and Bureaucratic Reproduction', *History and Anthropology*, 8 (1994), pp. 89-127.
15. Rabindranath Tagore to Mira Devi, 31 August 1927, in Tagore, *Java Jatrir Patra*, pp, 483-9.
16. The king himself, however, held that the rituals were inconsequential by comparison with the ultimate goal of striving for *nirvana* (salvation). See Suniti Kumar Chattopadhyay, 'Gleanings' in *Maha-Bodhi* 40, 8 (August 1932), 383-4.
17. Rabindranath Tagore to Rathindranath Tagore, 7 September 1927 and to Amiya Chakravarti, 9 September 1927, in Tagore, *Java Jatrir Patra*, pp. 489-501.
18. See Rabindranath Tagore's letters to Pratima Devi, 14 September 1927, 17 September 1927; to Amiya Chakravarti, 17 September 1927; to Rathindranath Tagore, 19 September 1927; to Nirmalkumari Mahalanobis, 20 September 1927; to Pratima Devi, 26 September 1927, in Tagore, *Java Jatrir Patra*, pp. 501-19.
19. Rabindranath Tagore to Mira Devi, 26 September 1927, in Tagore, *Java Jatrir Patra*, pp. 519-21.
20. Mukhopadhyay, *Rabindrajibani*, vol. 3, pp. 330-1.
21. Rabindranath Tagore to Amiya Chakravarty, 2 October 1927, in Tagore, *Java Jatrir Patra*, p. 526.
22. Mukhopadhyay, *Rabindrajibani*, vol. 3, p. 332.
23. Rabindranath Tagore to Nirmalkumari Mahalanabis, 1 August 1927, in Tagore, *Java Jatrir Patra*, p. 474.
24. Sugata Bose, 'The Spirit and Form of An Ethical Polity', in *Modern Intellectual History* (2007).

2

Multilayered Structures of Regionalism

SUDHIR T. DEVARE

CHRONOLOGY OF IMPORTANT EVENTS IN REGIONALISM IN SOUTHEAST ASIA

1947 Indian Council of World Affairs, under the leadership of Pandit Nehru hosts the Asian Relations Conference in Delhi.
1949 India hosts a 18-nation conference on the subject of independence of Indonesia.
1955 Afro-Asian Conference held in Bandung, Indonesia.
1967 ASEAN was founded in Bangkok with five Southeast Asian nations.
1976 ASEAN holds its first Summit in Bali, Indonesia.
1992 India becomes a Sectoral Dialogue Partner of ASEAN.
1994 ASEAN Regional Forum (ARF) holds its first meeting.
1994 Asia Pacific Economic Cooperation (APEC) holds a summit in Indonesia.
1995 India invited to ASEAN as Full Dialogue Partner.
1996 India becomes a member of ARF.
1997 ASEAN and China, Japan and South Korea set up ASEAN +3.
2000 India, Thailand, Laos, Cambodia, Myanmar and Vietnam enter into an agreement to form Mekong Ganga Cooperation.
2002 India holds first Summit with ASEAN in Phnom Penh.
2002 ASEAN and China sign a Declaration on Conduct of Parties in South China Sea.
2003 India and ASEAN enter into a Framework Agreement on Comprehensive Economic Cooperation.
2003 India and ASEAN issue a Joint Declaration to combat terrorism.
2004 India and ASEAN sign an agreement on Partnership for Peace, Progress and Shared Prosperity.
2004 First BIMSTEC Summit held in Bangkok.
2005 East Asia Summit (EAS) was established. India invited as a member.
2008 ASEAN adopts its Charter.
2009 India and ASEAN sign Free Trade Agreement.
2010 At its annual Summit in 2010 in Hanoi, ASEAN declares the goal of establishing an ASEAN Community.
2012 India will host first summit with ASEAN in December 2012.

Association of Southeast Asian Nations (ASEAN) has in recent years come to be known as one of the leading examples of regionalism. Along with the

European Union (EU) the ASEAN is recognized as a regional grouping which has made steady progress and is working towards creating a community of nations in Southeast Asia. ASEAN is still far from being a customs union or having a common currency. However, unlike EU it is not faced with the kind of challenges that the European Union is subjected to at the present time. The financial and economic crisis that the EU is going through has put the EU, the oldest and most successful regional grouping so far to a severe test. ASEAN had perhaps already passed that stage having suffered from an acute financial crisis in 1997-98 and survived its after effects.

REGIONALISM-TRANSFORMATION THROUGH GLOBALISM

Regionalism which is bringing about transformation of traditional international relations is relatively a new phenomenon. Whether this process is only symbolic or will decisively impact the nation state construct of the world remains to be seen. It is too early to predict the outcome and the jury is still out on the question. One fact is however evident, namely, that the winds of political globalism have begun to blow across the world. The discourse on limitations of a nation state in a rapidly inter-connected and inter-dependent world is raising questions about the permanence of national boundaries and validity of the principle of sovereignty. Human security is increasingly expected to assume the prime place on national agendas. Human rights and environment are being considered top priorities. These aspects are integral to political globalism which may over the years lead to a new global order. Regionalism is a major step on the path towards such universalism. Any regional grouping brought about by considerations of geographical proximity, cultural and ethnical commonalities or economic potentialities suggests an inevitable transfer of national sovereignty. What is its extent and whether does it indeed erode the concept of a nation state is still debatable. In the case of regionalism in the EU this question often comes to the surface as evident in the present financial crisis in the Eurozone. With respect to ASEAN this is much more so since the level of integration in ASEAN is still far less than that in the EU. Moreover, instances of bilateral disputes involving national boundaries or resources erupting among ASEAN members are quite common. That also raises the point about forms of regionalism and the subjects that a regional arrangement could cover. Regionalism can be based on geographical basis or it may be ideological; it may be for security cooperation or aimed at economic integration. In many cases of regionalism they may cover several aspects above making regionalism comprehensive. There are instances where inter-continental cooperation can lead to a trans-continental grouping as in the case of APEC (Asia Pacific Economic Cooperation); BRICS (Brazil, Russia, India, China and South Africa) etc.

EVOLUTION OF REGIONALISM IN SOUTHEAST ASIA

Regionalism in Southeast Asia has evolved over the past several decades. It may have been conceived with the idea of creating a politically cohesive grouping. But today it is comprehensive in terms of its scope involving strategic, economic and socio-cultural cooperation. It has the region of Southeast Asia as the geographical basis. In many ways, Southeast Asia is relatively a recent construct. It was in the early 1940s that Sardar Panikkar, a distinguished Indian scholar and statesman first described in his book on India and Southeast Asia in 1943 this region as Southeast Asia. During the 2nd World War, Lord Mountbatten had the headquarters of his Southeast Asian command in Kandy, Sri Lanka. ASEAN was formally established in 1967. Initially there was flexibility about membership in that even a South Asian state, Sri Lanka was invited to be a member. Interestingly the two important conferences namely, the Asian Relations Conference by the Indian Council of World Affairs in New Delhi in March 1947 and the Afro-Asian Conference in Bandung, Indonesia in 1955 had emphasized pan-Asian and pan-Afro-Asian causes and common aspirations. The emergence of the Non-aligned movement in 1961 signified the desire of newly independent and developing countries to come together on a global platform. Given a rich and active background of political thought-processes in Southeast Asia for a pan-Asian or even a pan-global grouping of like-minded nations it is significant that the region opted for a compact regional grouping such as ASEAN. The reasons for such an approach are not far to seek. Southeast Asia in the early 1960s was in the midst of the Cold War. The conflict in Vietnam was already getting deeper and violent. In Indonesia the division between the Communists and non-Communists had become explosive. Moreover, the confrontation between Malaysia and Indonesia threatened to throw the entire region into a violent situation even as Malaya and Singapore decided to separate and form independent countries. ASEAN as a regional grouping was looked upon by its leaders and people as a means to restore peace and stability to the conflict-ridden region. It may also be added that there was a pro-West orientation to the grouping as some of the member states were already in an alliance relationship with the United States while most Southeast Asian leaders had Western educational/political backgrounds.

ASEAN: MAIN ELEMENTS OF MULTI-LAYERED REGIONALISM

If ASEAN appears today a multi-layered structure of regionalism the progress in that direction has come about slowly and in an incremental manner. Right from its inception the ASEAN leaders had placed emphasis on mutual understanding and consensus. In fact 'muafakat' (consensus) and 'musyawarah' (consultation) are two key words in the ASEAN way. One of the first steps that was taken by this regional grouping was to end the 'confrontasi' between the two major constituents of ASEAN, namely, Indonesia and Malaysia. At the same time Indonesia's position as *primus pare*, 'first among equals' was accepted by all and Jakarta was agreed upon as the headquarters of ASEAN. While political understanding and commonality were agreed as the main pillars of ASEAN it took nearly nine years for ASEAN leaders to meet in a summit in Bali. The Vietnam War tested ASEAN's unity and sense of purpose. Some of the leading members of ASEAN were non-aligned and had strong differences with the Western powers over the conduct of the war. That the Summit took place in 1976 after the end of the Vietnam War and following patient deliberations among the member states shows that the foundation of political understanding had to be built slowly and surely. Economic cooperation and integration, which in subsequent years became the 'mantra' for ASEAN, was initially not a priority area on the agenda. It was progressively taken up only after ASEAN began stabilizing politically. That economic and socio-cultural issues came to dominate the ASEAN processes in the latter period points to the growing importance of geo-economics in the Asia-Pacific as also the practical and pragmatic approach of Southeast Asian nations have adopted in seeking to achieve what was readily possible.

ASEAN: SEARCH FOR IDENTITY AND POLICY PREFERENCE FOR DIALOGUE AND PARTNERSHIP

Regionalism in Southeast Asia has over the years acquired a multi-layered character. After years of deliberations the ASEAN adopted a Charter in Dec. 2008. The Hanoi Summit of ASEAN in 2010 placed before itself a time-bound agenda to become a community which will have Security, Economic and Social as three basic pillars. ASEAN is also scheduled to become a common market by 2015. The strategy of ASEAN in developing itself as a broad-based regional institution is quite clear. ASEAN is conscious of its strategic but also vulnerable geopolitical location in the Asia-Pacific region. (It can be said that today this region is home to seven major powers – Japan, China, Korea, the U.S, India, Australia and ASEAN. And perhaps for the first time in history several of these Asian powers are rising at the same time.) ASEAN is also aware of its military weakness and economic disparities and technological dependence on outside powers. In such a situation ASEAN believes that its regional identity can be best protected and preserved through an extensive process of dialogue and partnership. It also realized that its strategic location straddling northeast and South Asia and western and south Pacific, its demographic strength (ASEAN has approximately 600 million people) and enormous natural resources can be brought to bear only through its collective strength. Individually ASEAN members (barring Indonesia and perhaps Vietnam) may not be able to exert sizeable influence on the developments in their region.

Working towards unity through a broad-based consensus (howsoever diluted) is thus a *sine qua non* for preservation of identity for ASEAN.

INSTITUTIONALIZATION – KEY TO REGIONALISM

In their efforts to build a multi-layered structure of regionalism ASEAN has placed a great emphasis on institutionalization. And in this regard ASEAN showed considerable imagination and vision. Right from the 1980s ASEAN offered its platform to neighbouring major powers to come together for a dialogue and a cooperative agenda. ASEAN by itself was small and weak in terms of military or economic strength. But what they provided was a nucleus around which dialogues on security or free trade areas or economic cooperation could be built. Moreover, they were an acceptable group to large and powerful countries as they were no threat nor were they ideologically doctrinaire. In these respects they were unique in the region. ASEAN's role as an interlocutor with countries of the Asia-Pacific has been a positive contribution for the stability and economic integration of the region. In that it has exceeded the functions which a regional grouping is expected to perform. There is hardly any other example of regionalism in the world where the grouping has acted as an effective catalyst to bring together several major powers in institutionalized dialogues.

As stated earlier, ASEAN has managed to institutionalise a series of arrangements of security, economic, commercial or socio-cultural cooperation. The first and foremost requirement that is being increasingly realized by all members of ASEAN is with respect to the cohesion of ASEAN itself. While all members are regarded equal there is a great degree of difference in terms of economic and social progress between the original members and the new members, namely, CLMV countries – Cambodia, Laos, Myanmar and Vietnam. Bringing them to the same level as the original members is the priority. The adoption of the ASEAN Charter and declaration of the goals of achieving ASEAN Community in a time-bound manner are some of the steps taken by ASEAN with regard to concretizing their ideals. With regard to security, ASEAN had concerns about Vietnam – first during the Vietnam War and later in the Cambodian situation. It was only after the resolution of the Cambodian conflict at the Paris Peace Conference in 1992 that relations between Vietnam and ASEAN states began to normalize leading to Vietnam's entry in ASEAN. It is China which has continued to be the critical factor in ASEAN's engagements with outside powers. The uneasy relationship which China has had with several Southeast Asian countries prompted ASEAN to start a forum where matters of peace and security connected with China's outlook regarding these issues could be discussed openly with major powers including China. The dispute between China and four members of ASEAN – Malaysia, the Philippines, Vietnam and Brunei over the islands in the South

China Sea has been a highly sensitive issue that has confronted ASEAN for over two decades. The ASEAN Regional Forum (ARF) which ASEAN helped to set up to deal with security and peace issues in the Asia-Pacific has been found as a useful platform for discussion on the South China Sea issue. China has preferred to deal with this issue on a bilateral basis with the countries party to the conflict. In 2002 ASEAN and China had signed the Manila Declaration on finding a peaceful and mutually satisfactory solution to the dispute. However, a decade later the situation has not improved. China has reasserted its complete ownership of South China Sea rejecting the Philippines's claim over the Scarborough Shoal and Vietnam's claims over several islands and resources in the region. At the ASEAN Foreign Ministers' Meeting in Cambodia last week the issue came to a head with ASEAN Ministers for the first time in many years unable to have even a joint communiqué which would refer to discussions/progress on a draft code of conduct. That Cambodia, the host nation at the meeting refused to take a line against China's interests shows that the prospects of unity among ASEAN members on critical issues are not smooth and problem-free. This has also brought to the fore the fact that ASEAN has still to go a long way in following the path of consensus on intractable security issues.

LAYERS OF DIALOGUE IN ASEAN'S APPROACH

ASEAN in its bid to create another layer for security-related dialogue has formed ASEAN Defence Ministers' Meeting Plus (ADMM-Plus) where, *inter alia*, the issue of maritime security is being addressed in a priority manner. Given the current focus on South China Sea dispute ASEAN is anxious to get coherence on the question of peace and stability in the South China Sea in which this newly set-up forum could prove useful. India was invited to become a member of the ARF in 1996. In the South China Sea dispute India has taken the position that international laws with respect to freedom of navigation or exploration and exploitation of natural resources in South China Sea should be respected by all.

Yet another forum which ASEAN has been able to craft with a view to having a broad-based regionalism is the East Asia Summit (EAS) in 2005. The EAS was premised on the original concept of the East Asian caucus. However, the membership was expanded to include India, Australia and New Zealand. With the addition of the US and Russia last year the organization includes all major powers of the Asia-Pacific. ASEAN has managed to have its centrality recognized by all those interested in the membership. All prospective members are required to sign the Treaty of Amity and Cooperation with ASEAN as a pre-condition for membership to the EAS. The latter was projected as the prime over-arching regional organization which will encompass all possible areas of cooperation-security, economic, social and cultural. Indeed the EAS is an example of a super-structure of regionalism conceived and put up by ASEAN to create strong stakes for security, peace and economic growth in the critical Asia-Pacific region. For India, membership of the EAS offers a unique opportunity to interact and project its interests with major powers of East Asia on a multilateral and regular basis which was not previously available.

In developing multi-layered structures of regionalism ASEAN has welcomed all opportunities that came their way. In the middle of the 1990s the first major trans-continental organization, namely APEC (Asian Pacific Economic Cooperation) was established in which ASEAN states had played a major role. APEC's principle of voluntary trade liberalization and its detraction of focus from economic issues to security including terrorism may have led to its decline in importance. Another important forum for ASEAN has been ASEAN+3. Set up in the wake of the financial crisis of 1997-98 ASEAN+ 3 (China, Japan and Korea) is an active regional structure engaged in consultation in financial matters, trade promotion, investment, currency cooperation. Recently ASEAN +3 Finance Ministers agreed to double the size of the Chiang Mai Initiative (the swap line which can be tapped in times of serious financial difficulties), to tackle potential ramifications from the European financial crisis. In the area of economic cooperation ASEAN has come up with Dialogue Partnerships and Summits with major economies of Asia, Europe and North and Latin America. With India, sectoral dialogue partnership started in 1992. ASEAN and India will be also marking the 10th anniversary of their summit partnership which began in Phnom Penh in 2002. Dialogue meetings and Summits with ASEAN have now been institutionalized and are looked upon by leaders of all member states as important dates in their annual calendars.

ECONOMIC INTERDEPENDENCE – BINDING FACTOR IN REGIONALISM

Creating mutual stakes through economic interdependence and free trade agreements has been a global trend especially after the breakdown of the WTO Doha Round. In its search for structures for regionalism ASEAN has also pursued this path and has been engaged in forming FTAs with major economic powers and regional organizations. ASEAN and India signed an agreement on FTA in goods in August 2009. Currently negotiations are under way for an agreement on services and investment.

Presently the proposal of a Trans-Pacific –Partnership (TPP) is being pursued by a few countries on the two sides of the Pacific. While ASEAN as a whole has not supported it a few individual Southeast Asian states have joined this initiative.

India has supported the proposal of an Asian Economic Community which ASEAN countries also subscribe to. With the signing of Foreign Trade

Agreements (FTAs) among ASEAN and a number of major countries of Asia as also various bilateral FTAs among leading economies of Asia a web of interdependent economies is expected to come up in the near future. This will create a structure of regionalism in which member states will have a strong vested interest in its success.

INDIANIZATION AND ITS IMPACT ON SOUTHEAST ASIAN REGIONALISM

In the discussion over the civilizational dialogue between India and ASEAN (or rather Southeast Asia) it may be pointed out that Indianization of Southeast Asia which took place for several centuries has had a very useful imprint in creating a number of common bonds across the region. They related to religion, culture, architecture, tradition, language, literature, philosophy, textiles, etc. These common aspects may have contributed, indirectly or unwittingly, to forming a shared identity among the states of Southeast Asia. Thus the process of Indianization may be termed as a useful input in today's regionalism of Southeast Asia.

On another level, the civilizational dialogue and Indianization left a deep and longstanding footprint of India throughout Southeast Asia. This has been graciously recognized by the latter, which has resulted in India being invited to a large number of structures of regionalism which ASEAN have crafted in the past couple of decades. India's partnership of these regional organizations is an invaluable opportunity which India should value greatly. In many ways this has enabled India to return to Southeast Asia, a region with which it had a civilizational dialogue. This dialogue was based on areas of human creativity and excellence. There was no rivalry or military competition. In the knowledge-based world of today the dialogue should get further impetus. The collective strength generated in ASEAN through their multi-faceted regionalism should act as a very useful instrument in this regard.

SUGGESTED READINGS

Asian Development Bank. *Emerging Asian Regionalism: A Partnership for Shared Prosperity*. Philippines, 2008.

Devare, S.T. and Vibhanshu Shekhar., eds. *Delhi Dialogue III: Beyond the First Twenty Years of India-ASEAN Engagement*, New Delhi: Manohar, 2012.

———, Swaran Singh and Reena Marwah, eds. *Emerging China: Prospects for Partnership in Asia*. Delhi: Routledge India, 2012.

———. *India and Southeast Asia: Towards Security Convergence*. Singapore: ISAS, 2005.

Grare, Frederic and Amitabh Mattoo., eds. *India and ASEAN: The Politics of India's Look East Policy*. New Delhi: Manohar, 2001.

Kesavan, K.V. and Daljit Singh., eds. *South And Southeast Asia: Responding to Changing Geo-Political and Security Challenges*. New Delhi: K.W. Publishers, 2010.

Latif, Asad-ul Iqbal. *Between Rising Powers: China, Singapore and India*. Singapore: ISAS, 2007.

Ram, A.N., ed. *Two Decades of India's Look East Policy*. New Delhi: Manohar and Indian Council of World Affairs, 2012.

Rao, P.V., ed. *India and ASEAN: Partners at Summit*. New Delhi: K.W. Publishers, 2008.

Severino, Rudolfo. *Southeast Asia in Search of an Asean Community: Insights from the Former Asean Secretary General*; Singapore: ISAS, 2006.

Sridharan, Kripa. *The ASEAN Region in India's Foreign Policy*. Sudbury: Dartmouth Publishing Co., 1996.

3

Civilizational Dialogue between India and ASEAN: The Early 1920s

K. KESAVAPANY

INTRODUCTION

History is replete with examples of interaction between India and ASEAN countries in ancient times. The majestic temple complexes in Angkor Wat (Cambodia), Bagan (Burma), Ayutthaya (Thailand), and Luang Prabang (Laos) bear testimony to these past interactions. In addition, there are other sites like the Bujang Valley in Malaysia that shed light on connectivity between India and the Southeast region in the seventh to the eleventh centuries.

Much research has been undertaken on these ancient and early periods of interactions between India and the Southeast. Noteworthy is the work by scholars of the Greater India School who felt that the civilizational influences were one-way, from India to Southeast Asia. More recent work undertaken by researchers in the Nalanda Sriwijaya Centre, located in the Institute of Southeast Asian Studies, and elsewhere suggest otherwise. Professor Noboru Karashima, Professor Emeritus, Tokyo University, writes that "the unilateral concept of Indianization of Southeast Asia" advocated by the earlier scholars since the 1930s has been challenged in various ways over the last forty years. Recent archaeological discoveries in Southeast Asia and South Asia have revealed the interactions between these two regions extending back to even before the so-called Indianization of Southeast Asia began.[1]

In a similar vein and in the same book, Professor John N. Miksic, the well-known archaeologist of Southeast Asia, has written: "The study of intellectual exchange between South and Southeast Asia has lain almost dormant for the past 50 years. In the 1960s, the concept of "Indianization" which had long dominated the historiography of Southeast Asia was intellectually exhausted and scholars no longer found the assumptions underlying it credible." John Miksic adds: "The new studies emphasise the localisation of Southeast Asian cultural elements in Southeast Asia, what one might term the "Southeast Asianisation" of artistic, architectural, linguistic and religions as they crossed the Bay of Bengal and reached Southeast Asian shores". As Rabindranath Tagore was to put it, during his travels to the region, "I see India everywhere but I do not recognize it".

Against this background, conferences will no doubt lead to further interpretations of the ancient and historical ties between India and the ASEAN. However, even as we cast our eyes backwards and peer into the mist of history, we should also look at recent times, more particularly the early part of the twentieth century. It was this period that led to the modernization of the region and subsequently, to the liberation of our countries from the shackles of colonialism and imperialism. From this crucible of change emerged visionaries and leaders who helped shape the New Asia and guide the destinies of our peoples.

As the canvas is large and the scope for scholarship is immense, I would like to confine myself to four possible areas of interest:

(i) The legacy of Rabindranath Tagore.
(ii) The role of Indian women in societal change and their Southeast Asian connections.
(iii) The Effects of the Dravidian Movement in Malaya.
(iv) Malayan Chinese in India during World War II.

THE LEGACY OF RABINDRANATH TAGORE

Although the Nobel Laureate's literary genius and his many-sided accomplishments are well-known, it is his travels to Asia, including Southeast Asia, that are of interest vis-à-vis this paper. It is during these travels that Tagore spoke about "the idea of Asia" and a spirit of Asian universalism. As Professor Sugata Bose puts it "Rabindranath Tagore was one of the most creative exponents of an Asia-sense in the early twentieth century".[2] He notes that Asian universalism was in fact brought to India by two turn-of-the century ideologues – Okakura Kakuzo and Sister Nivedita, who established "a formidable cultural bridge between East and Southeast Asia".

In May 1916, Tagore decided to experience for himself this notion of Asian universalism and embarked on a series of voyages to Southeast Asia, including Malaya and the Indonesian Archipelago. The experiences gained from the voyages resulted in an outpouring of poems and letters, including the well-known "Sriwijaya Lakshmi" which, in Bose's words, celebrated "the renewal of a bond after a thousand year separation".[3]

It was in the course of these voyages that Tagore came face-to-face with the transformation of the Hindu epics *Ramayana* and *Mahabharata* into local idiom and values. And, in Thailand on 11 October 1927, he was to exclaim: "Today I will bear witness to India's glory that transcended its own boundaries. I will pay it homage outside India, at your door."

While the impact of Southeast Asia on Rabindranath Tagore might be known to the literary community, I dare say it is hardly known to anyone beyond that. It should therefore be the mission of ICCR and like-minded organizations in India to collaborate with counterpart organizations in ASEAN to undertake further research on this important personality who built bridges in his quest of a new Asia.

THE ROLE OF INDIAN WOMEN IN SOCIETAL CHANGE AND THEIR SOUTHEAST ASIAN CONNECTIONS

My attention to this topic was drawn by a paper written by a young Research Associate, Aparajita Basu. In a paper entitled "Envisioning an Anti-Imperial Asian Sisterhood: Indian Feminisms and their Southeast Asian Connections, 1930-65", Basu points out that "Pan-Asian idealism came to merge with anti-colonialism in the 1920s, fostering imaginaries of Indian culture and the nation state as located within the broader unit of a free Asia". Noting that there was no such study on Indian feminism, she sets out to question:

(a) Whether or not Indian women's rights activists engaged with discourses of Pan-Asianism in the period between 1930 and 1965; and
(b) To what extent they succeeded in fostering exchanges and collaborations with women's movements in parts of Asia (specifically Malaya and Indonesia) that were significant in shaping organizational strategies and legislation.

Although a study-in-progress, Basu's initial conclusions are that "there was often a flow of women reformers and ideas about women's issues between Singaporean women's groups and Indian activists and associations". She cites as an example of transnational feminism the story of Shirin Fozdar, the Bombay-born founder of the Singapore Council of Women. Basu adds: "Fozdar's unique exposure to both the tenets of Baha'ism and the ideologies of the formal Indian women's movement in the 1930s (as a delegate at the Lahore conference for example) enabled her to formulate a new Asian frame of reference for women's issues in post-World War II Singapore and to instigate cross-border exchanges between Singapore and other Asian women's groups in the years between 1952 and 1965".

In addition to Aparajita Basu, there are others like Nilanjana Sengupta, who, in a book on Subhas Chandra Bose entitled *A Gentleman's Word* has thrown light on the "liberation" of Indian women in Malaya in the 1940s. By enlisting in the Rani of Jhansi Regiment, the women's wing of the Indian National Army (INA), she not only fought for the freedom of a country that they had never lived in or visited but discovered that they could make a difference to their lives and the lives of others. The struggles and sacrifices of countless women like Lakshmi Menon, Janaki Nahappan and Rasammah, as well as their post-war contributions to the societies they lived in need to be made known.

THE EFFECTS OF THE DRAVIDIAN MOVEMENT IN MALAYA

Nineteenth century Madras Presidency gave birth to many social movements and these had their impact on migrants in Malaya and other parts of Southeast Asia. Religious reform, anti-caste reform, inter-caste marriages, anti-British agitations, the Ramakrishna Mission, Arya Samaj were all part of the social thoughts and civilizing influences that reached across the Bay of Bengal to Malaya and Southeast Asia. These had visible impacts on the South Indians who formed the majority of the Indians in Southeast Asia. Among the many social movements that made their impact in Malaya, was the self-respect movement begun by V. Ramasamy Naiker of Salem District in present day Tamil Nadu. He is fondly remembered as Periyar (the most respected person). The Dravidian movement he founded promoted self-respect through a breaking away from caste-based occupations, promotion of education and literacy and advocating the equality of women.

Periyar's speeches which were reported in a magazine called *Viduthalai* (Freedom) galvanised the Tamil population into establishing the Tamil Reform Association in Singapore. The Association launched a newspaper *Tamil Murasu* for propagating reform news among its readers. The paper remains, till today, the main organ for the Tamil community in Singapore.

These and other facets of the Dravidian movement, and the civilizing role it played in the early part of the twentieth century are hardly known to the younger generation of Tamils, let alone the wider community. Happily, Professor Veeramani, Vice-President, Ritsumeikan Asia-Pacific University, Japan and a well-known scholar on the Indian communities in Southeast Asia is working on a book which will throw light on this subject.

MALAYAN CHINESE IN INDIA DURING WORLD WAR II

This is a little-known saga about a group of Malayan Chinese who found themselves in India well before the Japanese invasion of Malaya and Singapore. Apparently this was part of the contingency planning by the British to use India as an evacuation centre in the event of any need to leave Singapore. In the event, the swift advancement of Japanese forces through the Peninsula led to the evacuation of about 5,000 persons from Malaya and Singapore, to India to avoid the war in Southeast Asia. According to Dr Geoff Wade, a scholar based in the Nalanda-Sriwijaya Centre located in the Institute of Southeast Asian Studies, part of the reason for this evacuation was the assessment by the British that some of these evacuees would be necessary "in the re-conquering and re-establishment of British control in Malaya and Singapore post-war". In the selection of the evacuees, the British paid special attention to business people, financiers and mining magnates who, it was felt, would be "key economic fulcrums in any efforts to re-establish British rule when peace returned to the region". Among them were prominent figures in Malayan society such as HS Lee, Tan Cheng Lock and Tan Chin Tuan.

With the end of the War, many of the Malayan Chinese were brought back and played key roles in business and politics in assisting the British to revive the economy and social organizations. Several of them went on to achieve even higher social status in post-war Malaya. HS Lee was a founder of the Malayan Chinese Association, the political arm of the Chinese community and later became the first Finance Minister of the Federation of Malaya. Likewise, Tan Cheng Lock became a leader of the community. Tan Chin Tuan was key in developing the Overseas Chinese Banking Corporation (OCBC) into one of the leading banks.

The interesting question to ponder is: What did these Chinese evacuees do during their time in India? How did they manage their loyalties between the British and the Kuomintang, which was also trying to attract them to their cause of liberating China from the Manchus. We know that at least one of them, Lee Choon Seng, bought a piece of land in Varanasi (near the Deer Park where Lord Buddha preached his sermon) and built a place of worship.

Scholarship on this episode of the Chinese in India would enhance an understanding of the connectivity that was brought about by the prevailing circumstances of World War II.

CONCLUSION

Much needs to be done to bring to light both the ancient and historical connections between India and Southeast Asia. As political and economic ties between India and Asia are being strengthened, it is important that the contemporary cultural connections underlying this important relationship are given the attention they deserve.

NOTES

1. *Early Interactions between South and Southeast Asia: Reflections on Cross-Cultural Exchanges.* Singapore: Institute of Southeast Asian Studies and New Delhi: Manohar, 2011.
2. 'Rabindranath Tagore and Asian Universalism', speech delivered at a conference in Singapore, 11-13 May 2011.
3. Ibid.

WORKS CITED

Ghoshal, Baladas. *India and Southeast Asia: Challenges and Opportunities.* New Delhi: Konark, 1996.

India-ASEAN Partnership in an Era of Globalization: Reflections by Eminent Persons. New Delhi: RIS and Singapore: ISEAS, 2002.

Panikkar, K.M. *India and the Indian Ocean: An Essay on the Influence of Sea Power on Indian History*. London: George Allen and Unwin, 1945.
Sarkar, Bidyut. 'India and Southeast Asia'. New Delhi: ICCR, 1968.
Vohra, N.N. (ed.). *Emerging Asia: Challenges for India and Singapore*. New Delhi: India International Centre and Manohar, 2003.

4

Normativity of Southeast Asia: Constraints and Options of Adapting to Global Change

RAZALI ISMAIL

Geographically, Southeast Asia is in two parts: a maritime Southeast Asia and a continental Southeast Asia. The former comprises countries like Brunei, Indonesia, Malaysia, Singapore, the Philippines and Thailand, while the latter includes countries like Cambodia, Laos, Myanmar and Vietnam.

While geography does not predetermine the history of Southeast Asia, it has had surprising influence on how it responds to external influence. Due to the accessibility from the sea-lanes – invariably, the Indian Ocean, the Gulf of Thailand, the Straits of Malacca, the Lombok Sea, and the South China Sea – the countries that constitute maritime Southeast Asia have had frequent contacts with foreign merchants, missionaries, and ultimately, military/naval delegations, as and when their intentions turned hostile. Maritime Southeast Asia became in history the confluence of strategic contacts and subsequent interaction on the basis of religion, e.g. Buddhism, Hinduism and Islam and Western colonialism and dominance. Also immigrant races Indians and Chinese came in search of work and settled in Malaysia and other parts. Today, maritime Southeast Asia is facing illegal trafficking of desperate peoples to the region or onwards to Australia.

Maritime Southeast Asia has had to contend with the strategies, designs and vagaries of the rise and fall of great powers at a far greater speed, and scale, than continental Southeast Asia, which essentially adopts foreign forms and practices at a far slower rate. Subsequently, this difference explains much of the religious and intellectual character of Southeast Asia.

Prior to the arrival of colonialism in 1509, marked by the fleets of Vasco da Gama that sailed from Goa in India, maritime Southeast Asia had known empires like Sriwijaya, Majapahit and Malacca. Each of these Buddhist, Hindu and Islamic dynasties had respectively exerted their influence and imprint on the region, especially in facilitating the import of different religious values and ideologies into their domains. When the thrones changed their religious beliefs, the followers and those that came under their influence, soon adapted to the new religion and creed as well.

To the degree there were any major differences, between one set of beliefs and the other, they were grafted into the next one. Invariably, it was not surprising to see maritime Southeast Asia sharing an easy mix of monotheistic belief with animistic reverence too. Moreover, the receptivity to foreign values came with the advent of Portuguese, Dutch and subsequently, British colonization. They reinforced the prior habits established by the previous indigenous dynasties.

In the same vein, when this geography became a promiscuous contest of European powers – with each trying to reach deeper into the heartland of the region – leaders and the people of Southeast Asia understood the vagaries and vicissitudes of power too. To the degree ostensible ownership over any part of maritime Southeast Asia switched hands, their fate were decided at the battlefields and balance of power in Europe. This is how the Dutch, fearing the rise of the French in the Napoleonic campaign, assigned the duty of protecting Malaya to the British in the mid-nineteenth century, while they concentrated on present day Indonesia. When the British abandoned their outpost of Singapore and Malaya to the Japanese Imperial Army in 1941 with nary a fight, Southeast Asia grew weary of foreign powers' affirmation to defend and alleviate the livelihood of the citizens, clear that as colonies, these Southeast Asian states were meant to enrich the imperial treasury and were part of the grand designs in the chess game among the colonizers.

Continental Southeast Asia, otherwise known as Indo-China, on the other hand, due to its rugged terrain, has had the form of colonial penetration that was originally less intense and direct. Even if the foreign powers wanted to make their presence felt in this part of the world, their influence had to be assiduously built. Indeed, when the local rulers imported religious systems and values from civilizational behemoths like India and China, they became an instant fixture to their local statecraft. This is because to the degree there were no major changes in the religious doctrines in India and China, local rulers in continental Southeast Asia did not feel impelled to change too, once they had imported the beliefs from these two civilizations. Thus, to the degree a dynasty or empire in Indo-China had adopted a religious faith from India and China, its subsequent belief system remained very much the same – unless a new ideology had already replaced the ones in India and China, or, had made major in-roads into the capital and heartland. Even that depended very much on the constellation of events in India and China. While communism was introduced in China in the early 1920s, it became a system of rule in 1949. Prior to 1949, continental Southeast Asia did not do much to change its religious and ideological leanings until the likes of China and India had begun to do so.

The point is continental Southeast Asia did not have a normative structure that was easier to change, as compared to those in maritime Southeast Asia. When this characteristic is further shaped by a political authority, such as the Communist Party, that is not given to easy manipulation, it is not surprising that events in continental Southeast Asia have moved slower than those in the maritime part of the region.

But the sustainability of the argument stops there. In an age of globalization, every country comes under influence to change to meet the demands and expectations of the international community and foreign investors, without which it faces the plausible risk of being dominated by more powerful and affluent neighbours like China and India whose size and scale far outweigh any country in Southeast Asia, even when combined. In other words, the inertia to stall has been removed from the political DNA of continental Southeast Asia.

To the extent the leadership in Cambodia, Laos, Myanmar and Vietnam has understood the imperative to change, there is no telling to which of the systemic forces with which they are responding first. The market exhortation is that globalization, democratization, digitization and deregulation have to be conducted swiftly to allow the economy and polity to catch up with the new standards of governance. Ironically these have to be done while powers like US, Japan and the European Union (EU) are all facing a diminution of their powers. Even the growth rate of China has dropped from 12 per cent per year to 9 per cent per year.

Myanmar, left behind for at least 20 years, likes to embrace change head-on, but due to low human capital, after five decades of neglecting the importance of basic, secondary and tertiary education, there is a dearth of talent in the country to actualize the reforms. The massive reforms which the country wants to undertake, especially under President Thein Sein, and jointly with Aung San Suu Kyi of the National League of Democracy (NLD), will begin to meet serious bottlenecks even as they begin in earnest with numerous "carpetbaggers" peddling technologies and instant solutions.

Maritime Southeast Asia, on the other hand, appears to want the same too, especially given the amount of energy and efforts they have vested in the creation of the ASEAN security, economic and cultural community. Indonesia, in particular, has encouraged all the member states in ASEAN to bring the regional organization into "the global community of nations" as encapsulated by the Bali Concord III.

But, as one may notice at the Bali Concord III, the world fawns to symbolism as much as it does to substance. During the ASEAN summit in Bali, in spite of the promise provided by Indonesia, almost everyone locked their sights on Myanmar, the most under-developed member state of ASEAN.

Southeast Asia has to respond to globalization not just in substance, but also in the symbolism that it avails. If the world demands greater respect for human rights, economic equity, gender respect, and ecological sustainability, it is incumbent on the region to do them, without which Southeast Asia would not be seen as anything other than a bastion of peace and prosperity merely. Important as the latter may be, they are not the stuffs that galvanize the attention of the international community, especially the West. The post industrial West likes to see comprehensive emphasis on good governance too, even if the Euro Zone is currently in crisis due to bad governance.

It is here where some of the most difficult issues in international relations have to be answered. Does a region buy into the need to be ideologically and intellectually consistent with the world – in order to impress the West – or does it do what it can to impress itself based on the templates and wisdom developed for several millennia in the East?

India, the home of non-alignment, is the best place to answer this question as it has sought to combine the best of the West and East. But India, in many ways, is also proving to be less of a model for Southeast Asia, in spite of New Delhi's efforts to Look East. First of all, India is a potpourri of cultures and influences that far exceed the richness and complexities of Southeast Asia. There is a limit to what Southeast Asia can learn from India just as there is a constraint to what India can teach Southeast Asia directly.

Secondly, India is the biggest democracy in the world. Southeast Asia is the biggest collection of diverse regimes. Thailand has a monarch that is almost a demi God who nonetheless encourages the people to choose the parliamentary process; Malaysia is a constitutional monarchy cum federation that has a strong Islamic undertone; Brunei is ruled by a Malay Sultan who has permitted limited debate in the parliament; Indonesia is a republic that has chafed at the idea of federalism only to allow Aceh to attempt its own Islamic autonomy; while Vietnam is a one party state that has adopted market reforms. The differences and inflections are enough to deter a quick comparison.

Thirdly, India is bent on being a secular democracy in spite of its religious diversity. Southeast Asia does not mind an institutional co-existence with Islam, Catholicism and Buddhism at all. Each of these differences makes for a difficult answer as to how much India's history and model can serve as a guide post to Southeast Asia. Invariably, how Southeast Asia marry the best of the East and West would be dictated by how they contain the contending forces of moderation and extremism.

Southeast Asia while significantly advanced in terms of national consolidation is, however, still the confluence of major powers' interests and strategy. The issue of the Spratly islands, claimants and contending forces is illustrative. The ascendance of China and India add to the mix. ASEAN is consolidated enough to withstand and take on opportunities, but there are vestigial remains of what can constitute future crisis, e.g. discontented areas of ethnic groups, dystopia, and resistance to assimilation due to flawed policies or neglect by central governments. And while Indonesia has set an important example in

ASEAN, it is not all clear how major countries from the area would conduct and manifest their national imperatives.

In this sense, the Global Movement of the Moderates (GMM) in ASEAN comes at a critical and vital time. Just as the Zone of Peace, Freedom and Neutrality (ZOPFAN) provided the parameters for the earlier members of ASEAN to keep the foreign powers from transforming Southeast Asia into a cockpit of super power rivalry, the region has to prevent extremists of any political or religious complexion from asserting themselves now and in future and overreaching ambitions of major powers from within and without.

GMM has to exert its influence on various global and strategic issues, even if the discourse is belaboured. GMM must also contribute to the greater cohesion of the region in the pursuit of moderateness. In this sense, GMM will constitute Southeast Asia's gambit to respond and consolidate without being overwhelmed by the forces and pressures of reforms, just as Southeast Asia tries to prevent 'reasons' for extremism and to temper and moderate extremities of major power interplay. The Global Movement of Moderates Foundation will take steps to gain understanding and support from the region and hopes to impact with bodies and governments globally.

WORKS CITED

Berkemer, Georg, Tilman Frasch, Herman Kulke and Jürgen Lütt, eds. *Explorations in the History of South Asia: Essays in Honour of Dietmar Rothermund.* New Delhi: Manohar and South Asia Institute: Heidelberg University, 2001.

Cooper, Nicola. *France in Indochina: Colonial Encounters.* Oxford, New York, 2001.

Manuel, Teixeira. *The Portuguese Missions in Malacca and Singapore (1511-1958).* Lisbon: Portugal: Agência Geral do Ultramar, 1963.

Roberts, Christopher B. *ASEAN Regionalism: Cooperation, Values and Institutionalisation* (*Routledge Security in Asia Pacific Series*). New York: Routledge, Taylor & Francis Group, 2012.

Sacks, Milton. *The Strategy of Communism in Southeast Asia, Pacific Affairs.* Pacific Affairs, University of British Columbia, 1950.

Schober, Juliane. *Modern Buddhist Conjunctures in Myanmar: Cultural Narratives, Colonial Legacies, and Civil Society.* Hawai'i: University of Hawai'i Press, 2011.

St. John, Robert Bruce, Clive H. Schofield, eds. *The Land Boundaries of Indochina: Cambodia, Laos and Vietnam* (Boundary and territory briefing ed.). Durham: IBRU, 1998.

Starling, Nicholas. *The Cambridge History of Southeast Asia.* Cambridge, UK: Cambridge University Press, 1991.

Steinberg, David Joel. *In Search of Southeast Asia: A Modern History.* Sydney: Allen & Unwin, 1971.

5

India-ASEAN Strategic Partnership

TAMALIA ALISJAHBANA

"Indonesia may trade with China but it sings and dances with India"

Recently, I overheard a conversation between a Japanese lady, from the Toyota Foundation, and an Indonesian. The Japanese lady asked about Indonesia's reaction to China's growing strength not only in the region but in the world. The Indonesian response was, "Yes, China is growing more and more powerful and we're afraid…. Our message to India is, "Please, get your act together – fast!" When asked about Japan's reaction to China's role her response was, "Ah yes, we're also a member of the 'We're afraid of China Club'."

Many ASEAN nations appear to share this fear, especially among those states sharing common borders with China. Perhaps "fear" is too strong a word. A more appropriate description would be to say that we have mixed feelings about China. On the one hand we enjoy trading with China and the economic prosperity that this brings but there is also a growing concern about China's rising power and future role in the region. China's aggressive stance towards several ASEAN members with regard to disputed oil and gas rich off-shore territories has fuelled these concerns. China claims sovereignty over nearly all of the resource rich South China Sea which is home to vital shipping lanes but ASEAN nations such as Malaysia, Brunei, the Philippines and Vietnam have claims there too.

In July 2012, for the first time in its 45 year history, after nearly a week of heated diplomacy ASEAN failed to produce its usual joint diplomatic statement. This in turn has held up progress on issuing a separate code of conduct for the South China Sea. Many ASEAN member states feel that these divisions have weakened ASEAN's ability to handle disputes jointly under an ASEAN banner rather than individual member states dealing with them in a bilateral fashion with China – which is in fact the approach that China has been demanding from the start.

During a panel discussion at the ASEAN Secretariat ASEAN-Indian Partnership in 2010, the Indian speakers spoke mostly about trade and security issues. In the talks given by the various speakers it emerged that one of India's main interests in ASEAN is a security interest. India is concerned that the sea lanes through Southeast Asia remain safe and open in the face of a possibly declining United States role in maintaining the security of Southeast Asian maritime routes, in the future – despite America's so called 'pivot to Asia' policy.

Many states look to India to play a balancing role in the region. Senior Singaporean statesman Lee Kuan Yew has used the metaphor of India and China as the two wings keeping the Asian continent afloat. This is of course only possible if India is able to focus its energies to match China both economically and politically.

There are nations who hope that India might fill the United States role of providing security to the Southeast Asian sea routes and the region in general in the face of China's growing military might. India meanwhile, has been expanding its military capabilities. With its Agni-5 intercontinental ballistic missile India has deterrence parity with China in that its missiles can strike anywhere within China. India's navy will soon also have a 50,000 ton carrier the *Vikramaditya* with MIG-29K attack aircraft on board, the Arihant ballistic missile carrying, nuclear submarine and the Akula-II submarine which is already part of the Indian Navy's Eastern fleet.

This is not to say that we are expecting India to lead a nuclear war. Warfare is highly costly and destructive both in terms of human life as well as material damage and a nuclear war could destroy the whole region. When a military option carries such grave consequences it may be time to look at alternative instruments of security which are not capable of producing such devastating after effects. Perhaps it is time to consider democracy as an instrument of security. If China were a democracy there would not be such security fears regarding the ASEAN sea lanes. Nations usually speak of military exercises and maneuvers when discussing security issues but democratic and pluralist societies are a far better guarantee of security. In this respect the more nations of Asia that are democratic the more India and Indonesia's security interests are served.

In the past India has remained tactfully silent about its democratic principles during Asian forums – partly because for too long India was one of the only democracies in Asia. In part, however, it is also because most Asian countries do not relish telling other governments how their countries should be run. However, if Gandhi and Nehru or Indonesia's Founding Fathers, Hatta and Syahrir were still alive today, they would undoubtedly be of the opinion that India and Indonesia have a moral duty to create a vision of a democratic Asia and that the two countries should work to ensure that that vision becomes a reality. Such a vision would include a democratic China, a democratic Middle East and a wholly democratic ASEAN. In this India and Indonesia have a prominent role to play.

India is the largest democracy in Asia as well as one of the Asian states that has consistently maintained a democracy for the longest period of time. Meanwhile, Indonesia is ASEAN's largest democracy. In the recent past however, democracy has not always been considered to be an Asian value. At the seminar held at the Indonesian Ministry of Foreign Affairs in 2010, Dr. Raja Mohan, Strategic Affairs Editor of the *Indian Express*, described how in the late 1990s the Singapore government was extremely voluble on the subject of 'Asian values', as, opposed to 'Western values' but how that whole discussion about 'Asian values' came to an abrupt end, when the people of Jakarta poured out into the streets demanding democracy in 1998. For India and Indonesia democracy is an accepted Asian value.

Even for nations with almost completely homogenous populations like Japan for example, an important aspect of democracy is also the protection and promotion of a pluralist society. Both India and Indonesia strongly support this aspect of democracy. It is a matter of little surprise therefore that both India and Indonesia also currently face extremist groups bent on establishing uniform, homogenous societies. Shyam Saran, former Indian Ambassador to Indonesia and later also Foreign Secretary of India has said that "Both India and Indonesia have a great stake in the flourishing of diversity and plurality that is under attack from terrorist and fundamentalist forces. We need to build resistance to these forces and on the first page is dialogue and engagement between our two countries."

India and Indonesia should form a strategic partnership for democracy. We share a long history. During India and Indonesia's struggle for independence the leaders of the two nations had a close relationship and frequently tried to assist each other in their fight for freedom. Gandhi and Nehru were profoundly inspiring figures not only for Indonesia's founding fathers but for the Indonesian people in general. In 1947 Nehru organized a conference of Asian nations in Delhi to support Indonesia's struggle for independence and provided a plane to fly Indonesian Prime Minister Sutan Syahrir through the Dutch blockade to Delhi for the conference. On its return flight to Indonesia the plane which was carrying Red Cross medical supplies and personnel was shot down by Dutch fighter planes as it was preparing to land. (Afterwards the Indonesian government erected a memorial at the site where the plane came down.) Later when India experienced famine Indonesian nationalist forces collected rice to send to India. Nationalist posters at the time cried out, "Help Mother India!" Indonesia was also one of the first nations to recognize Indian independence and Sukarno attended India's independence celebrations in Delhi. During the struggle for independence our founding fathers shared common goals, values and visions for India and Indonesia. A democratic and pluralist Asia would certainly have been a part of their long term vision. Makarim Wibisono, Indonesia's former Permanent Representative to the United Nations has remarked that, "Nehru and Sukarno in the past worked in partnership in norm setting. The task is now how we transform the accepted norm into real action for Asia."

Obviously, the governments of India and Indonesia are reluctant to lecture other nations about democracy, let alone try to coerce them into becoming democracies. To do so would be a grave mistake for democracy needs to grow from the people. So in creating a vision of a democratic and pluralist Asia it is the people who need to be given the opportunity to speak and act. Both India and Indonesia have active non-governmental organizations in the field of democracy and human rights. They should be encouraged to meet, exchange ideas and work together not only in the interests of India and Indonesia but also in building that vision of a democratic and pluralist Asia. Non-governmental organizations from Asian nations that are not yet democratic should be encouraged to participate in the dialogue and activities of such groups. Governments can provide forums and funding. It is not the governments of India and Indonesia that should be in the forefront of teaching other countries to become democracies but rather our civil societies should be given every opportunity to help non-governmental organizations of countries that are not yet democratic – should they ask for such help.

However, this is not to say that there is no role for governments. A prime example is Indonesia's active but quiet role in assisting the government of Myanmar in moving towards a more democratic regime. Behind the scenes the Indonesian government has encouraged Myanmar's military junta to release Aung San Suu Kyi and to hold democratic elections. Indonesia's retired General Agus Wijaya who sits on the Council of Advisors of the President of Indonesia and played a key role in Indonesia's own shift from military to civilian rule was sent to advise the military regime in Myanmar on the transition to civilian rule and on the role of the military in a democracy. Similarly India has assisted Afghanistan in holding free elections.

Civil society activities between nations in the interests of building up democracies should also include press exchanges because freedom of the press is one of the strongest pillars of democracy. When Aung San Suu Kyi recently went to Oslo for her acceptance speech of the Nobel prize, Indonesian journalist Bambang Harimurti was also asked to speak at the event. Bambang Harimurti was for many years editor-in-chief of Indonesia's main political journal *Tempo* and has played a significant role in the democratization of Indonesia's press. In Myanmar, Bambang has assisted the government in bringing about freedom of the press. In his civil society role during the many years Aung San Suu Kyi was under house arrest, Bambang sat on the board of the dissenting radio and television station Democratic Voice of Burma. Currently, Bambang is assisting Tunisia with its laws governing freedom of the press.

The governments of India and Indonesia should support the establishment of a continuous and lively dialogue as well as cooperation on issues of democracy, freedom of the press, human rights and national identity which of course, evolve around shared values. Such exchanges between India and Indonesia's non-governmental associations and groups would by themselves eventually lead to cooperation and action between the peoples of India and Indonesia and other Asian countries. This would help inspire other people to demand democracy. One should never underestimate the power of the people. One thing that the Indian and Indonesian governments can do to promote a democratic Asia is to work together to create an international forum or body to help Asian nations wanting to establish democratic institutions and finding solutions to problems of democracy in developing countries, as well as promoting democracy in Asia. Other democratic Asian states such as Japan, the Philippines and Thailand might well be interested in joining this effort.

An important element in creating and building democracies and pluralist societies is culture. Too often Indonesia through ASEAN has been grouped together with China but let us not forget although we may trade with China, we sing and dance with India – ideologically and culturally Indonesia remains closer to India. Through the centuries we have seen India's influence on our dance, our art, our temples, monuments and our music.

At the moment the Indonesian Ministry of Education and Culture is in the process of declaring 26 km of ancient Buddhist temple sites from the fourth till the twelfth century at Muaro Jambi as national heritage sites. In the past Muaro Jambi formed part of a triangle of great places of Buddhist learning with Tibet and Nalanda. It is an excellent opportunity for the University of Jambi to establish a special relationship with modern day Nalanda University.

India has through the ages touched Indonesia's inherent love of art and culture and inspired our creativity in both these fields. Even today, India still delights and entertains Indonesia with its Bollywood films. Throughout history Indonesians have cherished a deep and profound love for the arts and for culture. In Bali, Hinduism is not so much noted for producing deep cultural philosophies or religious thought, but rather the Balinese have taken the rituals of Hinduism and turned them into a most breathtakingly beautiful and rich art form. A noted Indonesian scholar once said, "Shiva left his ashes in India but he left his dance in Indonesia."

Indonesia's first meeting with Indians was not just an information and technology revolution it was a profound awakening of our creative soul that paved the way for great developments in the arts and in culture in many parts of Indonesia. Even today, India touches our hearts and inspires our creativity in a way that leaves the Indonesian soul deeply happy, for we do so love the arts. India and Indonesia should join hands to once again create together dances, dramas, textiles and stories as we did so many centuries ago. Why not create a Bollywood film together? It would be in the interests of both India and Indonesia for its governments to inspire a renaissance in the arts between the two nations, a renaissance that could spread to the whole of Southeast Asian cultural renaissance which includes the vision of a democratic Asia.

An important element in creating and building democracies and pluralist societies is culture. It is for these reasons that culture and the arts should be of interest to the governments of India and Indonesia. During the struggle for independence our leaders held similar values and visions but later in the 1960s, 1970s and 1980s our paths diverged. Now our paths appear to be converging again and democracy is one of our shared values. Let us start with a lively and continued dialogue between India and Indonesia. In the words of Dr Raja Mohan, "I believe that India and Indonesia can make a difference to the world. Once you bring people together you will see things begin to happen."

A part of that dialogue should be the vision of a democratic and pluralist Asia and for this India and Indonesia should form a strategic partnership. Hopefully, other ASEAN nations would in the future be in a position to join such a partnership for as an eminent Indonesian scholar once declared, "A nation that does not give its people the freedom to think and to express their thoughts is a nation that has not yet evolved out of its own tribalism."

PART 2

Tradition and Shared Regional Consciousness

6

Funan within the Buddhist Network of Asia: The Story of Mandra[1]

WANG BANGWEI

Historians of Chinese Buddhism know the importance of three biographic books of prominent monks, *Gaoseng Zhuan (The Biographies of Prominent Monks), Xu Gaoseng Zhuan (The Continued Biographies of Prominent Monks)* and *Song Gaoseng Zhuan (The Song Biographies of Prominent Monks).* The second one, *Xu Gaoseng Zhuan*, being called *Tang Gaoseng Zhuan (The Tang Biographies of Prominent Monks)* as well, covers the period from the beginning of the sixth century to the middle of the seventh century. It was written by Daoxuan, a well-known Buddhist monk-scholar, early in the Tang Dynasty. Though most of the figures in the book are Chinese Buddhist monks, in some chapters, particularly in the Chapter on *Text Translators*, a number of Buddhist monks from other countries are included. The experiences of these monks, either in their home places or in China, provide materials illustrating the connections between these countries and China. One example of these countries is *Funan.*

In Daoxuan's book the first biography is of Saṃghapāla, a Buddhist Master from the country of *Funan* of Southeast Asia. Attached to the biography of Saṃghapāla are three short biographies of which the first one is of Mandra, or Mantuoluo in Chinese transliteration. It says as follows:

> Early in the time of Liang, there was another Śramaṇa called Mantuoluo (Mandra) from Funan. In the language of Liang (i.e. in Chinese) his name means "sounding lightly". He brought a lot of Indian texts and presented them to the Emperor. The Emperor ordered him to join with Saṃghapāla in translating the texts of The Ratnamegha, The Dharmadhatu and The Mañjuśrīprajñāpāramitā. The texts they produced are all together in eleven scrolls. Although he was involved in the translation work, he did not know the language of Liang very well. So the meaning of the translations produced by him is not easily understood.[2]

And in the *Biography of Saṃghapāla* it says as follows:

> In the language of Liang the name of Saṃghapāla means "keeper of saṃgha" or "armour of saṃgha (Saṃghavarman?)". He is a native of Funan. He was very clever at an early age and inclined to Buddhism. At school age he joined the saṃgha. He was especially skilled

in studying the essays of Abhidharma. His great reputation was known all of the South Sea area. After being fully ordained he extensively studied the Buddhist Vinaya. He was so brave that he wanted to travel abroad and propagate Buddhism. Hearing that in the country of Qi (China) Buddhism was advocated; he got on a boat and arrived at the capital of China. He lived at the Monastery of Zhengguan and became a disciple of Guṇabhadra.[3] Under the guidance of Guṇabhadra he studied the Mahāyāna texts intelligently. Within a short time, he learned a lot and became competent in the scripts and languages of several countries. Just at this time the Dynasty of Qi fell and Buddhism was declining, but Saṃghapāla only cleaned his body, let his heart be quiet, and stopped connection with the outside. He stayed in his room and cultivated his own personality. While the Dynasty of the Great Liang was established, the government searched for the talents. Thus in the fifth year of Tianjian (506 CE), Saṃghapāla was invited to translate texts in the Hall of Shouguang, the Garden of Hualin, the Monastery of Zhengguan, the House of Zhanyun and House of Funan, all five places being located in Yangdu (Jiankang, the capital of the Liang, today's Nanjing). Until the seventeenth year of Tianjian (518 CE), he had translated eleven texts consisting of forty-eight scrolls. The titles include The Sūtra of King Aśoka, The Vimuttimagga and others. [4]

Through this we know that Mandra arrived in China a little bit late than Saṃghapāla and cooperated with the latter when he started the translating work. The texts translated by Mandra can now be found in the Chinese Buddhist Tripiṭaaka. Daoxuan also edited a bibliography called *Datang Neidian Lu (The Buddhist Text Catalogue of the Great Tang)*. In the forth scroll of this book we find the same account with some more details. The texts Mandra produced are listed as follows:

The Sūtra of Ratanmegha, in seven scrolls.
Fajie tixing wufenbie jing, in two scrolls.
The Prajñāpāramitāsūtra of Mañjuśri, in two scrolls.[5]

In the fourth scroll of another bibliography, *Gujin Yijing Tuji (The Pictures and Records of Texts Translation in Ancient Times and Today)* by another Buddhist monk-scholar, Jingmai, the date, the second year of Tianjian, in which Mandra arrived at Jiankang, the capital of Liang China, is provided.[6]

The second year of Tianjian of the Liang is 503 CE. This happened before Emperor Wudi of the Liang ordered Saṃghapāla to translate in the fifth year of Tianjian (508 CE). It appears that at that time Mandra did not know Chinese well and therefore needed Saṃghapāla to help him. Daoxuan's information is very likely from *Lidai Sanbao Ji (The Three Jewelries in History)*, a book by Fei Changfang of the Sui, i.e. just before the Tang. Fei Changfang again says Mandra finished the translation together with Saṃghapāla and the source texts were brought to China from *Funan* by Mandra. He also says that while Saṃghapāla translated in the Hall of Shouguang, the Monastery of Zhengguan and the House of Zhanyun, all the source texts Saṃghapāla used were brought to China by Mandra from *Funan*.[7] One of the prominent points that we have to pay attention to is that the Buddhist texts that Saṃghapāla translated all belong to the Mahāyāna tradition, and are not related to the southern Buddhist tradition, excepting the text of *Vimuttimagga*. The origin and the *nikāya* affiliation of these texts are definitely worth closer examination. As far as I know, this problem is almost totally neglected by scholars.

Fei Changfang also mentions two other catalogues of Buddhist texts a little earlier than his, the *Li Kuo Lu (The Catalogue by Li Kuo)* and the *Baochang Lu (The Catalogue by Baochang)*, from which his information was obtained, though both have been lost later. The accounts in the Buddhist texts catalogues after Fei Changfang and Daoxuan, for example, *Kaiyuan Shijiao Lu (The Buddhist Text Catalogue during the Reign of Kaiyuan)* by Zhisheng, are all based on the above narratives.[8]

Funan, or ancient Cambodia, was the largest country in Indo-China from the first to seven century.[9] The territory of *Funan* was larger than today's Cambodia. The Chinese name *Funan*, according to some scholars, is from an ancient Mon-Khmer word, *bnam*, meaning mountains. The connection between *Funan* and China had commenced quite early, in the time of the Three Kingdoms, that is, around the middle of the third century CE. During the Northern and Southern Dynasties a number of Buddhist monks arrived in China from *Funan*. Mandra and Saṃghapāla were two of them.

Though we have the above-mentioned accounts, there are still very few who know about the life of Mandra in China. However, in a book written by Annen, a Japanese Buddhist-monk scholar of the time of Heian, the name Mandra is mentioned. Annen edited a book called *Xitan Zang ((The Siddhaṃ-Piṭaka)* in 880 CE. In this book he discussed the so-called fourteen *svaras* or Sanskrit vowels and cited seven different explanations by various scholars. The sixth is related to Emperor Wudi of the Liang and Mandra. His text is as follows:

> The sixth explanation is that by Emperor Wudi of the Liang. The Emperor Wudi disputed with the above-mentioned masters. He says that the two scripts have been lost because it has been too long since the time of the great Saints. Now the great Saints have appeared again, how can it be said that the scripts are lost? (Guanding cites the points of Master Guan to dispute saying that) it is also a mistake by Master Zong as he takes the scripts of siddham to fill the gap. The siddham is just an auspicious symbol and has nothing to do with the fourteen svaras. (Next he cites the points of Master Guan again to dispute) the explanation of Duke Xie who added the last four scripts to fill the gaps, but this is just what Śarvavarman, a tīrthaka (heretical) teacher, taught the King of Śātavāhana. Śarvavarman added the last four scripts then it can become fourteen svaras. But in fact these four scripts are not of the svaras. How do we know this? This was said by Dhyana Master Mandra. The words of Mandra are as follows: The Kunlun people in the remote sea area do not understand this but learn under the influence of tīrthakas so that the Hīnayāna scholars of that country do the same. So we should not add the last four scripts to make it complete. Let us explain the four scripts: In (Fanxian's) translation of Mahāparinirvāṇasūtra in six scrolls, they are lü (ṛ), li (ṝ), lou (ḷ), lü (ḹ). Here in the translation of Mahāparinirvāṇasūtra (by Dharmakṣema) they are lu (ṛ), liu (ṝ), lu (ḷ), lou

(Ḷ). Both are criticized by Emperor Wudi. Of these two versions, the latter is a little bit better. The explanation is this: To add these four graphs in showing the fourteen svaras is that the tīrthaka scholar Śarvavarman taught the King of Śātavāhana. Why has he taught him in this way? It is said that this is because the tongue of the King was so stiff that he asked the King to recite them. [10]

Guanding was a well-known Buddhist monk-scholar in the time of Sui. Master Guan very likely refers to Huiguan in the time of Liu Song (420-79 CE). Master Zong was Sengzong of the Sothern Qi (479-502 CE). Duke Xie was Xie Lingyun, the most well-known writer and scholar of the time. Xie lived from 385 to 433 CE.[11]

Through this account we know that Mandra was a Chan Master and Mahāyānist as well. The story of Śarvavarman who taught the King of Śātavāhana can be found in two well-known Indian story collections *Kathāsaritsāgara* and *Bṛhatkathāmañjari*. In the story it is said that Śarvavarman was a minister under the King of Śātavāhana. He hoped to train the pronunciation of the King who had a stiff tongue.[12]

In this context Mandra says that "*Kunlun* people in the remote sea area do not understand this but studied under the influence of tīrthakas so that the Hīnayāna scholars of that country do the same." Here the sea means the South Sea and *Kunlun* was the name in ancient China for the aborigine people in the South Sea area. We find in *Jiu Tangshu, The Old History of Tang Dynasty*, this accounts: "Living to the south of the country of *Linyi*, the people are black and with curly hair on their heads. They all are called the *Kunlun*."[13] The words of Mandra show that the area during that time was not only under the influence of Buddhism but also under tīrthakas, that is, Brahmanism. The Buddhism in the area included both Mahāyāna and Hīnayāna, of course, both these were from India.

About the kingdom of *Funan* we can also find other accounts in Chinese literature. The most detailed is from *Lianshu, The History of Liang Dynasty*. It talks about the diplomatic relation between *Funan* and China:

After that the King of Funan was Kauṇḍinya. He was originally from a Brāhmaṇa family of India. As God said he would become king of Funan, he was happy and went to the country of Panpan in the south. When the people of Funan heard this, the whole of country was happy to support him to become king. They welcomed him and crowned him as their king. Then the new king changed the administrative system and adopted Indian laws. After Kauṇḍinya died, King Dhṛtavarman(?) succeeded. In the time of Emperor Wendi of the Song (424-453 C.E.), King Dhṛtavarman dispatched an envoy to China to present gifts. During the reign of Yongming (483-493 C.E.) King Jayavarman sent an envoy to present tribute. In the second year of Tianjian (503 C.E.), he sent an envoy to present corals, an image of Buddha and other aborigine products. The Chinese Emperor issued an edict saying: Kauṇḍinya Jayavarman, the King of Funan, living in the far sea area and ruling the South area for some generations, with great loyalty known far away, now presents tributes, through several times of translation. It should be accepted and he should be given the honour of the title of General Annan and the King of Funan.[14]

As Mandra arrived at Jiankang in the second year of Tianjian, it is very probable that he came together with the royal delegation of *Funan*. According to *Liansshu*, in the tenth, thirteenth, sixteenth years of Tianjian (511, 514, 517 CE), the first year of Putong (520 CE), the second year of Zhongdatong (530 CE), the first and the fifth years of Datong (535, 539 CE), each year there arrived one delegation from *Funan*. It shows how frequent the communication was between *Funan* and China. And this is why Emperor Wudi of the Liang decided to build a house called House of *Funan* in the capital particularly for the various people arriving from *Funan*. Meanwhile many books were brought by these people from *Funan* to China. In the Bibliography Section of *Suishu, The History of Sui Dynasty*, under the title of *Book of Brāhmaṇa Scripts* we find a record saying "there was a *Hu Scripts Book of Funan* kept in the Liang".[15] The *Hu Scripts Book of Funan* was obviously different from the *Book of Brāhmaṇa Scripts*, which was generally thought to be from India, though both unfortunately were lost quite long ago. To judge from the title *Hu Scripts Book of Funan*, it is very possible that it is a book written in the script of ancient Mon-Khmer language.

During the Liang Dynasty not only did Buddhist monks originally from *Funan* arrive in China and translated Buddhist texts there, just as Mandra and Saṃghapāla did, but there were also some Indian Buddhist monks who traveled to China through *Funan*. One example is the well-known Indian Buddhist monk-scholar Paramārtha. We find his biography also in Daoxuan's book *Xu Gaoseng Zhuan*. Paramārtha is also called Kulanātha in the biography. The text reads as follows:

> During the years of Datong (535-546 CE), the Emperor dispatched Zhang Fan, an officer of Zhihou, together with others to send the envoys of Funan back to their country. One of the delegation's task was to invite the well-known Buddhist scholars who knew the Tripiṭaka, the Mahāyāna texts and Zahua Jing and others. Paramārtha was widely known and his behavior was that of a saint. When the Chinese delegation searched for excellent scholars, wishing to benefit the people, Paramārtha was advised by the people of that country to come to China, bringing along with Buddhist texts, in accordance with the Emperor's order. Since Paramārtha already intended to do this anyway, he happily accepted the advice. He arrived at Nanhai (today's Guangzhou), on the fifth day of the eighth month of the twelfth year of Datong (546 C.E.). After that he spent two years before he arrived in the capital (of China) in the intercalary eighth month of the second year of Taiqing (548 CE).[16]

According to his biography Paramārtha was from Ujjayanī, a country in West India. He first arrived in *Funan* and was then invited to China. In China he translated a number of Buddhist texts and so became one of most prominent translators in Chinese Buddhist translation history. Though we do not know how long Paramārtha stayed in *Funan* before he came to China, his visit to that country, and the cases of Mandra and Saṃghapāla as well, all show that *Funan* was under very strong influence of Buddhism, particularly Mahāyāna Buddhism, at that time. We know of similar examples from other places like Kucha and Khotan on the so-called Silk Road in Central Asia.

In Chinese literature *Funan* is also called *Banan*. In the book *Naihai Jigui Neifa Zhuan* by the well-known Tang Buddhist pilgrim-monk Yijing, we find quite a great deal of information about the geographic and religious situation in the South Sea area.

Starting from Nālanda (in India), after one has traveled five hundreds yojanas east,[17] the whole area is called Eastern Frontier. At the farthest place, there is a mountain called Great Black Mountain, which is estimated to be on the southern boundary of Tibet. It is said if one travels from the south-west of Sichuan, after about one month, one can arrived at this mountain. Further to the south, near the seacoast there is a country called Śrīkṣetra. To the southeast of this is the country of Langjiashu. To the east of this is the country of Dvārapatī. At the extreme east is the country of Linyi. The people of these countries greatly rever the Three Jewels. Many of them hold firmly to the precepts of vinaya. The way of dhūta, that is begging, is a custom (for Buddhists monks) in these countries.[18]

And on the geographic situation, Yijing says:

Counting from the west there are Island of Polusi and Island of Maluoyu, which are now the country of Srīvijaya, then Island of Mohexin, Island of Heling, Island of Dada, Island of Penpen, Island of Poli, Island of Juelun, Island of Foshibuluo, Island of Ashan and Island of Mojiaman. There are more small islands which cannot all be mentioned here.[19]

And more on Buddhism:

In all these countries Buddhism is followed by the people and most of the Buddhists belong to Hīnayāna, except in Maluoyou where there are a few belonging to Mahāyāna. Among these countries some are of about a hundred Chinese lis in circumference, some are several hundred in circumference, and some measure about a hundred yojanas. Though it is difficult to calculate distances on the great ocean, those who travel in merchant ships know the approximate distance of these countries. Because the people of Juelun first visited Jiaozhou and Guangzhou, they were generally called by the name of "Country of Kunlun". Only these people of Kunlun have curly hair and black skin, the other countries are not different from China. It is their habit to have their legs bare and to wear ganman (a cloth). These things have been fully described in the *Nanhai Lu* (The Accounts of the Southern Sea). Setting out from Huanzhou, right to the south, one will reach Bijing after a journey of rather more than half a month on foot; if one travels by ship it takes five or six days. If one arrives at Champa in the south, that means he has arrived in the country of Linyi. In this country most Buddhists belong to the Sammitīyanikāya, and a few belong to the Sarvāstivādanikāya. Setting out southwestwards, one will in a month reach Banan, which formerly was called Funan. At first the people of the country lived naked and worshiped the devas (gods). Later on, Buddhism started to flourish there. However, now a wicked king has expelled and exterminated Buddhists and there are no Buddhist monks left at all. The adherents of tīrthaka (heretics) live intermingled. This area is the south corner of Jambudvīpa, not the islands at the sea.[20]

What Yijing describes is the situation he knew in the early time of Tang, about a hundred and thirty years late than the time of Liang. While the geographic condition was not much different from earlier times, the situation of Buddhism in *Funan* had changed a lot. That is, at about the middle of the seventh century the newly established *Zhenla (Chenla)* conquered and substituted *Funan* as a new Mon-Khmer country. The new king of *Zhenla* appears to have been unfriendly towards Buddhism but has suppressed it. Yijing's reports reflect this historical fact.

NOTES

1. This is a slightly revised version based on my paper which has been published in *International Comparative Social Studies*, vol. 24, with the title "The Buddhist Connection between China and Ancient Cambodia: Śramaṇa Mandra's Visit to Jiankang", Leiden-Boston: E.J. Brill 2010, pp. 280-91. However, I am grateful for the suggestions and comments of the participants of the conference of *Civilizational Dialogue between India & ASEAN* held from 20-22 July 2012 at Patna in India.
2. Taisho Tripitaka, No. 2060, p. 426b. 《續高僧傳》卷一《僧伽婆羅傳》：梁初又有扶南沙門曼陀羅者，梁言弘弱。大齎梵本，遠來貢獻。敕與婆羅共譯寶雲》、《法界體性》、《文殊般若經》三部合一十一卷。雖事傳譯，未梁言。故所出經文多隱質。
3. Guṇabhadra is a Buddhist master scholar from Central India. His biography can be seen in *Gaoseng Zhuan (The Biographies of Prominent Monks)*, Taisho Tripiṭaka, No. 2059, pp. 344a-355a.
4. Taisho Tripiṭaka, No. 2060, p. 426a-b.《續高僧傳》卷一《僧伽婆羅傳》：僧伽婆羅，梁言僧養，亦云僧鎧。扶南國人也。幼而穎悟，早附法津。學年出家，偏業阿毘曇論。聲榮之盛，有譽海南。具足已後，廣習律藏。勇意觀方，樂崇開化。聞齊國弘法，隨舶至都。住正觀寺，為天竺沙門求那跋陀之弟子也。複從跋陀研精方等，未盈炎燠，博涉多通，乃解數國書語。值齊曆亡墜，道教淩夷。婆羅靜潔身心，外絕交故。擁室棲閑，養素資業。大梁禦宇，搜訪術能。以天監五年被敕徵召于揚都壽光殿、華林園、正觀寺、占雲館、扶南館等五處傳譯，訖十七年。都合一十一部，四十八卷，即《大（阿？）育王經》、《解脫道論》等是也。
5. Taisho Tripiṭaka, No. 2149, p. 265c. 《寶雲經》七卷。（見《宋錄》），《法界體性無分別經》二卷。（見《李廓》及《寶唱錄》），《文殊師利般若波羅蜜經》二卷。（或有"說"字。見《李廓錄》）。右三部，合一十一卷。天監年初，扶南國沙門曼陀羅......共僧伽婆羅于楊都譯。
6. Taisho Tripiṭaka, No. 2151, p. 364b. 沙門曼陀羅......以梁武帝天監二年歲次癸未用以奉獻。
7. Taisho Tripiṭaka, No. 2034, p. 98c.（僧伽婆羅）以天監五年被敕徵召，於揚都壽光殿，及正觀寺、占雲館三處譯上件經。其本並是曼陀羅從扶南國齎來獻上。
8. Taisho Tripitaka, No. 2154, p. 537b.
9. For a general ancient history of the area of Southeast Asia, including Funan or Cambodia, see, for example, G. Coedès, *The Indianized States of Southeast Asia*, Canberra: Australian National University Press, 1975.
10. Taisho Tripitaka, No. 2702, p. 377c. 安然《悉曇藏》卷二：第六梁武解並彈前來諸師。彼彈前云：書缺二字者，爾時去聖久，所以缺二字。今聖人出世，何得言缺耶？（灌頂引觀師彈）次宗法師以“悉曇”足之者亦非。悉曇自吉祥，何關十四音耶？（引觀師彈）次彈謝公以後四字足之者。此是外道師名葉波跋摩，教婆多婆呵那王，以後四字是為十四音，實非音也。何以知之？此曼陀羅禪師傳述彼事，文云：邊海昆侖未體此旨，亦習外道之氣，乃至彼國小乘學者，亦複如此，故不得以後四字足也。下釋四字中云：六卷云履、梨、樓、呂（為樓許反），此中云魯、流、盧、樓。梁武並彈此兩處文，就兩文中，此中文小勝。有解云：以此四字足前為十四音，此是攝婆跋摩外道師教婆多婆呵那王。何故教之？舊云：彼王舌強，故令王誦此字也。

11. The so-called fourteen *svaras* is a very interesting topic. See Wang Bangwei, "Xie Linyun Shisi Yin Jikao" (Xie Linyun and his *Sishi Yin Xunxu*: The Earliest Approach to Indian Phonology in Mediaeval China), in *Guoxue Yanjiu (Chinese Classic Studies)*, vol. 3, Beijing: Peking University Press, 1995, pp. 275-300. Revised version in *Ershi Shiji Wenshi Kaoju Wenlu (The Collection of Papers of Historical and Literary Evidential Studies in Twentieth Century China)*, vol. II, Kunming: Yunan People's Publisher, 2001, pp. 1966-1980.
12. *Kathāsaritsāgara* and *Bṛhatkathāmañjari* both are based on another well-known Indian story collection *Bṛhatkathā* though the last one had been lost quite long ago. See the sixth taraṃga of the first lambaka of *Kathāsaritsāgara*, Sanskrit version in Devanagari scripts published by Motilal Banarsidass, Delhi, 1977, pp. 18-19. The English translation of the story can be found in *The Ocean of Story, being C.H. Tawney's Translation of Somadeva's Kāthā Sarit Sāgara*, by N.M. Penzer, London: Privately printed for subscribers only by Chas. J. Sawyer Ltd, 1926, vol. I, pp. 68-75. Some scholars mentioned this story while they discussed *Kātantra. See* B. Liebich, *Zur Einfuerung in die indische einheimische Sprachwissenschaft*, I. *Das Kātantra*, Heidelberg, 1919, pp. 3-4 and H. Scharfe: *Grammatical Literature, A History of Indian Literature*, edited by J. Gonda, vol. V, Fasc.2, Wiesbaden: Otto Harrassowitz, 1977, pp. 162-3. The story can also be found in the fifteenth chapter of Tāranātha's *rGya gar chos 'byung*, though with some revisions. The teacher was Vararuci, not Śarvavarman. See *History of Indian Buddhism,* the English translation by Lama Chimpa and Alaka Chattopadhyaya, Calcutta: K.P. Bagchi & Company, 1980, p. 111.
13. Zhonghua edition, Fasc. 16, p. 5270. 《舊唐書》卷一九七《南蠻西南蠻傳：“自林邑以南，皆捲髮黑身，通號為昆侖。”*Liyi* is the Chinese name for Champa, an ancient country in today's South Vietnam. For more references of *Kunlun*, see Wang Bangwei, *Datang Xiyu Qiufa Gaoseng Zhuan Jiaozhu (Biographies of the Prominent Monks Who Went in Search of the Law in the Western Regions during the Great Tang), by Yijing, with a newly collated and annotated text,* Beijing: Zhonghua Book Company, 1988, n. 2, pp. 82-3.
14. Zhonghua edition, Fasc. 3, pp. 789-710. 《梁書》卷五十四《諸夷傳》：其後王憍陳如，本天竺婆羅門也。有神語曰“應王扶南”。憍陳如心悅，南至盤盤。扶南人聞之，舉國欣戴，迎而立焉。複改制度，用天竺法。憍陳如死，後王持梨陀跋摩，宋文帝世奉表獻方物。齊永明中，王闍邪跋摩遣使貢獻。天監二年，跋摩複遣使送珊瑚佛像，並獻方物。詔曰：扶南王憍陳如闍邪跋摩，介居海表，世纂南服，厥誠遠著，重譯獻賝。宜蒙酬納，班以榮號，可安南將軍、扶南王。
15. Zhonghua edition, Fasc. 4, p. 945. 《隋書》卷三十二《經籍志》：《婆羅門書》一卷。（注）梁有《扶南胡書》一卷。Cf. Jao Tsung-I, "Shuo Funan Hushu" (On the Hu scripts of Funan), in his *Fanxue Ji (Papers on Sino-Indian Studies)*, Shanghai Classics Press, 1993, pp. 175-7.

16. Taisho Tripiṭaka, No. 2060, p. 429c. 《續高僧傳》卷一《拘那羅陀傳》：大同中，敕直後張泛等送扶南獻使返國。仍請名德三藏、大乘諸論、《雜華經》等。真諦遠聞行化，儀軌聖賢。搜選名匠，惠益民品。彼國乃屈真諦，並齎經論，恭膺帝旨。既素蓄在心，渙然聞命。以大同十二年八月十五日達於南海。沿路所經，乃停兩載。乙太清二年閏八月，始屆京邑。
17. Literally *yojana* means a distance traversed in one harnessing or without unyoking, thus it was used as a measure of distance in ancient India which is said to equal about 18 or 13 or 7 km according to various explanations.
18. Taisho Tripiṭaka, No. 2125, p. 205b. 從那爛陀東行五百驛，皆名東裔。乃至盡窮，有大黑山，計當土蕃南畔。傳云是蜀川西南，行可一月余，便達斯嶺。次此南畔，逼近海涯，有室利察呾羅國，次東南有郎迦戍國，次東有杜和缽底國，次東極至臨邑國。並悉極遵三寶，多有持戒之人。乞食杜多，是其國法。For more discussion on this account, see Wang Bangwei, *Nanhai Jigui Neifa Zhuan Jiaozhu (Accounts of the Inner Law Sent Home from the South Sea), by Yijing, with a newly collated and annotated text,* Beijing: Zhonghua Book Company, 1995, pp. 13-17.
19. Ibid. 從西數之，有婆魯師洲、末羅遊洲，即今尸利佛逝國是；莫訶信洲、訶陵洲、呾呾洲、盆盆洲、婆里洲、掘倫洲、佛逝補羅洲、阿善洲、末迦漫洲；又有小洲，不能具錄。
20. Ibid. 斯乃咸遵佛法，多是小乘，唯末羅遊少有大乘耳。諸國周圍，或可百里，或數百里，或可百驛。大海雖難計裏，商舶串者准知。良為掘倫，初至交廣，遂使總喚昆侖國焉。唯此昆侖，頭卷體黑。自余諸國，與神州不殊。赤腳敢曼，總是其式。廣如《南海錄》中具述。驩州正南，步行可餘半月，若乘船纔五六朝，即到匕景。南至占波，即是臨邑。此國多是正量，少兼有部。西南一月，至跋南國，舊云扶南。先是裸國，人多事天，後乃佛法盛流。惡王今並除滅，迥無僧眾，外道雜居。斯即贍部南隅，非海洲也。

WORKS CITED

Annen, *Xitan Zang (The Siddhaμ-Pi aka),* Taisho Tripitaks, No. 2702, 安然，《悉曇藏》

G. Coedès, *The Indianized States of Southeast Asia*, Canberra: Australian National University Press, 1975.

Daoxuan, *Xu Gaoseng Zhuan (The Continuous Biographies of the Prominent Monks)*, Taisho Tripitaka, No. 2060, 道宣，《續高僧傳》

———, *Datang Neidian Lu (The Buddhist Text Catalogue of the Great Tang)*, Taisho Tripitaka, No. 2149, 道宣，《大唐內典錄》

Fei Changfang, *Lidai Sanbao Ji (The Three Jewelries in History)*, Taisho Tripitaka, No. 2154, 費長房，《歷代三寶記》

Huijiao, *Gaoseng Zhuan (The Biographies of the Prominent Monks),* Taisho Tripi aka, No. 2059, 慧皎《高僧傳》

Jingmai, *Gujin Yijing Tuji (The Pictures and Records of Texts Translation in Ancient and Today)*, Taisho Tripitaka, No. 2151, 靜邁，《古今譯經圖記》

Kathāsaritsāgara, Sanskrit version in Devanagari scripts, Delhi: Motilal Banarsidass, 1977.

B. Liebich, *Zur Einfuerung in die indische einheimische Sprachwissenschaft*, I. *Das Kātantra*, Heidelberg, 1919.

Liu Xu, *Jiu Tangshu (The Old History of Tang Dyanasty)*, Zhonghua edition, 劉昫，《舊唐書》

Yao Silian, *Lianshu (The History of Liang Dyanasty)*, Zhonghua edition, 姚思廉，《梁書》

Jao Tsung-I, "Shuo Funan Hushu" (On the Hu scripts of Funan), in his *Fanxue Ji (Papers on Sino-Indian Studies)*, Shanghai Classics Press, 1993, pp. 175-7, 饒宗頤，"說扶南胡書"，《梵學集》

H. Scharfe: *Grammatical Literature, A History of Indian Literature*, ed. by J. Gonda, vol. V, Fasc.2, Wiesbaden: Otto Harrassowitz, 1977.

Tāranātha, *rGya gar chos 'byung, History of Indian Buddhism*, English translation by Lama Chimpa and Alaka Chattopadhyaya, Calcutta: K.P. Bagchi & Company, 1980.

Wang Bangwei, *Datang Xiyu Qiufa Gaoseng Zhuan Jiaozhu (Biographies of the Prominent Monks Who Went in Search of the Law in the Western Regions during the Great Tang)*, by Yijing, with a newly collated and annotated text, Beijing: Zhonghua Book Company, 1988, 王邦維，《大唐西域求法高僧傳校注》.

———, *Nanhai Jigui Neifa Zhuan Jiaozhu (Accounts of the Inner Law Sent Home from the South Sea)*, by Yijing, with a newly collated and annotated text, Beijing: Zhonghua Book Company, 1995, 王邦維，《南海寄歸內法傳校注》

———, "Xie Linyun Shisi Yin Jikao" (Xie Linyun and his *Sishi Yin Xunxu*: The earliest approach to Indian Phonology in Mediaeval China), in *Guoxue Yanjiu (Chinese Classic Studies)*, vol. 3, Beijing: Peking University Press, 1995; revised version in *Ershi Shiji Wenshi Kaoju Wenlu (The Collection of Papers of Historical and Literary Evidential Studies in Twentieth Century China)*, vol. II, Kunming: Yunan People's Publisher, 2001, 王邦維，"謝靈運十四音訓敘輯考"

Wei Zheng et al., *Suishu (The History of Sui Dynasty)*, Zhonghua edition, 魏徵等，《隋書》

7

Reception and Assimilation of the 'Buddha-nature' Idea in East Asian Buddhism

SUNG-DOO AHN

There have been multiple cultural exchanges between India and ASEAN on the one hand, and between India and East Asian Countries on the other. In the latter case, the Indian influence on East Asian Countries was largely through the medium of Buddhism, particularly from the second century CE to the eighth century CE.

Possibly the cultural influence of Indian Buddhism contributed to expanding the new horizon of human experiences of the East Asian people, and it was the first cultural event in the history of mankind that was peaceful and non-violent. In world history, Buddhism has played a unique role as the first religion which began the creation and transmission of a new international culture with its accompanying cultural transformation and synthesis throughout Asia. This process of the synthesis and its mediums is not explainable by the simple transmission of technologies or techniques. It could be traced mainly through the translation, interpretation, and reception of the classical Buddhist texts. This process has been accompanied and accomplished by the transmission of the upper structure, namely, of the texts, and is widely recognized as unique. This has created the problem of translation and interpretation for the first time in the dimension of cultural studies, whose solution has required the hermeneutical work called "ko-i" (格義. "matching the concepts" of Buddhism and Confucianism or Daoism) for a long time in the history of Chinese Buddhism. This work has not been simply to change the original Buddhist terms into the appropriate terms of the target language. That is, the receptive history of Buddhism in China could not have achieved any success without the remolding of the epistemological frames of the original terms into the epistemological frames of the target language. In the importation and indigenization of humanistic systems, it is very important not to ignore the fact that the concepts and terms used in them presuppose their own historicity and social backgrounds, whose deep understanding is indispensable for the appropriate digestion of their humanistic systems. Moreover, historicity and sociality are so closely linked with the epistemological network of the whole society that it is not feasible to accommodate and integrate them to our own systems partially.

What I want to deal with and sketch out in this regard is how the 'Buddha-nature (*tathāgatagarbha*)' idea was adopted and reinterpreted in East Asian Buddhism. It has generally been supposed that the Buddha-nature idea played a minor role in Indian *Mahāyāna*-Buddhism, but when the idea was imported to East Asian Countries, it soon dominated Buddhist views on reality and was regarded as the highest Teaching of the Buddha among the followers in East Asian countries. The so-called "sinologized" Buddhist Schools of the latter period could demonstrate their superiority by reinterpreting and assimilating this idea with other mahāyānic theories. For this purpose, I want to investigate some basic concepts related with the 'Buddha-nature' idea, and to show how these concepts were reshaped by East Asian Buddhists.

'BUDDHA-NATURE' IDEA IN INDIAN BUDDHISM

David Seyford Ruegg, the leading Western scholar on the 'Buddha-nature' idea, thinks that it "is used to denote the 'buddhamorphic' Base or Support for practice of the Path, and hence the motivating 'cause' (*hetu: dhātu*) for attainment of the Fruit (*phala*) of Buddhahood".[1] This shows that the 'Buddha-nature' idea was a religiously motivated movement in the *Mahāyāna* circle. However, in Indian *Mahāyāna*-Buddhism, the representatives of which are the *Madhyamaka* school and the Idea-Only school, the epistemological and ontological issues played an important role in the soteriological concern.[2] In this regard, the 'Buddha-nature' idea had quite a different perspective. It seems that the *tathāgatagarbha* idea of Indian Buddhism stressed the pervasiveness and innateness of *tathāgatagarbha* from a religious viewpoint, but did not show any fundamental interest in its ontological aspect. From this, we can infer why the *tathāgatagarbha* idea did not develop into an Indian Buddhist school, but remained in India as a spiritual vision for attaining the ultimate reality transmitted from teacher to student, not from an official teaching program at monastery universities. So, we can raise the question whether it is appropriate to establish the *tathāgatagarbha* idea as an independent school comparable with the Madhyamaka or Idea-Only school. Though that is very relevant to East-Asian Buddhism, in the context of Indian Buddhism, it would be far from reality. The division of Indian Buddhism of SNS in three stages clearly shows that there was no proper place for the *tathāgatagarbha* idea in the history of Buddhist thought.

The difference of the practices observable in Indian *tathāgatagarbha* idea can be understood properly to be "positive-mystical current" using the phraseology of Schmithausen (1981: 224 etc.). Though this term was originally used to characterize calm meditation (*śamatha*) in contrast to 'insight-meditation (*vipaśyanā*)', we may reserve the same expression for the *tathāgatagarbha* idea because of its positive characterization with regard to ultimate reality. To take an example: according to the traditional accounts, ultimate reality can be realized when the spiritually negative elements in one's mind are totally extinguished. Only through getting rid of the defilements, in other words, by way of the negative approach to the ultimate reality, can one see the reality as it really is. In contrast, the *tathāgatagarbha* idea suggests a totally different approach to reality. If living beings are the "Embryo-Essence" (*garbha*) of the *tathāgata*, as the word *tathāgatagarbha* itself implies, then it would be hard to apply the negative approach consistently to the Buddha-like essence, which was endowed with so many positive and invaluable Buddha-qualities. Furthermore, if the Embryo-Essence of the *tathāgata* is innate in all living beings, there is no reason but to give full credit to our Buddha-like nature and to approach it *via positiva* in order to realize it.

This idea found some expressions in the early stage of Indian Buddhism. In the following section, I would like to describe the various aspects of the *tathāgatagarbha* idea and related ideas with it in three texts.

1. *The Meaning of tathāgatagarbha in the Tathāgatagarbhasūtra*

It is often mentioned that the 'Buddha-nature' idea can be traced back to the canonical materials. As an indication for it, one can refer to a famous passage in *AN* I.10.11-12 which declares that the mind is originally pure, but because of fortuitous defiling factors becomes impure. Though this passage is also cited in other *Mahāyāna* texts, for example, *Aṣṭasahasrikā*, *Madhyāntavibhāgaṭīkā* etc., I think the meaning of it may be best explained from the perspective of the 'Buddha-nature' idea. However, the *tathāgatagarbha* texts seem to be written after Nāgārjuna (*c.* 150-250), the founder of *Madhyamaka* school. The first text expounding the *tathāgatagarbha* idea is *Tathāgatagarbhasūtra,* which appeared around 250 CE.[3] After this text, some other important texts follow: *Śrīmālādevīsiṃhanādasūtra*, *Aṅgulīmālika* and Māhāyanist *Mahāparinirvāṇasūtra*, etc.

Because the word *tathāgatagarbha* was used for the first time in the *Tathāgatagarbhasūtra*, it would be relevant to examine its precise meaning. According to Michael Zimmermann, the compound *tathāgatagarbha* can be theoretically interpreted in three ways: as dependent compound (*tatpuruṣa*), as adjective compound (*bahuvrīhi*), and as "born from a *tathāgata*" (2002: 41-5). Among them the most 'natural' interpretation of the word *tathāgatagarbha* in the *Tathāgatagarbhasūtra* is to understand it as an adjective compound (*bahuvrīhi*). Whether or not the last word of the compound *garbha* means '*Mutterleib*' or 'embryo' or simply 'inside, middle or interior of anything', or one step further 'essence, central part', the compound *tathāgatagarbha* is understood as an adjective to *sarvasattva* (all living beings), and means: (1) "living beings have an embryo of a *tathāgata*" or (2.1) "Living beings have a tathāgata in their womb (garbha)", or (2.2) "Living beings have a tathāgata as an embryo (*garbha*)", or (3.1) "Living beings have the tathāgata-core", or (3.2) "Living beings have a tathāgata at their core" (2002: 44). Zimmermann thinks that "the grammatically adequate interpretation serving as the basic one of the compound *tathāgatagarbha* is that of a *bahuvrīhi* meaning "containing a tathāgata"" (2002: 45). Though this interpretation is well attested in the first similes (Buddha in the lotus) of the *tathāgatagarbhasūtra,* maybe the latest addition among the similes, "because it covered the whole variety of themes illustrated in the similes", he calls attention to the other interpretation of the *tathāgatagarbha* as a *tatpuruṣa*. In this case one can see in the rendering growing tendency to interpret the term "as a separate entity found in living beings in the sense of "store of a tathāgata" or "essence of a tathāgata", which may be supported by the synonym *buddhadhātu* in the Māhāyanist *Mahāparinirvāṇasūtra*" (2002: 46).

Now, keeping in mind this basic meaning of the *tathāgatagarbha*, let us examine the sentence in the *Tathāgatagarbhasūtra* propounding the religious meaning of *tathāgatagarbha.*

Sons of good family, just as these unsightly, putrid, disgusting and no [longer] pleasing lotuses, supernaturally created by the Tathāgata, and the pleasing and beautiful form of a tathāgata sitting cross-legged in [each of] the calyxes of these lotuses ... in the same way, sons of good family, also the Tathāgata, the Honorable One and perfectly Awakened One, [perceives] with his insight (*prajñā*), knowledge (*jñāna*) and tathāgata-vision that all the various sentient beings are encased in mytriads of defilements, [such as] desire (*rāga*), anger (*dveṣa*), misguidedness (*moha*), longing (*tṛṣṇā*) and ignorance (*avidyā*). And, sons of good family, [he] perceives that inside sentient beings encased in defilements sit many tathāgatas, cross-legged and motionless, endowed like myself with a [tathāgata's] knowledge and vision. And [the Tathāgata], having perceived inside those [sentient beings] defiled by all defilements the true nature of a tathāga (*tathāgatadharmatā*) motionless and unaffected by any of the states of existence, then says: 'Those tathāgatas are just like me!' Sons of good family, in this way a tathāgata's vision is admirable, [because] with it [he] perceives that all sentient beings contain a tathāgata (*tathāgatagarbha*). (Zimmermann 2002: 102-105)

It may be obvious that the above statement is more religiously oriented, rather than philosophical. Irrespective of the various interpretations of the presence of *tathāgatagarbha* in living beings, the text makes it clear that there is a capacity for them to become a Buddha. The problem arises when we ask for the meaning of the presence of *tathāgatagarbha*; can it be understood only as a Base in the sense of the defilement-covered, causal level or as an already perfected state in the sense of full Enlightenment? It may be safe to say that in the context of the *Tathāgatagarbhasūtra* the *tathāgatagarbha* idea was suggested to encourage humans to strive for the realization of perfect Buddhahood because it contains as a spiritual Base a *tathāgata*. In addition,

I think the introduction of the *tathāgatagarbha* idea is closely related with the Mahayanist self-consciousness that their spiritual goal of the Buddha is superior to the Arhat-ideal, as is strongly suggested in the passages of the *Śrīmālādevīsimhanādasūtra*.

2. *Some problems in the statements of the 'Buddha-nature' of related texts*

The immanence of a Buddha in a living being may not be in direct contradiction with the Buddhist practices of the path, in so far as it is understood to be a spiritual Base or element, with the help of which one can travel on the path leading to the full realization of one's capacity to become a Buddha. However, it would be spiritually very dangerous, if the 'Buddha-nature' theory is regarded as being opposed to the well-known criterion for the Buddhist soteriological goal, namely to the criterion of the non-self (*anātman*) theory. The mainstream Buddhist schools did not only accept this criterion, but they also emphasized its indispensability in reaching the highest goal. So, in this viewpoint, we could not but inevitably raise the question whether the presupposed immanence of the Buddha in the *tathāgatagarbha* idea can eventually be in line with the non-self theory or not. It appears hard to find a gap-bridger between these opposing tendencies. It became far more complicated, when some texts, representative of the *tathāgatagarbha* line of thought, describe the *tathāgatagarbha* in highly positive terms. Mahayanist *Mahāparinirvāṇasūtra*, for example, attributes four positive qualities, permanent (*nitya*), immutable (*dhruva*), blissful (*sukha*) and eternal (*śāśvata*), to *tathāgatagarbha*, and even mentions that the *tathāgatagarbha* is self. These qualities were usually "epithets that one would expect to relate to the Absolute – indeed, *prima facie*, to a substantial Absolute" (Ruegg 1989: 19). As Ruegg suggested, "the parallelism between the *tathāgatagarbha* and the Vedāntic *ātman* is quite striking". However, in order to avoid the misunderstanding of simply identifying the *tathāgatagarbha* with *ātman*, the author(s) of the *Mahāparinirvāṇasūtra* warn(s) us that the meaning of the statement of Buddha should not be understood on the surface level, but its proper meaning can be realized, only when we recognize the intention (*abhiprāya*) of Buddha well. The intention of Buddha is his compassion to lead the non-Buddhists to the Buddhist goal. He allures them to convert to and follow the Buddhist path by suggesting similar theories in outlook.[4] So, the *tathāgatagarbha* is in reality nothing but non-self.

But, there arose an important question in this respect: what is the status of the *sūtra* disclosing the *tathāgatagarbha* line of thought? According to the Buddhist hermeneutical device of 'definitive meaning' (*nītārtha*) and 'provisional meaning' (*neyārtha*), the assertion that the value of the statement of Buddha is dependent on his intention belongs to the category of 'provisional meaning'. Then, these *sūtras* should have only provisional, not definitive value. In this regard, however, Ruegg points out that this criterion "had to be handled with care and restraint ... in order not to be tainted with arbitrariness and disregard for all canonical corpus" (1989: 35). In addition to the first solution to the hermeneutical problem of provisional and definitive meaning of the *tathāgatagarbha*, he suggests as the second solution that this doctrine has to be reviewed "in relation to the doctrine of non-substantiality (*nairātmya*) and Emptiness (*śūnyatā*), which is generally accepted in the Mahāyāna" (Ruegg 1989: 35). In the following section, I would like to deal firstly with some passages of the *Ratnagotravibhāga* (hereafter, *RGV*), where the *tathāgatagarbha* is defined in three points, and with the other passage, in which the *tathāgatagarbha* is identified with 'emptiness'.

According to the *RGV* 21, 8-10, Thusness is divided into the following two: the Thusness free from impurities (*nirmalā tathatā),* which is called the *dharmakāya*, characterized by the Transformation of the bases (*āśrayaparivṛtti*), whereas the Thusness accompanied with impurities (*samalā tathatā)* means the *tathāgatagarbha* as a causal factor [for becoming the Buddha] not separated with the receptacle of defilement. The former designates a resultant aspect, and the latter only capacities to become a Buddha. It is here interesting to note that the *tathatā* is used explicitly to designate the cause of Buddha.

With regard to the *samalā tathatā*, the *RGV* explains the meaning of the *tathāgatagarbha* in three points: (i) because the *dharmakāya* of the *tathāgata* penetrates [all living beings]; (ii) because the Thusness (*tathatā)* of the *tathāgata* is not differentiated from [that of the living beings]; (iii) because the germ (*gotra*) of the *tathāgata* exists [in all living beings].

Of these three points the *RGV* (v. I.145) divides the *dharmakāya* in two: pure *dharmadhātu* and Teaching flowing from the pure *dharmadhātu.* There are also two types of *tathatā* as mentioned earlier. And the *gotra* is also classified into two types: *gotra* staying in its original state and *gotra*, which is cultivated (*RGV* v. I.149). Through the interplay of these three points from one side, and every two types of these three from the other side, the *RGV* sets forth the meaning of 'all living beings contain the *tathāgara* as essence' in various aspects and establishes its religious significance. There is no space in this paper to give a deeper illumination on these points, but it may be enough to say that in the *tathāgatagarbha* idea in India the religious motivation dominates, not the metaphysical or ontological interest.

However, we can find in the *RGV* some passages, where the inclusion of emptiness in the *tathāgatagarbha* is stated. The *RGV* I.155-6, for example, makes it explicit that the *tathāgatagarbha* is empty of adventitious impurities, but not empty of incalculable Buddha-qualities. In this regard, it should be mentioned that the use of the concept 'emptiness' in the *RGV* does not coincide with the *Mādhyamika* usage of emptiness, what is clearly demonstrated in the famous citation of 'well-grasped emptiness' in the *RGV* 76, 9-10. At any rate, we assume that by restricting the emptiness the *RGV* seems to declare the superiority of the *tathāgatagarbha* over the purely negative understanding of emptiness.

3. *Criticism against the 'Buddha-nature' idea in other Mahayanist Schools*

The concept of the *tathāgatagarbha* appeared, though very rarely, several times in the *Yogācāra* and *Mādhyamika* texts. In some *Yogācāra* texts, *MSA*, two commentaries on *MSg*, namely *MSgBh*, *MSgU*, and *LAS*, the word *tathāgatagarbha* are mentioned directly or in similar form. Let's briefly discuss them.

In the *MSA* IX. 37d, the expression *tad-garbhāḥ sarvadehinaḥ* is used.[5] It goes without saying that *tad* in *tad-garbhāḥ* is *tathāgata,* as the prose-commentary makes explicit. So, the wording of the sentence has to be understood as an adjective compound, meaning that "all those who have the body have the *tathāgata* as Embryo". The reason for this understanding is explained in the former part of the same verse (IX. 37abc). It reads: "the state of the *tathāgata* is the purified Thusness (*tathatā),* though undifferentiated with all [living beings]." This interpretation goes on around the two concepts of *tathatā.* Here, the relation between three factors, *tathāgata, nirmalā tathatā* and all [living beings] can be clearly explained in the sense of two kinds of *tathatā,* i.e., *nirmalā* and *samalā tathatā,* in the *RGV.* It will suffice to indicate the differences of *MSA* with the *RGV* in this context that the latter expands the usage of the *tathāgata* into *dharmakāya, tathatā* and *gotra,* whereas the former restricts the usage of the *tathāgatagarbha* to *tathatā* alone.

The restriction of the usage of *tathāgatagarbha* to *tathatā* is also true for the *MSgBh* (*P*: Li 180a6f.) and *MSgU* (*P*: Li, 282b1f.). As the *Mūla*-text of these commentaries, *MSg* deals with the problem of hermeneutical interpretation of the *Mahāyānasūtras* before the introduction to the Three Natures *(trisvabhāva)* and how these could be arranged for the 'provisional' or "definitive' meaning. In this context, these two commentaries on *MSg* regard the four kinds of purity as intending the Perfected Nature, and enumerate the synonyms of the first purity, *prakṛti-viśuddhi,* as follows: *tathatā, śūnyatā, bhūtakoti, ānimitta, paramārtha* and *dharmadhātu.* Among them, the *tathatā* is equated in these two commentaries with the *tathāgatagarbha.* The tendency to explain the *tathāgatagarbha* in line with the *tathatā* is, as we saw above, only connected with the non-differentiation of *tathatā* in all states, whether in its fully actualized state or in its latent form in living beings. And, if the *tathāgatagarbha* is definable within the framework of the *tathatā*, it means that the *tathāgatagarbha* should be related with an objective aspect, not with the knowledge-aspect.

So far, we discussed the meaning of the *tathāgatagarbha* presented in the Commentarial treatises. Now, we turn to the description of the *tathāgatagarbha* in *LAS* 220, 1-239,10, which left a mark on Chinese Buddhism more strongly than these commentaries; the description, which relates the *tathāgatagarbha* with the *ālayavijñāna*. Here the passage reads:

> The *tathāgatagarbha* has the beneficial and unbeneficial [factors] as cause, is the agent (*kartṛ*) leading to all rebirths and existence-forms (*gati*), comes to existence like a dancer in the dangerous existence-forms, and is free from the [concept] 'I' and 'Mine'. Because of non-realization of that, [the *tathāgatagarbha*] comes to existence, when it unites with the operation of the conditions resulting from the combinations of the three [factors]. The Non-Buddhists do not realize [this], and attach to the [eternal] cause (*kāraṇa*), and ... is called '*ālayavijñāna*'. (*LAS* 220,9-14)

The most innovative idea in the citation is the equation of the *tathāgatagarbha* with the *ālayavijñāna*. In so doing, however, the *tathāgatagarbha* has to be endowed with the characteristics of the *ālayavijñāna*, and as a result, the inevitable question arises about the ontological status of the *tathāgatagarbha*. And, connected with it, many dogmatic problems would arise, such as: Can the *tathāgatagarbha* be regarded as real existent, just like the *ālayavijñāna* is accepted as the Dependent Nature to be the Base of *samsaric* existence and Nirvana? According to the above equation the *tathāgatagarbha* would mean the Dependent Nature, but how does this statement coincide with the other statement (in *LAS* 68,1) that the *tathāgatagarbha* is the Perfected Nature?

In the other *Mahāyāna* school, *Madhyamaka* school, the *tathāgatagarbha* idea was not included as an essential part of its system. It was marginally dealt with by the great exponents of the school. Candrakīrti, for example, mentions the *tathāgatagarbha* when he evaluates it in the frame of 'provisional' and 'definitive' meaning. In *MA* 196, 12-198, 13 Candrakīrti citing the *LAS* 77, 13-79, 12 seems to regard it as a 'provisional meaning', in that the statement of Buddha on the *tathāgatagarbha* can be properly understood in dependence upon Buddha's intention. Also in Bhāvaviveka's *Tarkajvālā*, "the all-pervasiveness of the *tathāgatagarbha* has been taught for the sake of certain persons who have not freed themselves from the dogmatic postulation of a self (*ātmagrāha*)."[6] Apart from their Tibetan successors, the Indian *Mādhyamikas* treated the *tathāgatagarbha* within the theory-evaluating context.

'BUDDHA-NATURE' IDEA IN EAST ASIAN BUDDHISM

In contrast to the minor role played by *tathāgatagarbha* in Indian Buddhism, it left a deep and long-lasting impact on East Asian Buddhism particularly since the Southern-Northern Dynasty period onward. As a representative of the 'mystical-intuitive' approach to ultimate reality, the claim that all living beings contain the *tathāgata* as Embryo, was recognized as a highly universal soteriological declaration. That this theory was highly celebrated from its inception in East Asian Buddhism than in the other Indian *Mahāyāna* schools was convincingly illustrated in some episodes. Daosheng (355-434) was said to have established the theory of the 'Buddha-nature' against the theory of the *icchantika*, who does not have any spiritual capacities to become a Buddha, successfully in East Asian Buddhism.[7] Also Zuercher (2007: 249) reported the story of a famous Buddhist master of the Southern-Northern period, 慧遠 who was convinced of the unchangeability of the Buddha, though at that time the teaching of the eternality of *Nirvāṇa* was not handed down to Chinese Buddhism. Another story was concerned with the doctrinal conflict of the *tathāgatagarbha* idea with the *Yogācāra* Germ (*gotra*) theory. It was well-known in the fifth century that the *Yogācāras* advocated their five *gotra*-systems. The persons are classified into five sorts according to their family: Those who belong to the *Bodhisattva-gotra*, to *Pratyekabuddha-gotra*, to *Śrāvaka-gotra*, those whose *gotra* is not determined and finally those who have no *gotra* (*agotraka*). The last one, also called '*icchantika*', was said to have no capacities at all to become a Buddha. There were fierce controversies among Buddhist fellows over whether an *icchantika* can achieve *Nirvāṇa*. The debates waned after the Mahayanist *Mahāparinirvāṇa* was translated, which demonstrated the existence of the *tathāgatagarbha* in all living beings in explicit expression.

These two stories show respectively the tendency among Chinese Buddhists to evaluate the *tathāgatagarbha* idea higher than the *Madhyamaka* or *Yogācāra* system. In due course, the *tathāgatagarbha* idea was finally regarded as an independent *Mahāyāna* school, still more, far higher located in their hierarchical evaluations. As a result, the most important exponents of Chinese Buddhism at that time spoke in favour of the *tathāgatagarbha* and it had a very important role beyond comparison in the history of Chinese Buddhism. As a consequence of this, the development of an independent Chinese Buddhist system gradually emerged. I think the Dilun school paved the way for and contributed heavily to this development.

Now, I want to give a short introduction about the Dilun school. The founder of this school was the famous Indian *Yogācāra* Master and translator Bodhiruci, who arrived in China around 508 and died around 535(?). Though the Dilun school, named after Bodhiruci's translation of the *Daśabhūmika-Bhāsya* of the great Indian Master Vasubandhu, flourished and survived only during the sixth century, its influence over other Buddhist schools and thought in his time was uncontestable. All the famous and influential Thinkers and schools of that time, such as Tiantai, Huayen, the Shelun school of Paramārtha, San-chieh Chiao 三階教, Chi-tsang of Sanlun school 三論宗 were all concerned about the implication of Bodhiruci's translation. Moreover, the Dilun school was, more or less, credited to the compilation of the famous 'The Awakening of Faith in *Mahāyāna*' (Dasheng qixinlun, 大乘起信論), one of the most important and influential writings throughout East Asian Buddhism. In this sense, the Japanese scholar Otake, who has studies around this school, advanced an opinion that the *Yogācāra* ideas of the Dilun school should be regarded as the basic and common inheritance of that time in Northern Dynasty (2010: 90).

1. *Characteristics of Bodhiruci's Translations and Thought*

As mentioned earlier, the characteristic development of East Asian Buddhism may be reduced to the enforcement of the *tathāgatagarbha* idea, to the result that this idea exercised dominant power in East-Asia over the two main Indian *Mahāyāna* schools. And, the role of Bodhiruci and his follows was decisive for the later development of the other schools, regardless of whether they resulted from the misunderstanding of Bodhiruci or not. Bodhiruci is said to have translated the Indian *Yogācāra* texts from his own perspective and method. He supplemented the original text with his own ideas, ideas that showed the integration of two systems: *Yogācāra* and *tathāgatagarbha* thoughts. The best example is his translation of the Jingang Xianlun 金剛仙論, which is now regarded as the annotated translation of Vasubandhu's Commentary on *Vajracchedikā Prajñāpāramitā*.[8] Depending on his translations, his pupils elaborated somewhat creative theories of mind and about Dependent origination, etc.

There were two sub-schools in Dilun school, called the Southern division and Northern division. According to the Chinese Buddhist Historiography, Kaiyuan Shijiao lu (開元釋教錄 *T*55: 540b), the two Indian Masters, Bodhiruci and Ratnamati, gathered together in order to translate the *RGV*. However, there arose between two Masters the dissention as to the interpretation of the *RGV*, and in consequence, the *RGV* was translated separately. Usually, the followers of Bodhiruci were called the 'Northern division of the Dilun', and the followers of Ratnamati the 'Southern division of the Dilun'. Their differences lie mainly in the fact that the 'Northern division' gave more attention to the defiled aspect of the Mind, the centrality of which is, without doubt, around the concept of the *ālayavijñāna,* whereas the 'Southern division' focused on the pure aspect of the Mind, namely, *tathāgatagarbha*.

2. *Structure of the Mind arranged by Bodhiruci*

Undoubtedly, Bodhiruci as an Indian monk-scholar must have known the *Yogācāra* theory of eight kinds of Mind established in Asaṅga's *Mahāyānasaṃgraha*. As is well-known, the eight kinds of Mind are the six kinds of consciousness (*vijñāna*), Defiled Ego-consciousness (*kliṣṭaṃ manas*) and the Storehouse consciousness (*ālayavijñāna*). However, curiously enough, Bodhiruci's arrangement of the Mind is different from the authentic *Yogācāra* view. He seemed to arrange the Mind into seven types, with the elimination of *kliṣṭaṃ manas*. Much more confusing is the transmission of his theory of the Mind.

In order to give a clear picture, Otake (2010: 66-9) suggested that Bodhiruci's theory of Mind can be classified into two kinds: the one is the theory that sees the seventh consciousness in *ādāna-vijñāna*, and the other is the theory that requires the 8th consciousness and names it as the *ālayavijñāna*. But, this *ālayavijñāna* does not have the function of consciousness, for it is only a designation for the 'Emptiness-principle' 空理. As Otake suggested, the first kind is related with and stems from the *SNS*. Because the *SNS* which he also translated calls the seventh consciousness as *ādāna-vijñāna*; here without mentioning the *kliṣṭaṃ manas* the text identifies the *ādāna-vijñāna* with the *ālayavijñāna*. As for the second kind of explanation, it may well have its origin in the *LAS*, as the above citation of it (*LAS* 220, 9-14) shows; here, the *tathāgatagarbha* is equated with the *ālayavijñāna*! So, the attribution of the 'Emptiness-principle' to the *ālayavijñāna* (in reality, to the *tathāgatagarbha*) is formally accomplished on the base of this equation. The problem is that the 'Emptiness-principle' still demands some other teachings for expanding the meaning of *tathāgatagarbha* further into Emptiness. In this regard, I think the explanation of the *RGV* was presupposed in Bodhiruci's schema of the Mind. At any rate, it would be clear that Bodhiruci's schema of the Mind allows many dogmatic theories to interplay on the same level, though they had different origins and contexts.

It is not clear why Bodhiruci raised his own theories of the Mind. The decisive point in his theory is that it lacks the defiled Ego-consciousness. Otake (2010: 66), pointing out this omission, assumed that the Indian *Yogācāra* group, to which Bodhiruci belonged, did not recognize the authority of Asaṅga and refused to accept the Defiled Ego-consciousness as an independent consciousness. Though he did not give any further evidence to support his assumption, I think his idea is worthy of reconsideration and research in a wider perspective. The unfamiliar theory of the 9th consciousness of Paramārtha as well seems to suggest that there were in Indian *Yogācāra* of that period many competing theories on the nature of the Mind and its structure. I think the reason why Bodhiruci did not recognize the independent existence of the Defiled Ego-consciousness is closely connected with the fact that its existence would come in conflict with the *tathāgatagarbha* idea, particularly when the *tathāgatagarbha* is understood as an essence of a living being. Therefore, Bodhiruci did not pay attention to the verse of the *LAS* (II.106) which clearly presupposed eight kinds of consciousness, including *manas* as the 7th consciousness.

Now, I turn to the meaning of the 8th *ālayavijñāna*, which is no more than the 'Emptiness-principle' for Bodhiruci. For this purpose I consult the passage in the *Vijñptimātratā-śāstra* 唯識論, translated by Bodhiruci as well. The passage divides the Mind into two sorts: associated Mind and unassociated Mind. It reads: "In so far as the Mind is associated with the latency of the defilements and the other mental factors like feeling, perception and formations etc., it is called associated Mind; therefore, [the expression,] *citta-mano-vijñāna-vijñapti*[9] is of the same meaning, though the naming is different."[10] We may point to Bodhiruci's peculiar usage of the word 'association of Mind'. With the expression 'association of mind' all the aspects of the mind are subsumed, whether it is in latent form or in manifest form, as the passage implies. If we think of the importance of the distinction between latent and actual state for Indian *Yogācāra* tradition, we can say that Bodhiruci's idea was far from the authentic *Yogācāra* position.

In contrast to the associated Mind, Bodhiruci regarded the "unassociated Mind as ever-lasting and unchanging ultimate Truth, because of the purity of the Mind by nature. Therefore, what belongs to the Three spheres, is nothing but the Mind".[11] Here, the non-association of the Mind seemed to be understood as an original purity, never under the domain of cognitive apprehension. What is interesting is that this non-association of the Mind is connected with the state expressed in the famous passage of the *Daśabhūmika* VI.[12] It is worthwhile to notice that the mind in the verse was understood to be momentary and evanescent from the viewpoint of Indian *Yogācāra*. But, Bodhiruci regarded it as unchanging reality, because "the Mind does not have external things as its object, but has only internal mind [as its object]".[13]

If we put this distinction into the structure of mind, the 8th will be tantamount to the 'unassociated Mind', and the other seven forms of mind to the 'associated Mind'. This would be supported in the translation of *LAS* by Bodhiruci (*T*16: 556c). It reads: "the *tathāgatagarbha* does not exist in the *ālayavijñāna*, therefore, seven kinds of consciousness come to and fro, but the *tathāgatagarbha* is without change".[14] If my juxtaposition is right, how can we understand Bodhiruci's idea on the *tathāgatagarbha*? If the *tathāgatagarbha* is totally different from the other associated form of Mind, how is it possible to bridge the gap between them? This is not the proper place to give a satisfactory answer to these questions, but I am of the opinion that the point of departure may be for Bodhiruci to secure the Base or Support for the spiritual training and eventually Awakening.

3. *Classification of Buddhist Scriptures and Theories of Dependent Origination*

As an important contribution of the Dilun school to the development of East-Asian Buddhism the theories of Dependent origination and the classification of Buddhist scriptures, or doctrinal taxanomies, are to be mentioned first of all. For these two were related with each other, it is necessary to discuss them. On these issues, I want to introduce and summarize some important researches, which have been recently done in Japan and Korea, etc.

It was reported that the classification of the Dilun school exercised much influence upon the other classificatory attempts of the Tiantai school or Huayen school in that period. The Dilun school divided the class of the scriptures usually into the following three: (a) Distinct Teaching for three vehicles 三乘別教, (b) Shared Teaching 通教, and (c) Shared Essence 通宗. Further,

(c) was subdivided also into three Teachings: (c1) Gradual Teaching 漸教, (c2) Sudden Teaching 頓教, and (c3) perfect Teaching 圓教.[15]

To (a) belong the Teachings of the Abhidharma-school, and to (b) the Teaching of the *Prañāpāramitā Sūtra* and *Yogācāra*. The term 'Perfect Teaching' invented for the first time in East-Asian Buddhism by the Dilun masters was used to designate the *tathāgatagarbha* Teaching. What is referred to by the Perfect Teaching is that all the distinctions, such as that between pure and impure, etc., appear harmoniously to the mind of those who realize the Teaching of the *tathāgatagarbha*. The breaking off of all dichotomies was understood to be the sign of the highest Teaching, and as such, the *tathāgatagarbha* thought had to reveal this kind of reality over the simple Base or Support for the realization. In order to express such ideas, the Dilun school, particularly the Southern division, developed the terminologies which want to show that the phenomena and noumena are one and the same.

As the classification of the scriptures shows, the masters of the Southern division regarded the *tathāgatagarbha* as the highest Teaching, which was idiomatically expressed like this: "'Buddha-nature' is eternal, and exists by nature". If the 'Buddha-nature' is, however, eternal and unchangeable, then the old problem reappears again: how can we avoid the risk of identifying the *tathāgatagarbha* with the brahmanical *Ātman*, and of degrading the Teaching into the status of provisional meaning? But as far as I know, the distinction between 'provisional' and 'definitive' meaning did not play a major role in East-Asian Buddhism. In contrast, it was more and more important to understand whether the *tathāgatagarbha* is already existent in the present or will be realized in the future. In this question, the Southern division of the Dilun held the former position in the sense that the 'Buddha-nature' is the *dharma-kāya* immanent in living beings. The Northern division, on the contrary, held that the claim of the *tathāgatagarbha* thought that 'all living beings contain the *tathāgatagarbha* as their essence' is to be understood in the sense of the declaration of future cultivation.[16] This idea of the Northern division seems to be more similar to the original Indian idea of *tathāgatagarbha*. It is, however, interesting to note that the new interpretation of the Dependent Origination of the Southern division is very relevant to their understanding of the *tathāgatagarbha*.[17]

The Southern division was using their own term (yuan ji, 緣集) to describe the different functions of the Dependent Origination. It was divided into three kinds: Dependent Origination of the Conditioned 有爲緣集, Dependent origination of the Unconditioned 無爲緣集, Dependent Origination of the Self-Essence 自體緣集. This theory was first formulated by the Master Fashang (495-580). For him, the first kind means the usual sense of the Dependent Origination, whereas the second one is the Dependent Origination of the pure factors, leading to the *Nirvāna*. For the Southern Division these two originate from the Self-Essence (=*tathāgatagarbha*). Through the simple juxtaposition the *tathāgatagarbha* became the Base of defiled and pure factors. Still more, this idea led to the well-known concepts of Essence 體 and Activities 用. Later, the Dependent Origination of the *dharmadhātu* 法界緣集 was added as the fourth, and was regarded as the highest interpretation which explains the relation between the phenomenal things and noumenal principle. It became the trademark of the theory of the Dependent Origination of the Huayen school.

CONCLUDING REMARKS

In the present paper an attempt is made to show in the historical and religious context, though very sketchily, that how and in what measures Indian Buddhist ideas have transformed the worldview of East Asian Buddhists. For this purpose I chose the *tathāgatagarbha* theory, which reflected the different soteriological milieu between two countries most effectively. As was well-known, the *tathāgatagarbha* played very important role in East Asian Buddhism. But, it differed much when we look at the intellectual interplay of Indian Mahayana Buddhists. They showed no significant influence from the side of the *tathāgatagarbha.*

However, when we deal with the Chinese texts of the same or a little later period as in Indian sources, then, we find that the spiritual atmosphere changed dramatically. In East Asian Buddhism of the sixth century, the *tathāgatagarbha* thought played the decisive role in the sinologized understanding of Buddhism and through it in the further development of East Asian Buddhist thought. Focusing on the Dilun school in sixth century, the founder of which was the Indian Master Bodhiruci, I dealt with some peculiar characteristics of the Dilun school, which consisted, above all, in the complex of the structure of Mind and creative interpretation of the Dependent origination. These aspects were partly received and partly criticized by the later schools. In any cases their criticism shows that the Dilun idea left deep marks behind their system-building.

At any rate, I hope the present paper contributes to the understanding that the 'new' cultural and spiritual dimensions would not come to existence without cultural contacts. In ancient time, the contact between India and East Asian countries was advanced mostly by the selfless endeavors of Buddhist Monks. Through their activities they could construct the world, which I think was once praised by Rabindranath Tagore in his poetry "Gitanjali".[17]

> Where the mind is without fear and the head is held high;
> Where knowledge is free;
> Where the world has not been broken up into fragments by narrow domestic walls;

Where words come out from the depth of truth;
Where tireless striving stretches its arms towards perfection;
Where the clear stream of reason has not lost its way into the dreary desert sand of dead habit;
Where the mind is led forward by thee into ever-widening thought and action—
Into that heaven of freedom, my Father, let my country (or, rather: our Asia!) awake.

ABBREVIATIONS

DaBh	*Daśabhūmikasūtra* (ed. Rahder), Leuven, 1926.
LAS	*Laṅkāvatārasūtra* (ed. Nanjo), Kyoto, 1923.
MA	*Madhyamakāvatāra* (*Candrakīrti*), ed. L. de la Vallée Poussin, 1907-1912.
MSA	*Mahāyānasūtrālaṅkāra* (*Maitreya*), ed. S. Lévi, Paris 1907.
MSg	*Mahāyānasaṃgraha* (*Asaṅga*), ed. Nagao (攝大乘論). Tokyo 1982.
MSgBh	*Mahāyānasaṃgraha-bhāṣya* (*Vasubandhu*).
MSgU	*Mahāyānasaṃgraha-upanibandhana* (**Asvabhāva*).
P	*Peking-Edition of Tibetan Tripiṭaka.*
RGV	*Ratnagotravibhāga* (ed. Johnston), Patna, 1950.
SNS	*Saṃdhinirmocanassūtra* (ed. E. Lamotte), Louvain, 1935.
T	*Taisho Shinshu Daizokyo*

NOTES

1. Ruegg 1989: 18-19.
2. Williams 2000: 161.
3. See Zimmermann 2002: 79.
4. For the discussion and explanation of the differences between tathāgatagarbha with ātman, see Ruegg 1989: 21-6.
5. *sarveṣāṃ aviśiṣṭhāpi tathatā śuddhim āgatā /*
tathāgatatvaṃ tasmāc ca tadgarbhāḥ sarvadehinaḥ // MSA IX.37.
6. Cited in Ruegg 1989: 40; originally *Tarkajvālā* iv, f. 169a8 (see fn. 59 of the same page).
7. For this, see Tokiwa 1944: 177ff.
8. See Otake 2001: 49. He also suggested that the text may be originally the lecture-note of Bodhiruci, and was compiled by many Chinese assistants (2001: 68).
9. It is not clear why the word *vijñapti* appears as the last member in sequence.
10. 唯識論 (*T*31: 64b24-27): 心有二種 何等為二 一者相應心 二者不相應心 相應心者 所謂一切煩惱結使 受想行等 諸心相應 以是故言 心意與識及了別等 義一名異故.
11. 唯識論 (*T*31: 64b27-29): 不相應心者 所謂第一義諦 常住不變 自性清淨心故言三界虛妄 但是一心作 是故偈言 唯識無境界故.
12. Daśabhūmika VI. E (ed. Rahder): *cittamātram idaṃ yad idaṃ traidhātukam.*

13. 唯識論 (*T*31: 64b19-21): 如大乘經中 說三界唯心 唯是心者 但有内心 無色香等外諸境界.
14. 入楞伽經 (*T*16: 556c11-13): 如來藏識 不在阿梨耶識中 是故七種識 有生有滅 如來藏識 不生不滅. It should be noted that the Sanskrit texts (*LAS* 221, 12-13) has different meaning; see for it Otake 2010: 68.
15. For the classification of the Teaching in the Dilun school. See Aoki 2010: 62ff.
16. Aoki 2010: 47.
17. The following explanation is based on Aoki's paper (in: Aoki 2010: 81ff.).

WORKS CITED

Ahn, Sung-doo. *The Annotated Translation of Ratnagotravibhāga*. Seoul: Np., 2011.

Aoki, Takeshi. 'The Formation of the Doctrines of the Dilun School as Seen in Dunhuang Manuscripts'. *Formation and Transformation of the Dilun Thoughts*. Tokyo, Np., 2010.

Otake, Susumu. 'Problems of the Formation of Jingang Xianlun' (Japanese), in 佛教史學研究 44-1, Np: Np. 2001.

Otake Susumu. 'The Consciousness-Only Doctrine of the Dilun School' (Japanese), in *Formation and Transformation of the Dilun Thoughts*. Tokyo, Np., 2010.

Ruegg, David Seyfort. *Buddha-Nature, Mind and the Problem of Gradualism in a Comparative Perspective*. London: Heritage Publishers & SOAS, 1989.

Schmithausen, Lambert. 'On Some Aspects of Descriptions of Theories of "Liberating Insight" and "Enlightenment"', in *Studien zum Jainismus und Buddhismus: Gedenkschrift für L. Alsdorf*. Wiesbaden: Franz Steiner Verlag, 1981.

Williams, Paul. *Buddhist Thought*. London and New York: Routledge, 2000.

Tokiwa, Daijo. *Studies of the Buddha-Nature* (Japanese). Tokyo, Np., 1944.

Zimmermann, Michael. *The Tathāgatagarbhasūtra: The Earliest Exposition of the Buddha-nature Teaching in India*. Tokyo, International Research Institute for Advanced Buddhology: Soka University, 2002.

Zuercher, E., *The Buddhist Conquest of China: The Spread and Adaptation of Buddhism in Medieval China*. Leiden: Brill, 2007.

8

India and Southeast Asia: The Sanskrit Linkage

SATYA VRAT SHASTRI

There is wide presence of Sanskrit in the vast stretches of land going by the name of Southeast Asia with a variety of languages and dialects and sub-dialects. This is a standing testimony to the close cultural links between India and Southeast Asia.

The absorption of so much Sanskrit must have been a gradual process, spanning several centuries of acculturation. It may well be argued that language is not the only link between countries and regions. There could be, and indeed there are, other links as well, like links of ethnicity, history, religion, mythology and so on. But it is the linguistic link which is the most important, for its being the most basic one pertaining to expression, something through which an individual gives expression to their thoughts, ideas and feelings.

That Sanskrit could make such deep inroads into the languages of Southeast Asia speaks volumes for its expressiveness which must have provided the need to the speakers of these languages over the ages to adopt words from it. In the case of languages like Thai the adoption is an ongoing process. A similar phenomenon is being witnessed in the case of English in India these days which has resulted in the adoption of enormous number of words from it by Indian languages, English words having been accepted as much as the original Indian words. Their attempted translations in many cases have remained moribund with people merrily using English words even in their vernacular conversation for want of better equivalents, something that had happened in the case of Persian and Arabic words from which it had percolated, in large numbers in Indian language, in ages gone by. What is happening in the case of English, or had happened earlier in the case of Arabic and Persian in India, happened in Southeast Asia as well. Words of Sanskrit that 'migrated' from India are no longer Sanskrit words at present. They are local words now. They have been assimilated into the respective languages, given their phonological form in an overwhelming number of cases and assigned even their own meaning. This has resulted in the evolution of an interesting phenomenon of 'connect' and 'disconnect': the words do maintain some connection, however, indistinct with their originals to make their identification with them possible, yet they are not the same, having assumed a different from in accordance with the phonology of the languages into which they have been assimilated.

Once integrated into the mainstream of the respective languages, these foreign words give up their foreign tag and become part and parcel of the current coinage. To the Sanskritists of India they may be Sanskrit words, if they are *tatsams*, of the form resembling to Sanskrit or words of Sanskrit origin if they are *tadbhavas*, derived from Sanskrit. To ordinary men and women who speak the language they are the words of their own language and not words coming from any other source, words that are borrowed and assimilated. They are their words reflecting very much as they do their ethos.

In this connection I am tempted to recount my own experience. It is some two decades ago that I was going to Kuala Lumpur from Bangkok by train. I had with me the name and address of a person I was to meet there. As the train was nearing Kuala Lumpur I took out the address book. It carried the address "*Uttara Long*", Kuala Lumpur. Unable to make sure as to what *Uttara Long* was, whether it was the name of a locality or a road or a street, I enquired of the conductor of the compartment. He looked at the address book and said: *uttara* is a Malaysian word which means "north". His remark both amused and delighted me. Well, *uttara* is Malaysian. As is with *uttara*, so with other Sanskrit words. They are at present either Malaysian or Cambodian or Lao or Thai or Indonesian.

A close look at the words of Sanskrit origin of Southeast Asia reveal that some of them are sometimes more expressive and better suited being less heavy and more direct than their counterparts' in use in India. A couple of instances would bear it out. For the English word "prejudice" the Malay word is *pūrvaśaṅkā* (written as *pūrvasaṅgkā*) which in any case is a trifle more catchy that the *pūrvāgraha* of Hindi. In the same category are the words *wārtawān*, Sanskrit *vārtavān* for journalist and *beritautama*, Sanskrit *vārtāuttama* or *uttamavārtā* for headlines which are more expressive and to the point than *partrakār* and *surkhiyāṅ* (Urdu word meaning those in red) in use in Hindi. Similarly more simple and direct and certainly less heavy is the word *anekprasong*, Sanskrit *anekaprasaṅga* of Thai for multi-purpose than its Indian counterpart *bahūddeśyīya*. Other words falling in the same category are *lokasattva* of Bahasa Indonesia for animals and *dhanāgāra*, pronounced as thanǡkhān (literally meaning House of Money) of Thai for bank or *dūralekha*, pronounced as *thoralek* of Thai for telegram.

An observation that may be of interest here is that in a few languages – it is particularly relevant in the case of Thai – the Sanskrit quotient goes up with changing hierarchical order. There is more of Sanskrit among elites, the nobility, than among the common folk. For son-in-law, the Thai elites would use the word *jāmatā*, pronounced as *chāmadā*, a derivative of Sanskrit *jāmātā* while the common folk would prefer *lookkhoey*. Similarly the common word for marriage in Thai is *taengṅān* while among the elite it is *vivāhamoṅkhon*, Sanskrit *vivāhamaṅgala* or *monkhonsomrot*, Sanskrit *maṅgalasamarasa* or just *vivāha*. Added to this is the observation that the locals while adopting words from Sanskrit have not often imparted them an aesthetic look. To celebrate the 50th anniversary of the coronation of the present king the Thais used the word *kāñcanābhisek(a)* rather than the *suvarṇajayantī* of *abhiṣeka* which would have been used in India.

There is a whole lot of technical terms, educational, economic and political drawn from Sanskrit, particularly in Lao and Thai, a study of which could be revealing. They could provide a good material to a researcher in this field. For him a work like the present one could be of inestimable value. So will it be to one who wants to take up the socio-cultural study.

Sanskrit words in the languages of Southeast Asia are found in four forms: One, in their original Sanskrit form, i.e. *vipāka*, Cambodian, consequence; *āgama*, Indonesian and Malay religion; *gaja*, Indonesian, elephant; *put(e)ra*, *put(e)ri*, Indonesian, son and daughter respectively; *yāpana*, Lao, life maintenance; *yāmika*, Lao, watchman; *nāga*, Lao, a noble man; *nandī*, Lao, happiness, rejoicing; *alpa*, Malaya, careless, negligent; *dayā*, Malay, force, deceit, cunning; *aneka*, Malay many; *dāna*, Malay, charity, gift; *prārthanā*, (pronounced as prathanā, *r* is silent), Thai, desire; *velā*, Thai, time; *nālikā*, (Sanskrit *nāḍika*, *ḍ* and *l* are interchangeable in Sanskrit) Thai hour; *vivāh(a)*. Thai, marriage; Two, with negligible change in sound like the loss of final vowel, the dentalization of palatal *s* and cerebral *ś* and *n*, the *o* form of *a* (a common feature even in eastern even in eastern part of India), the *w* form of *v*, the insertion of *g* before a nasal, the deaspiration of aspirates like *bh* which is pronounced as *b* in Indonesian and Malaya or *p* and *ph* in Lao and Thai respectively, the appearance of anaptycal vowel among conjunct consonants and so on, e.g. *bhasa*. Thai and Lao, *bahasa*, Cambodian, Malay and Indonesian, *bhāṣā* language; *nayok*, Thai, *nyak*, Lao *nayaka*, chief leader; *kāy*, Cambodian, Malay and Thai, *kāya*., body; *dharmaniam*, pronounced as *dhamniam*, Thai *dharmaniyama*, a custom; *sāsana*, Thai and Lao, religion; *wanitā*, Indonesian, *vanitā*, woman; Three, with phonetic variation of Sanskrit words according to local pronunciation, e.g. *ākāt* (interestingly written as ākāsa) Thai, *aṅgkās*, Malay and Indonesian, *ākāśa*, sky, space; *khana*, Cambodian, *kṣaṇa*, moment; *khana*, Thai, *gaṇa*, group (vide *khanabody*, dean of the faculty), *dontrī*, Thai, *tantrī*, music; *phan*, lao and Thai, *bandha*, things, objects; *cuaca*, Malay, *svaccha*, clear and so on; Four, (a) in combination with another word, a synonym, a combination seemingly superfluous, carrying the same meaning for which either of the two would have sufficed, e.g. *mit(d)sahāy*, Lao and Thai, *mitrasahāya*, friend; *citacet*, Lao, *cittacetas*, mind; *kamalāg*, Lao, *kamarāga*, sexual passion; *nained*, Lao, *nayananetra*, eye; *nitinai*, Lao, *nitinaya*, by law, dejure; *phalaphon*, Lao, *phalaphala*, fruits, big and small; *vanudyān*, Lao *vanaudyāna*, forest preserve; *supamoṅggon*, Lao, *śubhamaṅgala*, good luck, welfare; Lao, *sukhaksema*, happiness; *sūnyākād*, Lao, *śūnyākāśa*, vaccum; *kulavaṅgsa*, Malay, *kulavamśa*, family; *kiyattiyot*, Thai, *kīrtiyasas*, fame (b) in combination with a synonymous Sanskrit word, the combination yielding an altogether different meaning, *hedkān*, Lao *hetukārana*, proceedings, situation event; (c) in combination with a local word, both of them meaning the same, e.g. *rāṅgkāy*, *rāṅg* = body, Thai *kāy* = *kāya*, Sanskrit, *raṅgkāy* = body, (d) in combination with a local word both having separate meanings (this category has larger number of words), e.g. *orang bisaya*, *orang*, Malay, *bisaya*, Sanskrit, *viṣaya*, a person from *śrīvijaya*, *pañcalima*, *pañca*, Sanskrit, lima, Malay, *pañcalima* = jugglery; *pelasarī*, *pela*, *phala*, Sanskrit, *sarī*, Javanese, *pelasarī*, a plant with yellow scented flowers; *bāṅgrāk*, *bāṅg*, place, Thai, *rāk*, Sanskrit, *rāga*, *bāṅgrāk* = a place for love; *namtān*, *nam*, Thai, water (extract or juice), *tāl* (prounced as tan), Sanskrit *tāla*, *namtān*=sugar; *phollomai*, *phala*, Sanskrit, *mai*, Thai, *phollomai* = fruit; *tonmai*, *ton*, Sanskrit *tarū*, *mai*, Thai, *tonmai-tree*; (e) in combination with a non-local word, wargaduniā, Malay, *warga*, *varga*, Sanskrit, *duniā*, world, Arabic, *wargaduniā*=a stateless person; *mahāmilia*, Malay, mahā, great, Sanskrit, *milia*, Arabic, *mahāmilia* = highness.

In many cases the Sanskrit words in Southeast Asian languages have undergone change in meaning. Thus in Thai *prārthanā*, already noticed, means desire; *karunā* means please; *pramān* (*pramāna*) means approximately; *viniccaya*, Sanskrit *viniścaya* in Cambodian means, judgement; *kaṣīṇa āyu*, Sanskrit *kṣīṇa āyu*, in Lao means one who is eighteen year or over eighteen years old; *bītha*, Sanskrit *pītha*, in Lao means to hurt, to kill, *saṅgketa* in Lao means agreement, condition; *cercā*, Sanskrit *carcā* in Malay means abuse, *saṅg kat*, Sanskrit *saṅgata* in Lao means similar; comparable, *saṅgked*, Sanskrit *sanketa*, means abuse, revile; *nāḍī*, Sanskrit the same, in Malay means wrist; *peribhāsā*, Sanskrit *paribhāṣā*, in Malay means proverb, idiom; *remaja*, Sanskrit *ramya*, in Malay means adolescent, youth; *perwara*, Sanskrit *pravara*, in Malay means court damsel; *laksamana*, Sanskrit *lakṣmaṇa*, in Malay means a naval admiral, *ajita*, Sanskrit the same, in Indonesian means undependable; *anartha*, Sanskrit the same, in Indonesian means, poor, needy; *asvāsa*, Sanskrit *āśvasa*, in Indonesian means whiteness; *cāmara*, Sanskrit the same, in Indonesian means, bull, male cow; *candāla*, Sanskrit the same, Indonesian means a person in exile; *sāmanta*, Sanskrit the same, in Indonesian means neighbor; *sārathi*, Sanskrit the same, in Indonesian means, vehicle, carriage; *svāhā*, Sanskrit the same, in Indonesian means heaven; *pāpa*, Sanskrit the same, in Indonesian means, difficulty, bad luck; *pradātā*, Sanskrit the same, in Indonesian means, judge, lawyer, server of justice; *prajā*, Sanskrit the same, in Indonesian means grandchild; *pratāpa*, Sanskrit the same, in Indonesian means discussion, negotiation; *sampāna*, Sanskrit *sopāna*, in Balinese (Indonesian) means high wall, barricade.

From what has been stated above it should be clear that Sanskrit is one of the strongest of the links between India and the ASEAN, and the people who have owned it and made it an inseparable part of their vocabulary. It is not something that belongs only to the past. In the Royal Institute of Thailand in Bangkok, scholars are busy exploring Sanskrit for its potential for coining new words for new objects and ideas. These are all Thai scholars who have devoted their lifetime to the study of Sanskrit, a few of whom are involved with the Sanskrit study centre, set up in Bangkok not too long back, and the only one of its kind in the whole of Southeast Asia.

The names of cities, towns, villages, roads, lanes, squares, buildings, shops and offices, Government and private, hills and mountains and the name of individuals, both male and female and practically everything (from the human, animal and plant life), which are based on Sanskrit, run into legions providing evidence, if ever that was to be needed, of the strong bonds that Sanskrit, one of the most ancient and the proudest of the heritage of India, has forged between the people of India and the ASEAN.

9

The Depiction of the Avalokiteśvara in Vietnamese Buddhism

NGUYEN NGOC QUYNH

FEMININE CHARACTERISTIC OF VIETNAMESE BUDDHISM

The Buddhist culture is an important part of Oriental culture. It is also the main content of the Vietnamese religious culture. Buddhism in Vietnam has its own characteristics, which are easily perceptible to any one who visits the country. The most noticeable characteristic is the existence of Goddesses in Vietnamese Buddhism.

Vietnam is located in Southeast Asia. From early times, it had got its own cultures of wet-rice cultivation. This culture pays more attention to fecundity and women are representatives of that characteristic. Thus worship of Goddesses is understandable. Furthermore, it can be said that the most ancient belief that appeared in Vietnam is the worship of the goddesses.

Because of its geographical position, Vietnam was influenced by two great cultures, India and China, at different historical stages by various means. Indian culture was brought to Vietnam by traders and missionaries. It came and stayed peacefully in daily life of the Vietnamese people. Facing these two cultures, Vietnam had different ways of receiving and localizing them. The most perceptible and special feature is in the field of religious beliefs of the common people. Indian Buddhism came to Vietnam and after it mixed with indigenous faith in goddesses, belief in "Tu phap" (Four Dharmas: Cloud, Rain, Thunder and Lightning) appeared. This belief can be said to be the result of the acculturation and localization reflected via cultural exchanges between India and Vietnam.

After over 1,000 years of domination, China also did leave many traces in Vietnamese religions. Vietnamese Buddhism is under great influence of Chinese – Han Buddhism. Vietnamese Buddhism is, however, different from Chinese Buddhism because of the existence of many indigenous goddesses on its pantheon and full of traits of folk beliefs.

Like many other peoples in the world, there existed the faith in great Mother or Goddesses in Vietnam of ancient times. However, despite the growing influence of the patriarchal ideology, the faith in Mother and Goddesses has always been maintained along with national history. Because the role of women has been dignified so the worship of Avalokiteśvara has been accepted and popularized widely in the agricultural countries.

THE WORSHIP OF AVALOKITEŚVARA IN VIETNAM

It is believed that Buddhism came into Vietnam quite early, at around the commencement of the Common Era. Since Buddhism entered Vietnam directly from India, Theravada Buddhism was more prevalent in those days. However later, in the fourth-fifth centuries, Mahayana Buddhism became more popular due to Vietnam's proximity to China. Buddhism, in Vietnam, progressed rapidly during the reigns of the Ly (1009-1225 CE) and Tran Dynasty (1225-1400 CE). During this period Buddhism attained the status of state religion. However, the succeeding period in which Vietnam was ruled by the Le Dynasty (1428-1527 CE), Buddhism suffered a setback with the emergence of Confucianism.

The most striking feature of Buddhism in Vietnam is the integration of Buddhist, Taoist and Confucian traditions. The religion reflects the rituals, beliefs and notions of all the three faiths in a balanced manner. Also, the two step development of Mahayana and Theravada Buddhism in the country is a defining feature. The two schools are representative of the two different forms of influences, one from India and the other one from China.

Avalokiteśvara ("Lord who looks down") is a Bodhisattva who embodies the compassion of all Buddhas. She is one of the more widely revered Bodhisattvas in mainstream Mahayana Buddhism. The original name for this Bodhisattva was *Avalokiteśvara*. The Chinese name for Avalokiteśvara is *Guānshìyīn Púsà* 觀世音菩薩, which is a translation of the earlier name "Avalokiteśvara Bodhisattva." This Bodhisattva is variably depicted as male or female, and may also be referred to simply as *Guānyīn*. In Sanskrit, Avalokiteśvara is also referred to as *Padmapāni* ("Holder of the Lotus") or *Lokeśvara* ("Lord of the World"). In Cambodia, this Bodhisattva is called *Lokesvara*; in China and in Vietnam she is called *Guan Yin*; in Japan, her name is *Kanon* or *Kazeon*; in Sri Lanka, she is called Lokanatha. From among Vietnam, Laos and Cambodia, Mahayana Buddhism is popular only in Vietnam. Despite the fact that Indian Theravada came to Vietnam first. Meanwhile, Buddhism in Vietnam is mainly Mahayana brought from China. Belief in Bodhisattva is the main focus of Buddhism in both China and Vietnam. Among beliefs in Bodhisattva, the most popular form is the practice of Guan Yin (Avalokiteśvara) worship.

In Thailand, Cambodia and Japan, statue of Avalokiteśvara sometimes has mannish figure, sometimes has a female one. In Vietnam and in China the statue of Avalokiteśvara has a female figure.

Avalokiteśvara is one of four great Bodhisattvas. Avalokiteśvara has various statues and names. The image of Avalokiteśvara is very close to Vietnamese people and Avalokiteśvara is worshipped in many Asian countries. In each country, the image of Avalokiteśvara has its special features to adapt to native cultural tradition. When entering in Vietnam, the image of Avalokiteśvara (Goddess of Mercy) was totally transformed into the image of a female god. The Vietnamese believe that Avalokiteśvara is a benevolent goddess. There are many types of Avalokiteśvara statues in Vietnam temples.

According to writer Nguyen Duy Hinh: "Avalokiteśvara as well as other Bodhisattvas who have multi-arms were influenced by Hinduism. The influence began to emerge from 4th century to 8th century. At that time Hinduism developed powerfully the kind of statue with multi-eyes and arms was born on the basis of dancing – statues of Siva belief. Not only Avalokiteśvara has multi-eyes and arms but many deities of Buddhism have multi-eyes and arms to show their supreme power."

According to Vietnamese people, Avalokiteśvara is at the head of other Bodhisattvas in relieving sufferings and misfortunes particularly of women and children. In Vietnam, there are two Buddhist sects which respect Avalokiteśvara. They are the Pure Land and Mantrayana.

The Pure Land sect advocates outside force. When the believers of this sect pray to Avalokiteśvara for help, they only pray to her name. Many the Northern and Central Buddhist temples follow the Pure Land sect. The statue of Avalokiteśvara that is worshiped in the Northern and Central Buddhist temples are the statue of the Amitabha trinity including Amitabha trinity (in the middle), Avalokiteśvara (on the left side) and Mahasthamaprapta (on the right side). Avalokiteśvara and Mahasthamaprata manifest mercifulness and intelligence of Amitabha. On behalf of Amitabha, Avalokiteśvara preaches Buddhist law and comes to the aid of all people.

Thanks to Buddhist prayers we know that Avalokiteśvara are present everywhere to save and come to the aid of all people. Avalokiteśvara herself can change into various shapes. She has 500 various names and 33 shapes so there are many statues of Avalokiteśvara.

The Mantrayana sect has serious regulations. According to prayers of Mantrayana, there are seven images of Avalokiteśvara:

- Arya Avalokiteśvara
- Ekadasa Mukha Avalokiteśvara
- Amoghapasa Avalokiteśvara
- Sahasrabhuja Avalokiteśvara
- Hayagriva Avalokiteśvara
- Cinatamini-cakra Avalokiteśvara
- Cundī Avalokiteśvara

Vietnamese Buddhist temples worship various statues of Avalokiteśvara. Some Buddhist temples worship a single statue of Avalokiteśvara. However, other temples worship many statues of Avalokiteśvara. The statues of Avalokiteśvara which are worshipped in many Buddhist temples are statues of Cundī-Avalokiteśvara, of Avalokiteśvara holding her baby; of Avalokiteśvara with a thousand – hands and a thousand – eyes. . . . In recent years, in the Northern and in Southern Buddhist temples there are the statues of Avalokiteśvara of the South Sea.

In plastic art, the statue of Avalokiteśvara is a combination of Chinese and Indian sculptures. These sculptures harmonize with cultural traditions in Vietnam so the statue of Avalokiteśvara is close to Vietnamese people's thought.

SOME IMAGES OF AVALOKITEŚVARA UNDER THE INFLUENCE OF VIETNAMESE POPULAR CULTURE

The mercifulness of Avalokiteśvara corresponds with religious spirit of Vietnamese people particularly Vietnamese women. It is mainly Vietnamese women who take part in activities in Buddhist temples. The female characteristic of Vietnamese agricultural culture also influences the image of Avalokiteśvara in Vietnamese Buddhist temple. So Avalokiteśvara is worshipped in almost all Vietnamese Buddhist temples. The following statues of Avalokiteśvara are influenced by Vietnamese popular culture:

******The statue of Avalokiteśvara holding a baby*. It is called *Quan am tong tu.*

According to folk tale *Thi Kinh* was a good natured woman. Because of misunderstanding, she became the victim of her husband's unfounded suspicion. She then dressed in disguise as a man called *Kinh Tam* and entered monkhood at a temple. A girl named *Thi Mau* fell in love with *Kinh Tam*, but was rebuffed resolutely. Later on, *Thi Mau* abandoned her baby born out of wedlock at the temple claiming that *Thi Kinh* was the father of the child. *Thi Kinh* endured all indignities, looked after the child and finally became Avalokiteśvara. The statue of *Thi Kinh* depicts a fine woman carrying a child with a parrot by her side. The parrot is the reincarnation of her husband.

Some researchers think that the statue of *Quan Am Thi Kinh* is influenced by a fairy tale of Korea. The statue of *Quan Am Thi Kinh* is worshipped in many Vietnamese Buddhist temples.

**Hư'o'ng Pagoda (Perfume Pagoda) Avalokiteśvara*

Huong Pagoda Avalokiteśvara is a well-known Avalokiteśvara in the system of Avalokiteśvaras. She was a princess of King Dieu Trang Vuong. She left honour and wealth to become a nun. Then she became a Buddha in Huong Tich Cavern.

In Huong Tich Cavern there are stalactites with special shapes. Many people believe that when they pray for help of Avalokiteśvara, they should rub on stalactites and pray. *Huong pagoda* (Perfume Pagoda) is where people pray for child. That is why so many people go to Huong pagoda.

These two stories of Avalokiteśvara are popular in Vietnam. Through two stories we can find that Vietnamese people were open to Avalokiteśvara's belief and image. In Vietnam Avalokiteśvara's belief and image were changed in accordance with Vietnamese society. In the process of historical changes there were some Avalokiteśvaras who had Vietnamese characteristics. These Avalokiteśvaras were believed to be born in Vietnam and defended the holy rights of the nation.

** The worship of Avalokiteśvara outside Buddhist temple*

The statue of Avalokiteśvara is not only worshipped in Buddhist temples but also in the altar of the family. The worship of Avalokiteśvara is a more popular phenomena. In the present conditions, as economic life is developing so spiritual need is increasing more and more. Many rich families build shrines for worshipping Avalokiteśvara in their precincts. Some families worship Avalokiteśvara in their ancestral altars but in the highest place. We can also see many great statues of Avalokiteśvara in public places.

CONCLUSION

It is a well-known fact that belief in Bodhisattva is the main feature of Buddhism in both China and Vietnam. Among such beliefs, the most popular form is the practice of Avalokiteśvara worship in both the countries. It is noticeable that in Vietnam, the depiction of the image of Avalokiteśvara is somewhat changed into the image of a female goddess since the Vietnamese believe that Avalokiteśvara is a benevolent goddess. In Vietnamese temples the images of Avalokiteśvara have been depicted in many forms. Some of these images of Avalokiteśvara have been changed under the effect of Vietnamese traditional culture. In Vietnam one finds that some of the images of Avalokiteśvara holding a baby are called "*Quan Âm tống tử*" or "*Quan Âm Thị Kính*". Thus we find that in the process of historical changes the images of some of the Avalokiteśvaras have been influenced by the culture of Vietnam and have also been endowed with the Vietnamese characteristics. These Avalokiteśvaras were believed to be born in Vietnam and defended the holy rights of nation.

The image of Avalokiteśvara is presented in folk literature of Vietnamese people to dignify female feature. It is a special characteristic of Vietnamese Buddhism. In plastic arts, many researchers think that the image of Avalokiteśvara in Vietnam accepted some elements of Indian deities. Through Champa culture and the standards of plastic arts of China, the image of Avalokiteśvara has changed and been created to harmonize with Vietnamese culture.

At present, the image of Avalokiteśvara is worshipped in Vietnamese Buddhist temples as well as in altars of some Vietnamese families. The worship of Avalokiteśvara becomes popular because Vietnamese people believe in her power of saving humans from sufferings and misfortunes. The worship of Avalokiteśvara is not only popular in Vietnam but also in many Asian countries. In Vietnam, the image of Avalokiteśvara has changed to correspond with Vietnamese people's mind. The worship of Avalokiteśvara always harmonizes with Vietnamese customs and belief and especially dignifies female features.

WORKS CITED

Chu Quang Chú. *Vietnam's Ancient Statues with Ethnic Tradition of Sculpture.* Np: Arts Publishing House, 2001.

Thích Viên Đúc (translated). *Tantricism.* Ho Chi Minh: Ho Chi Minh City Publishing House, 1996.

Trang Thanh Hiến. *The Image of Thousand-armed and Thousand-eyed Guan-yin in Việt Nam.* Hanoi: Culture and information Publishing House, 2005, 27.

Nguyễn Minh Ngọc, Nguyễn Mạnh Curòng, Nguyễn Duy Hinh. *Avalokiteśvara Bodhisattva in pagodas in the Red River Delta region.* Hanoi: Social Sciences Publishing House, nd., 474.

Nguyễn Duy Hinh. *Thought of Vietnamese Buddhism.* Hanoi: Social Sciences Publishing House, 1999.

———. *Philosophy of Vietnamese Buddhism.* Hanoi: Culture and Information Publishing House, 2006.

Hồ ngọc Liên. 'Multi armed Bodhisattva's statue in Vietnam Museum of History in Ho Chi Minh City'. *Journal of Arts and Culture,* No. 2, 2003.

Bá Trung Phụng. 'Lokesvara's Image in Cham Sculptural Art'. *Journal of Religious Studies,* No. 6, 2006.

Viên Trí. *Concept of Avalokiteśvara Bodhisattva.* Hanoi: Religion Publishing House, 2003.

PART 3

Travelling Texts, Histories, Culture

10

The Significance of Vietnam-India Cultural Exchanges for India-ASEAN Development

VO VAN SEN

Dating back to thousands of years, the relationship between India and Southeast Asia has been thriving with the passage of time. Especially in the new millennium, India's Look-East policy, as a civilizational and cultural link, proves to be a solid bridge in connecting India and Southeast Asia.

The exchanges of cultures and dialogues amongst civilizations help to foster the implementation of feasible strategies for the development of Indian Studies communities, to navigate research orientation and to assess and evaluate the current status of this relationship. Typically, activities of Vietnam-India cultural exchange and civilizational dialogues firmly contribute to cementing the bond within Asia, by improving cross-cultural communication skills, by an inter-civilizational engagement to consolidate familiarity of local customs, by sharpening the ability to adapt and be flexible to new circumstances, by constructively coping and dealing with differences and by enhancing transnational competencies.

THE RELATIONSHIP BETWEEN INDIA AND SOUTHEAST ASIA FROM TIME IMMEMORIAL – A BRIEF HISTORY OF INDIAN-ASEAN RELATION EVOLUTION FROM A WIDE VARIETY OF ASPECTS

Throughout the course of history, cultural exchanges and cultural acculturation have been an integral part in the history of mankind, in the development of interaction, dialogues and cooperation. In fact, India has had cultural ties with Southeast Asia since ancient times. Typical of many ancient Indian classical works was *Ramayana* which strongly referred to Southeast Asia. As one of the most important works of ancient India which became popular in Southeast Asia during the eighth century and was represented in literature, temple architecture, dance and theatre, the *Ramayana* has exerted profound impact on art and culture in Southeast Asia. Moreover:

> Indian notions of divinity, cosmology, administration, law and kingship blended with local cultures and enriched local civilization can still be seen today. Great temple complexes

of Asia filled with carvings and inscriptions reflecting India's reach, the walls of Cambodia's Angkor Thom enlivened by Panoramic battle scenes from the Ramayana or Indonesia's great spriraling temple – Borobodur – ringed with the vivid scenes from the life of Buddha, affirm the unmistakable existence of Indian influences to the development of Asian nations.[1]

To add:

Indonesia's shadow-puppet theater features all-night performances of Indian epics. Even modern places and institutions preserve Indian names and symbols. The name "Singapore" comes from the Sanskrit simha (lion) and pura (city).[...]Names like Indochina and Indonesia incorporate an Indian root. Indonesia's national airline is named for Garuda, the sacred bird that carried the god Vishnu.[2]

As for Buddhism, Buddha's teachings spread far and wide on the Indian subcontinent and from there throughout Asia. At present, however, two major forms survive: one Hinayana, known as Theravada, in Southeast Asia, and two Mahayana, namely the Chinese and Tibetan traditions. The Theravada tradition spread from India to Sri Lanka and Burma in the third BCE, and from there to Yunnan in southwest China, Thailand, Laos, Cambodia, South Vietnam and Indonesia. The Chinese form of Mahayana later spread to Korea, Japan and North Vietnam. Another early wave of Mahayana, mixed with Shaivite forms of Hinduism, spread from India to Nepal, Indonesia, Malaysia and parts of Southeast Asia starting in about the fifth century.

Demand for Eastern goods also had the effect of stimulating Indian trading along the Malay Peninsula,[3] which helped to spread Indian cultures in that area, and in return, was affected by native culture. As an outcome, one of the greatest phenomena was "Indianization and de-Indianization". Indianization can be regarded as an Indian initiative with large-scale migrants setting up and forming colonies in Southeast Asia, bringing with them original cultural features and making significant social changes. Indian interests in Southeast Asia increased when India and China began to trade with each other in the second century BCE. Indian merchants searched for a water route, and they found it in Southeast Asia's seas. The trip through the Malacca Strait between Malaya and Sumatra was the quickest and easiest way to travel between Asia's two main centers of civilization and the expansion of Hinduism in Southeast Asia soon took place. Indeed, from about the first century CE, India started to strongly influence Southeast Asian countries. Thanks to Indian merchants, Hinduism and Buddhism were introduced into Southeast Asia via the sea route.

The historical ties between India and Southeast Asia are rooted in the maritime contacts across the Indian Ocean and the Malacca Strait, which date back to thousands of years.[4]

For more than a thousand years, Indian Hindu/Buddhist influence was therefore the major factor that brought a certain level of cultural unity to the various countries of the region. From the fifth to the thirteenth century, Southeast Asia had very powerful Indian colonial empires and became extremely active in Buddhist architectural and artistic creation. Basically, de-Indianization was a peaceful process as it did not take place in political and military expansion, but mainly through commerce and religion. Therefore, de-Indianization in Asia was a process of localization with normal cultural exchanges. Throughout history, Indianization and de-Indianization enriched cultures from nations in South Asia, especially Southeast Asia. Singapore's former Foreign Minister and Deputy Prime Minister Professor S. Jayakumar emphasized the cultural dimension in Indo-Singapore and India-ASEAN relations when he said:

> In our cooperation with each other, we are fortunate to enjoy close historical and cultural ties. This promotes mutual trust and confidence, which makes for good rapport between our peoples. As we focus on developing economic and political links, it is important that we continue to strengthen our cultural links.[5]

A BRIEF LOOK AT THE DEVELOPMENT HISTORY OF MAJOR ASEAN-INDIA COOPERATION PROGRAMS

The Mekong River not only connects the countries it borders but also constructs a subregion having a lot in common, which enables cooperation in virtually all fields such as economy, culture, foreign policy, social issues, education, etc. In today's globalized world, Southeast Asian countries find it both a challenge and an opportunity for the sustained growth of India's economy and its increasing competitiveness.[6] Therefore, generating investments in education and technology transfers between India and Mekong countries, to share development experiences, will ultimately strengthen capacities in Mekong countries and enhance India-ASEAN solidarity.

In the words of honourable Manmohan Singh, the Indian Prime Minister:

> I reiterate India's commitment to work with ASEAN and other East Asian countries to make the 21st century truly an Asian century.[7]

have been truly justified by some of the landmark developments between India and ASEAN as follows.

In November 2004, at the Vientiane summit, the documents 'ASEAN-India Partnership for Peace, Progress and shared Prosperity', and 'Plan of Action to Implement the ASEAN-India partnership for Peace, Progress and shared Prosperity' were signed. In October 2003, at the Bali summit, 'the Framework Agreement on Comprehensive Economic Cooperation between ASEAN and India' was signed. In the ministerial meeting of the Mekong river – the Ganges in 28 July 2001 in Hanoi, Vietnam, the six ministers from Cambodia, India, Laos, Myanmar, Thailand and Vietnam signed a landmark document of the relationship in this area 'Action Plan on cooperation Mekong-Ganga' which was triggered by specific action plans in such fields as culture, education, economy, transport etc. In the education realm, the Mekong-Ganga focused on the promotion of education linkages in all aspects such as distance education, information technology applications to increase and enhance capacity building in key areas of electronic industry and research, planning, education as well as foreign language training. In the year 2000, India, Thailand, Laos, Cambodia, Myanmar and Vietnam signed an agreement in Vientiane to form the Mekong Ganga Cooperation. In 1995, ASEAN at the Bangkok summit of Full Dialogue Partnership the connection with India was announced.

LOOK-EAST POLICY

India, a vast sub-continent in South Asia, is a fast emerging economic and political force to be taken into thorough consideration. In this light, Indian leadership came up with a concept of ideas which is then called India's "Look-East Policy" [Eric Koo Peng Kuan 2011], which accurately justified the words of Indian Prime Minister Dr. Manmohan Singh

> I believe that the East Asian Community is a natural extension of the ASEAN-India engagement process.[8]

If his words prove to be true and for India's Look-East Policy is to bear fruit, then India must act East!

To begin with, a dynamic economic policy of commitment, with Southeast Asia was carried on which sought to promote trade links with individual partners and then provide foreign employment for India's own expanding work force. For this purpose, India's Look-East Policy was launched in 1992 just after the end of the Cold War, which was a strategic policy decision made by the government of India in its policy of foreign affairs. Thanks to the formulation of the Look-East Policy, this region's significance has been given more weight.

> It was also a strategic shift in India's vision of the world and India's place in the evolving global economy (Prime Minister Manmohan Singh).

Therefore, the birth of this Policy was a turning point in India's foreign relations. The Look-East Policy has been given a significant push from the turn of the twenty-first century. India's search for a new fresh look in the relationship with Southeast Asia is no longer encouraged by the globalization phenomenon, but rather to facilitate development by increasing its connectivity to the world of Southeast Asia. Since the time of adoption of the Look-East Policy, India and ASEAN, with an interdisciplinary approach, have embarked upon multiple bilateral, regional initiatives for the flourishing pursuit of the Look-East Policy, which so far has made great strides and achieved impressive outcomes.

In the economic area, for example, India has many ties with countries such as Singapore, Malaysia, Thailand, Indonesia, and the Philippines. Adopting key strategies to strengthen the commercial trade in Cambodia, Myanmar, Laos and Vietnam would allow ASEAN-India trade to take off. In this context, Vietnam will become a focal attention in the Look-East Policy, first of all by a long tradition of friendly relations between the two countries, and then, by promising a long-term partnership. The Indian Prime Minister Manmohan Singh said:

> In India's Policy, in order to promote regional integration, India pays special attention to Cambodia, Laos, Myanmar and Vietnam. India considered the cooperation with Vietnam an important role in the process of integration into the region.

MEKONG-GANGA PROJECT

The Mekong-Ganga Cooperation was launched with the Vientiane Declaration on 10 November 2000 in the capital city of Laos, Vientiane with the primary thrust to expand solidarity, harmony and cooperation in all sectors, especially tourism, culture and education for the purpose of rapid social and economic development of India as well as Mekong countries. The notion of the Project was first proposed by Thailand's Foreign Minister Dr. S. Pitsuwan.[9] Since the Ganga and the Mekong are considered two of the greatest rivers in Asia, creating and nurturing a strong linkage between the two civilizations is a great need with the additional goal to publicize the determination to solidify the bonds between India and the Mekong countries.

With the help of the Mekong-Ganga Cooperation, joint research in various fields has been promoted, gatherings for experts have been held in literature, performing arts, women's empowerment, health and nutrition and the conservation, preservation and protection of heritage sites and artifacts. The Mekong Ganga Cooperation Project also encourages the establishment of networking and arrangements among universities in the region for diversified cooperative programs such as translation of classics of Mekong Ganga Countries into other Mekong region languages, etc.

GREATER MEKONG SUBREGION

Since 1992, six countries in the Greater Mekong Subregion (GMS) – Cambodia, PRC, Lao PDR, Myanmar, Thailand, and Vietnam, participated in a comprehensive program of economic cooperation including transport, energy, telecommunications, resource development, resource management and environment, trade facilitation, private investment, tourism and agriculture.

The aim of the Greater Mekong Subregion Program is to help create significant benefits for the countries sharing the Mekong River. The opportunities and economic growth lie in the three goals, i.e. poverty reduction through sustained and equitable economic growth, sustainable management of shared environmental resources, and nurturing human and social capital for sustainable development and MDG (Millennium Development Goals).[10] The effective integration and connectivity between the economies and sub-region will provide solid potential to broaden interests in the all-round economic resurgence of Asia. Also with the Greater Mekong Subregion Program, India is fast penetrating ASEAN markets by enhancing mutual economic benefits, keeping up with the development of transportation as well as infrastructure, etc.

VIETNAM AND INDIA IN THEIR ENDEAVOURS TO FOSTER THE RELATIONSHIP

Vietnam and India hold a traditional friendly long-standing relationship which thrives in every page of history. These relations are said to have been formulated about 2,000 years ago with the arrival of Buddhism brought in by the Chinese people, and of Hinduism by the Indian people [Geetesh Sharma, 2006]. At that time, Indians from the South also came to Vietnam for commercial purpose. These events are still engraved in Vietnamese stories, folk tales and historical records. In addition, Cham people in MySon, in central Vietnam claim to be descendants of Indian ancestors. They migrated to the central of Vietnam to settle down and built government mechanism for their kingdom of Champa from the second to fifteenth centuries. As early as the first century BCE, Vietnam and India began their commercial activities.

India's influence today can still be clearly seen in literature, religion, philosophy, art and architecture in Vietnam, in which Cham Tower is one of the most typical examples. However, from 111 BCE to 938 CE, for over 10 centuries, Vietnam was dominated by Chinese feudalism. This period saw the process of strong Sinicization and de-Sinicization in the history of Vietnam. To successfully escape from the assimilation plot of Han Hegemonism, the Vietnamese people cleverly based themselves on two factors: preservation and strengthening of their Van Lang – Au Lac cultural identities; simultaneously, a reception of the best in Indian culture.

Indianization process took place in peace as a normal cultural exchange. Representing the profound penetration of Indian culture was the deep taking-on of Buddhism (including by way of communication through China and directly from India to Northern Vietnam), taking India as firm foundation for the realization of "Tam giao dong quy" – the combination of the three religions Buddhism, Confucianism and Taoism in Vietnamese culture. The process of Indianization – deindianization in Vietnam can be said to be one of the decisive bases for Vietnam to fully get rid of Chinese assimilation! **In** the two wars against France and America, the Vietnamese people always got whole-hearted support from India.

Vietnam also consistently supports India's stance. During the Cold War, the friendship between India and Vietnam stood the test of time, being not only the outcome but also the driving force directly contributing to the friendly relations between India and Soviet and socialist China – a relationship which backed the geopolitical balance of India in a bipolar world order. Vietnam always supported India's point of view for unification, recognized Kashmir[11] as a division of Indian territory, supporting India to become a standing member of the United Nations Security Council. Vietnam and India shared the views on issues of regional and international scales with geostrategic interests throughout historical periods being consistent with each other, which is the profound foundation for sustainable relations between the two peoples.

The period from early 1990s up to now, after the socialist regime in the Soviet Union collapsed, the Cold War ended, and the new world order was forming, India has implemented the Look-East Policy (from New Zealand to Southeast Asia up to Northern Asia). As India's strategic partner from the beginning of the Cold War to now, Vietnam actively supports the successful implementation of India's Look-East Policy.

The full diplomatic relations between Vietnam and India, established on 7 January 1972,[12] have covered many major strategic areas, based on mutual trust and confidence. India is committed to promoting mutually beneficial cooperation in varied areas from military training, military medicine to English training and from cultural activities to senior officer exchanges. Now moving forward from their respective ideological linkages, both countries are endeavoring to refurbish their relations according to the requirements of economic globalization. India and Vietnam are members of the Mekong-Ganga Cooperation. Moreover, Vietnam actively builds positive partnerships between India and the Mekong sub-region countries such as Myanmar, Thailand and Cambodia, Laos and Vietnam to focus on tourism, culture, education and communication. The scope can be expanded to industrial, commercial and economic cooperation. The importance of Vietnam in Southeast Asia dramatically increases in terms of strategy as well as economy. Vietnam seems well poised to emerge as the new economic hub of Asia-Pacific region to attract investors from other nations. Therefore, India needs to exploit its traditional relationship with Vietnam to further increase trade in the region. To this end, Vietnam backs the important relationship and role between India and the Association of Southeast Asian Nations (ASEAN) and its negotiation of an Indo-ASEAN free trade agreement. Vietnam also supports India in its peaceful use of nuclear energy, and backs India's bid for a permanent candidature in an expanded United Nations Security Council. In return, Vietnam received India's support for entry into the World Trade Organization. Vietnam and

India work closely together in organizations like ASEAN, and Mekong-Ganga Cooperation (MGC) and Vietnam are also expected to help India in gaining membership of organizations like Asia Pacific Economic Cooperation (APEC) and Asia Europe Meetings (ASEM).[13]

Vietnam and India have always enjoyed good political relations and exchanged many high-level visits. For example, President Rajendra Prasad visited Vietnam in 1959. Subsequent visits were paid by Prime Minister Rajiv Gandhi (1985, 1988), President R. Venkataraman (1991), etc. Most recently, in the meeting between Vietnamese Prime Minister Nguyen Tan Dung and E. Ahamed, Indian Minister of State for the Indian Ministry of External Affairs and Human Resources Development during his visit to Vietnam on 6 January 2012,[14] E. Ahamed confirmed that

> India stands committed to forging closer relations with Vietnam both bilaterally and within the framework of ASEAN as part of the 'Look East Policy' of Indian Government. Indeed, Vietnam is a critical pillar of this strategy. Vietnam's membership of ASEAN has added a new and important dimension to the two sides' relationship. The two countries enjoy a strategic understanding at regional and multilateral forums, including ASEAN, East Asia Summit, ASEM, ARF and international organizations like WTO and UN. As two developing countries with a young dynamic population's stake in the future, Vietnam and India should take advantage of the bilateral synergies to jointly face emerging challenges and also to exploit new opportunities.

The last forty years have witnessed successful diplomatic relations between the Socialist Republic of Vietnam and the Republic of India. Over these past forty years, the relation between the two countries has steadily strengthened and achieved remarkable outcomes in various areas such as politics and foreign affairs, economic relation and commercial exchanges, cultural and educational exchanges. In reality, the relationship and cooperation between Vietnam and India strongly developed in various fields as both nations show high appreciation and determination to bring the bilateral relationship and comprehensive cooperation to a new height with stability and sustainability in the interests of the two peoples and for the sake of peace, stability, cooperation and development. The relations between the two countries, especially on defence ties, benefited extensively from India's Look-East Policy.[15] Bilateral military cooperation includes sale of military equipment, sharing of intelligence, joint naval exercises and training in counterinsurgency and jungle warfare.[16] India is helping Vietnam to build capacity for repair and maintenance of its defence platforms. In this strategic partnership, Vietnam and India extensively cooperate on developing *nuclear power*, enhancing regional security and fighting *terrorism*, transnational crime and *drug trafficking*. A professor of Defence studies at King's College, London – Professor Harsh V. Pant stated in his paper, *The India-Vietnam Axis*[17] that:

> The two nations also have stakes in ensuring sea-lane security.... Naval cooperation,

however, remains the focus. Vietnam has given India the right to use its port of Nha Trang in the south, and the Indian Navy has already made a port call.

So far, the two countries have signed various important bilateral treaties and agreements such as Trade Agreement, Bilateral Investment Promotion and Protection, Avoidance of Double Taxation Agreement, Consular Agreement, Culture Agreement, Tourism, Air Service, Agreement on Cooperation in Science & Technology. In addition, the two sides have also concluded many other MOUs in specialized sectors.

Hence, bilateral relations between the two nations have been constantly consolidated and developed in almost all areas, harvesting positive outcomes and encouraging achievements. In fact, the relationship has developed into multifaceted phase, spanning over diverse areas. In a globalized and integrated world, these bilateral relations guide the way towards economic growth and prosperity for both countries, and are therefore elevated to the level of a strategic partnership through closer engagement and stronger commitment.

THE FOLLOWINGS ARE SOME OF THE TYPICAL SUCCESSFUL COOPERATIVE ACTIVITIES BETWEEN VIETNAM AND INDIA

The two countries established the India-Vietnam Joint Commission for Economic, Scientific & Technical Cooperation on 18 December 1982. This is a very important mechanism for the two sides to review and promote cooperation in all fields, including the formulation of an Action Plan for every three years.

In the economic linkages, bilateral trade has increased rapidly since the liberalization of the economies of both Vietnam and India.[18] India is the 13th-largest exporter to Vietnam, with exports have grown steadily from US $11.5 million in 1985-6 to US $395.68 million by 2003.[19] Vietnam's exports to India rose to US $180 million, including agricultural products, handicrafts, textiles, electronics and other goods.[20] The list of major Indian export basket to Vietnam includes animal feed, pharmaceuticals, medicinal materials, plastic, iron and steel, seafood chemicals, chemical products, machinery and equipment, leather and leather garments, motorcycle parts, fertilizers, and automobile parts. Between 2001 and 2006, the volume of bilateral trade expanded at 20-30 percent per annum to reach US $1 billion by 2006.[21] Continuing the rapid pace of growth, bilateral trade is expected to rise to US $2 billion by 2008, two years ahead of the official target.[22] In 2010, bilateral trade exceeded US $2.7 billion, reaching US $2.38 billion for the period of January-August 2011, an increase of 43 percent over the corresponding period in 2010. The two countries have set a bilateral trade target of US $7 billion by 2015. Indian companies have invested in oil and gas, steel, spices, pharmaceuticals, edible oil, steel furniture, sugar, plastics, coffee, consumer products and other sectors.

In his paper 'India-Vietnam Strategic Partnership: The Convergence of Interests', Dr. Subhash Kapila clearly stated that:

> India and Vietnam are both geostrategically important countries, vital to all major nations [.....] Vietnam is strongly placed to help India in the energy sector both in terms of oil supplies and further joint prospecting for oil and gas. India has adequate experience in oil and gas prospecting, especially in offshore deposits.

There are about 35 representative offices of Indian pharmaceutical companies here, and about 50 other representative offices in many areas in Vietnam in various sectors, including agriculture, rubber, coffee, cashew nut, carbon black and tea. Particularly, India is undertaking a US $5 billion steel plant project by Tata Steel in the northern province of Ha Tinh.

India's FDI to Vietnam was 580 million US $ in 2006. There are significant changes in Indian direct investment to Vietnam in 2007 with Essar Group signing an MOU in January 2007 for setting up a hot rolling steel mill worth 527 million US $ in Ba Ria-Vung Tau and Tata Steel signing an MOU to set up a steel complex in Thach Khe-Ha Tinh with estimated investment of US $3.5 billion. These projects make India among top-10 investors in Vietnam and Vietnam as the biggest receiver of Indian direct investment in ASEAN.

As far as defence is concerned, the cooperation is one of the key points of the strategic partnership and has significantly developed in a multilateral manner. In the security arena, India and Vietnam cooperate under the mechanism of the ASEAN Regional Forum (ARF).

In the sectors of science, technology and space science, agreement on bilateral cooperation in Science & Technology was first concluded in 1976, and renewed in 1996. A Joint Committee on Science & Technology was established in 1997. India-Vietnam Protocol on Information Technology was signed in 1999. Moreover, the Government of India, through its two grants, is helping Vietnam in setting up of an Advanced Resources Centre in IT in Hanoi and also assisting in human resources and bio-technology development in IT in the country. As one of the leading players in information technology sector in the world, India has set up an Advanced Resource Centre in Information and Communications Technology in Hanoi City. The Government of India is also working towards the gifting of a supercomputer to Vietnam, and also collaboration of national *space programmes.*

In terms of education and training, India annually provides about 100 scholarships both short and long-term. During 2006-7, India provided 70 ITEC scholarships to Vietnam under ITEC Assistance and programmes. India also provides 20 scholarships under Cultural Exchange Programme (CEP) and 10 scholarships to Vietnam annually under the MGC scheme. More and more self-financed Vietnamese students go to India these days because of reasonable fees and English teaching advantage. The number amounts to around 100 every year. India has also established an English language training centre VICELT, in Da Nang and an Entrepreneurship Development Centre in Hanoi and plans to establish a vocational training centre in Ho Chi Minh City.

On the cultural front, India has recently taken a decision to open an Indian Cultural Centre in Hanoi to bring the Indian cultural traditions closer to the locals. Besides, the Archeological Survey of India has decided to carry out a restoration of the Cham monuments at MySon.

From these active interactions and cultural exchanges, Vietnam has learned advanced models for economic development. Vietnam is on the way up from a backward agricultural country to the application of modern sciences and technology. With positive outcomes, with the increasing potential in cooperation, Vietnam-India cultural exchanges will certainly become a strong part of the multilateral ties where our commitment today will be the solid foundation to further develop the relation and collaboration among the members of the multicultural community in which cultural diversity has much to offer to modernization and to enrich our diversified regional worlds.

Vietnam-India relations can justify that in a complicated changing world, two countries can build an all-round thriving strategic relationship. An multifaceted relationship based on a long-standing traditional interrelation stemming from both countries' strategic concern for peaceful development in the world.

Experiences have shown that frequent visits of high-level delegation, dissemination of information about each other to improve mutual understanding of the countries are critical requirements. Currently, the knowledge of Vietnamese people on the potential development of Indian economy, culture, literature and education is still limited. Vice versa, India's knowledge on Vietnamese aspects is also limited.

In the new historical setting, deriving from strategic interests of both countries, Vietnam-India relations will surely undergo all-round and powerful development in the twenty-first century to become Nam-Nam model – a typical strategic partnership.

THE SIGNIFICANCE OF INDIA-ASEAN RELATIONSHIP

Indian history encompasses a long succession of intercivilizational encounters, including those that exerted Indian influence on other regions. In fact, the spread of Buddhism and the Indianization of Southeast Asian countries did diversify their inherently rich cultures. Therefore, India-ASEAN relationship is the key to harmonize these cultures, thus promoting understanding among, tolerance, and acceptance of each other's culture. Thanks to this relationship, Indian-ASEAN peoples treasure the benefits of cultural diversity within the broad rubric of unity and community harmony.

Secondly, with the spread of Indian culture into Vietnam in particular, the resistance power of Vietnam cultural values is strengthened. In reality, although the Buddhist kingdoms of Southeast Asia maintained extensive contact with China for some time, Confucian values which struck firm roots in northern Vietnam did not flourish further south. Since India's cultural influences were more compatible with local norms and beliefs than China's, they spread far and wide and were deeply absorbed into Vietnamese ground. This shows harmonization, acceptance of positive and suitable cultural features to diversify its own culture rather than assimilation. Therefore, Indian culture, to some extent, enhances a thriving and harmonious life with such other cultures as Champa and Funan in the South of Vietnam.

Thirdly, in the journey further South of Vietnam, Indian values did not spread by means of war at all. In fact, they did not characterize any direct political control over the place. India's thoughts always proved to be gentle with the peaceful and moderate nature of Buddhism in Southeast Asia stemming from the inherent gentleness, from the peaceable nature of the Indian religions and cultures that spread to the region.

> Another legacy is the Sanskrit element in many Southeast Asian languages, together with the Indian origin of the alphabets in which those languages are written. By 500 A.D., Sanskrit had become the hallmark of civilization in much of Southeast Asia and was frequently the official language of the court. Once again, this form of Indian influence arrived in the form of culture and religion, not by the sword.[23]

Last but not least, Vietnam plays an integral part in various aspects including geo-political matter as, from geostrategic perspective, Vietnam in Southeast Asia plays the role of an extremely critical "chain link" in India's Look-East Policy. Vietnam's geo-strategic location, its demonstrated military prowess and its national will-power gives it a critical place in the strategic calculus of Southeast Asia. In general, Vietnam acts as a solid bridge for India to firmly step into Southeast Asia, being a potential regional power with great political stability and a successful economic performer.

SOME SUGGESTED DIRECTIONS FOR FUTURE GROWTH

Since India is in the immediate neighborhood of ASEAN, there is an increase in understanding on the need to cooperate on a wide range of issues at the regional and global level as there is a vast untapped potential. These are to foster closer academic linkages and educational opportunities and to enhance cultural cooperation. Each country should develop special schemes to prioritize activities with specific timelines for implementation.

Furthermore, to give greater visibility to cooperation, India and ASEAN countries should embark on a cultural programme approach with clear strategic thrusts to meet the objectives of the relations and could be multi-year in nature. For example: setting up a joint task force on education and cultural exchanges with a specific plan of action. To facilitate successful collaborative efforts, India and ASEAN countries should establish a common academic network of policy think tanks to strengthen policy coherence on international academic and cultural issues. More specifically, the task force will address all issues on higher education, cultural exchanges between the country members. The task force would plan a course of action which deals with each and every field to serve the competitive advantage of the countries involved. The task force also prepares for cultural exchanges to allow students' visit, home-stay, and field trip in a member country; for academic transfer to allow flows of students from one educational institution to another among member countries. The task force should survey the markets and explores possible solutions, to properly meet the requirements of the job-market in advance and structure courses in a manner that will help their students well prepare for jobs available in the huge employment market. To this end, a specific Plan of Action for culture, education, and people-to-people exchanges should be established in due time.

SETTING UP A CULTURAL HUB OF REGIONAL NETWORKS BETWEEN INDIA AND ASEAN COUNTRIES

To attract students from other continents, India-ASEAN Cooperation Project should include setting up a cultural hub between India and ASEAN countries. This hub will spin around an inter-related and an inter-linked India-ASEAN community, generating opportunities for young generations.

In order to achieve this goal, the key strategies include improving the mission of education in order to spread cultural values of other countries, fully supporting education cooperation to meet international standards, facilitating regulations for international cooperation and development, paving the way for better international awareness and cooperation, and enhancing the education market in the area. Moreover, the cooperation strategies for cultural activities at the bilateral, multilateral, and international level should be tailored to the cooperation strategies between India and ASEAN countries in the world at multilateral level.

In addition, India should

- reinforce regional integration into ASEAN countries through well-balanced development of the region.
- attain sustainable economic growth to vitalize the academic potential of the ASEAN region. In this case, in addition to economic development, human resources investment should be paid close attention to.
- expand approaches: India and ASEAN countries are expected to explore broader approaches world-wide to promote all aspects such as trade, investment and the exchange of experts in the region.
- strengthen understanding on India and ASEAN countries by making robust cultural and educational connections possible by organizing

courses on the culture of the two regions. In his paper,[24] Prashanth Parameswaran clearly stated:

> In the field of education, for instance, offereing courses that emphasize the common cultural heritage of South and Southeast Asia would be a more effective method of creating affinity rather than existing initiatives that merely dole out scholarships.

To facilitate all the key strategies initially set up, leaders from ASEAN countries and India should exchange more high-level visits to express a willingness to share skills in all sectors possible, to strategically think about long-term avenues for boosting connectivity, to formulate broader scope of cooperation, and to deepen existing cooperative activities.

In this light, the robust cultural and civilizational connection between India and ASEAN in general, between Vietnam and India in particular, will, without doubt, bring India and the ASEAN countries into a multi-dimensional cooperative network. To make the most out of the network, all the member countries should bear the sense of responsibility and build cooperative spirit, and nurture mutual confidence. There is a heightened sense of urgency for the completion of the "road" connecting India and ASEAN as both can thrive only on tight multi-faceted cooperation toward an all-round sustainable development.

NOTES

1. Ellen L. Frost, *Why India belongs in "East Asia".*
2. Ibid.
3. Patit Paban Mishra (2001). 'India-Southeast Asian Relations: An Overview'. Teaching South Asia – An internet Journal of Pedagogy
4. Sudhir Devare, 2006: 89
5. S. Jayakumar's statement at the first ASEAN-India Dialogue Session, Jakarta, 24 July 1996.
6. Sudhir Devare, 2006.
7. Keynote Address by Dr. Manmohan Singh, Indian Prime Minister at a special leaders dialogue of ASEAN business advisory council, in May 2005 on "Make 21st Century truly an Asian Century", retrieved from http://newasiaforum.org/speech_pm.htm
8. Keynote Address by Dr. Manmohan Singh, India Prime Minister at special leaders dialogue of ASEAN business advisory council, in May 2005 on 'Make 21st Century truly an Asian Century', retrieved from http://newasiaforum.org/speech_pm.htm
9. Sayantani Sen Mazumdar, 'Mekong-Ganga Cooperation – A Brief Overview', accessed electronically at www.globalindiafoundation.org
10. UNEP Regional Resource Center for Asia and the Pacific. *Sustainable Development Strategy Case for Greater Mekong Sub-region.*
11. Kashmir is the northwestern region of the Indian subcontinent. Until the mid-19th century, the term *Kashmir* geographically denoted only the valley between the Great Himalayas and the Pir Panjal mountain range. Today *Kashmir* denotes a larger area that includes the Indian-administered state of Jammu and Kashmir (the Kashmir valley, Jammu and Ladakh), the Pakistani-administered Gilgit-Baltistan and the Azad

Kashmir provinces, and the Chinese-administered regions of Aksai Chin and Trans-Karakoram Tract. In the first half of the first millennium, the Kashmir region became an important center of Hinduism and later of Buddhism; retrieved on 8 February 2012 from the world wide web http://en.wikipedia.org/wiki/Kashmir

12. Vietnam – India: 40 Years of Developing Bilateral Cooperation. Retrieved January 2012 from the world wide web http://www.vccinews.com/news_detail.asp?news_id=25074 (Vietnam Business Forum interviewed Sir Rajit Rae, Ambassador of India to Vietnam in December 2011).
13. Yogendra Singh, Research Scholar, Jawaharlal Nehru University. 'India-Vietnam Relations: The Road Ahead'. Retrieved January 2012 from the world wide web www.ipcs.org
14. 'India is committed to continued comprehensive cooperation with Vietnam'. Retrieved January 2012 from the world wide web http://www.qdnd.vn/qdndsite/en-US/75/72/183/161/202/172270/Default.aspx; Vietnam News Newspaper, January 7, 2012 (*Ties with India a Priority for Vietnam*).
15. Prakash Nanda. *Rediscovering Asia: Evolution of India's Look-East Policy*. Lancer Publishers, 2003.
16. Blank, Stephen. *Natural Allies?: Regional Security in Asia and Prospects for Indo-American Strategic Cooperation*. DIANE Publishing.
17. Retrieved January 2012 from the world wide webhttp://online.wsj.com/article/SB10001424053111903791504576584653465899250.html
18. 'India and Vietnam in Changing East Asia'. Institute of Peace and Conflict Studies. Retrieved January 2012 from the World Wide Web. http://ipcs.org/southeastasia_publications2.jsp?action=showView&kValue=2278&country=1016&status=article&mod=a.
19. 'India – Vietnam Economic and Commercial Relations'. Federation of Indian Chambers of Commerce and Industry. Retrieved January 2012 from the world wide web http://www.ficci.com/international/countries/vietnam/vietnamcommercialrelation.htm.
20. 'India-Vietnam: Developing a Strategic Partnership'. *Asian Affairs*. Retrieved January 2012 from the world wide web http://www.asianaffairs.com/may2008/cdrfiles/india_vietnam.pdf.
21. 'Vietnam favours FTA with India'. *The Hindu*. 7 July 2007. Retrieved January 2012 from the world wide web http://www.hindu.com/2007/07/07/stories/2007070761171600.htm. and "Vietnam PM urges greater trade ties with India". *The Hindu Business Line*, 7 July 2007. Retrieved January 2012 from the world wide web. http://www.thehindubusinessline.com/2007/07/07/stories/2007070752021000.htm.
22. 'Trade with India to reach US $2 billion in 2008'. *Vietnam Business Finance*. 3 May 2008. Retrieved January 2012 from the world wide web. http://www.vnbusinessnews.com/2008/05/trade-with-india-to-reach-us2-billion.html.
23. Frost, *Why India belongs in "East Asia"*.
24. Prashanth Parameswaran (May 2010), 'Strengthening ASEAN-India Relations in the 21st Century', retrieved from www.project2049.net.

WORKS CITED

Arnason, Johann. P. *Understanding Intercivilizational Encounters*. Thesis Eleven, 2006.

Chakraborti, Tridib.Trans Nguyen Ngoc Thuy. *Quan he An Do-Vietnam: mot Tinh ban huong Dong da duoc thu thach qua thoi gian* (India-Vietnam relationship: a Look-East Friendship which stood the Test of Time). *Southeast Asian Studies Magazine*, no. 5, 27-35, 2003.

Choshal, Baladas. 'India's Look-East Policy and Vietnam'. Mainstream, vol. XLVII, no. 40, 19 September 2009.

Dang Ngoc Hung. *Viet Nam va An Do: hop tac kinh te, thuong mai va khoa hoc cong nghe* (Vietnam and India: Cooperation of Economy, Trade, Science and Technology). *Southeast Asian Studies Magazine*, no. 51, 19-26, 2001.

Devare, Sudhir. *India and Southeast Asia – Towards Security Convergence*. ISEAS, Singapore. New Delhi: Capital Publishing Company, 2006.

Dinh Trung Kien. *An Do hom qua va hom nay (India – Yesterday and Today)*. Np: National Political Publisher, 1995.

Do Thu Ha. *Hop tac Vietnam - An Do trong linh vuc Van hoa Giao duc nhung Nam gan day* (Cooperation between Vietnam and India in the field of Culture and Education in recent Years). Southeast Asian Studies Magazine no. 51, 58-60, 2001.

Fadia. B.L. *India Government and Politics*. Agra: Sahitya Bhawan Publications, 2008.

Frost, Ellen, L. *Why India belongs in "East Asia"*. Retrieved July 2012 from www.american.edu/sis/aseanstudies/upload/Why-India-Belongs-in-East -Asia.pdf

Eric Koo Peng Kuan. 'India's Look-East Policy'. Retrieved July 2012 from www.whstsindia.com/editorials/wis200501019-India's-look-East-Policy.html

Foreign Affairs. *The Rise of India*. 2006. Retrieved July 2012 from http://www.foreignaffairs.com/features/collections/the-rise-of-india

Foreign Policy Reseach Center (no. 8, 2011). *Focus: India's Look-East Policy*. New Delhi.

Hoang Thi Diep. *Nhung Nhan to Khach quan Chi phoi viec Thiet lap Quan he Ngoai giao Viet Nam va An Do nam 1972* (Objective Factors Dominating the Establishment of Vietnam-India diplomatic relations in 1972). Southeast Asian Studies Magazine no.5. 69-72, 2003.

——. *Ve moi Quan he Truyen thong Vietnam - An Do* (About Vietnam-India Traditional Relationship). Southeast Asian Studies Magazine, no.1, 54-60, 2005.

Indian Business Chamber in Vietnam, *Membership Directory 2007*, HCM City General Publishing House.

Dixit, J.N. 'Across Borders: Fifty years of India's Foreign Policy'. New Delhi, Picus Books, 1998.

Mishra, Patit Paban. *India-Southeast Asian Relations: An Overview. Teaching South Asia – An internet Journal of Pedagogy*, 2001.

Nguyen Canh Hue. *Quan he Viet Nam - An Do tu 1945 den nay – Thanh tuu, Kinh nghiem va Van de dat ra* (Vietnam-India relationship since 1945 – achievements, experiences and issues to be solved). *History Studies Magazine*, no. 7, 44-49, 2000.

——. *Vai Nhan xet ve Quan he Viet Nam - An Do tu 1945 den nay* (Some Remarks on Vietnam-India Relations since 1945). *Southeast Asian Studies Magazine*, no. 51, 61-63, 2001.

——. *Vai net ve quan he Viet Nam - An Do* (A brief Look at Vietnam-India Relationship). *History Studies Magazine*, no. 3, 50-58, 2004.

Nguyen Huy Hoang. *Nhin lai 30 nam Quan he Kinh te Vietnam-India* (A Review of 30-year Vietnam-India Economic Cooperation). Southeast Asian Studies Magazine no. 51, 13-18, 2001.

Nguyen Tat Giap, Nguyen Thi Thuy. *Vai net ve Quan he Viet Nam - An Do trong nhung nam dau the ky XXI* (A brief Look on Vietnam-India Relations in the early 21st Century). *International Studies Magazine*, no. 58, 12-19, 2004.

Nguyen Thu Huong. *Vi tri cua An Do tren Truong Quoc te va Quan he An Do – Viet Nam Nam* (India's Position in the World and India-Vietnam Relationship). *Vietnam-India Relationship*, no. 42, 13-21. 2001.

Pham Quyet Thang. *Quan he Viet Nam - An Do trong thap ky 90 the ky XX* (Vietnam-India Relations in 1990s). *Southeast Asian Studies Magazine*, nos. 51, 54-57, 2001.

Pham Thanh Ha. *Quan he Viet Nam - An Do trong Boi canh Toan cau hoa hien nay* (Vietnam-India relations in the current setting of globalization). *Africa and Middle East Studies Magazine* no. 7, 43-50, 2009.

'Relationship between India and Southeast Asia – A strategic Commitment or Regional Intergration. Proceedings of the International Conference' 1st USSH – MAKAIAS INTERNATIONAL SCIENCE CONFERENCE by the University of Social Sciences and Humanities, Vietnam National University – Ho Chi Minh City in cooperation with Maulana Abul Kalam Azad Institute of Asian Studies, India in May 2009.

S. Prasamrajan. 'Ahoy Hanoi: With India and Vietnam reviving old bonds, the chances of a strategic tie-up become stronger'. India Today: 20 November 2000, New Delhi, 50.

Sharma, Geetesh. *Cac Quan he Vietnam-India tu the ky I den the ky XXI Publisher* (Vietnam-India Relations from the first Century to the 21st Century). Ho Chi Minh City: Publisher Lao Dong, 2006.

——. Cac Quan he Vietnam-An Do tu The ky I den The ky XXI, translated from "India-Vietnam Relations. First to Twenty First Century" by Ha Duy in 2006. Ho Chi Minh City: Lao Dong Publisher, 2006.

Special reference Material. *Quan he quoc phong Viet Nam - An Do va yeu to Trung Quoc* (Vietnam-India defense cooperation and the Chinese factor) 1-4, 2011.

Subhash, Kapila. 'India-Vietnam Strategic Partnership', *The Convergence of Interests*, no. 177.

Sultan, Shahin. 'India's "Look East" Policy Pays off'. *Asia Times*. Retrieved July 2012 from http://www.atimes.com/atimes/South_Asia/EJ11Df05.html

Thu Tam. *Kha nang hop tac giua An Do va Vietnam trong lanh vuc dao tao Quan tri Kinh doanh* (the Cooperative Capacity between India and Vietnam in the field of Business Administration Training). *Information-Argument Magazine*, no. 11, 59-61, 2000.

Tran Dinh Thien. *Lien ket kinh te ASEAN – Van de va Trien vong (Economic Partnership – Problems and Prospects)*. Np: World Publisher, 2000.

Tran Thi Ly. *Su dieu chinh chinh sach cua Cong hoa An Do tu 1991-2000 (The Republic of India's Policy Regulations in 1991-2000 Period)*. Np: Social Sciences Publisher, 2002.

UNEP Regional Resource Center for Asia and the Pacific. *Sustainable Development Strategy Case for Greater Mekong Sub-region*.

Vo Xuan Vinh. *Viet Nam trong chinh sach huong Dong cua An Do* (Vietnam in India's Look-East Policy). *Southeast Asian Studies Magazine*, no. 2, 46-52, 2005.

——. 'ASEAN trong Chinh sach huong Dong cua An Do' (ASEAN in India's Look-East Policy). *Communist Magazine*, no. 5, 125, 2007.

——. *Vi the cua Viet Nam trong Chinh sach huong Dong cua An Do xet tu goc do cac Muc tieu Chinh sach* (Vietnam's Standing in India's Look-East Policy from the Perspective of Objectives and Policies). *Southeast Asian Studies Magazine*, no. 9, 32-38, 2010.

Vu Duong Huan. *Thuc trang va trien vong quan he huu nghi va hop tac truyen thong Vietnam*

-*An Do* (Current situation and prospects of Vietnam-India Friendship and Traditional Cooperation). *International Studies Magazine*, no. 43, 3-15, 2001.

Vu Van Luu. *An Do dieu chinh chinh sach doi ngoai da dang va thuc te* (Regulations of Indian foreign Policy – Diversity and Practicality), 1991.

WEB SITES

ASEAN-India Dialogue Relations. Retrieved July 2012 from the World Wide Web http://www.aseansec.org/14802.htm

AsiaInt Special Reports, p.1. 'India's "Look East" Policy: Changing the Asian Strategic Landscape.' (Avail. at http//www.AsiaInt.com)

Asian Affairs. 'India-Vietnam: Developing a Strategic Partnership'. Retrieved January 2012 from the world wide web http://www.asianaffairs.com/may2008/cdrfiles/india_vietnam.pdf

Blank, Stephen. 'Natural Allies?: Regional Security in Asia and Prospects for Indo-American Strategic Cooperation', DIANE Publishing.

Federation of Indian Chambers of Commerce and Industry. 'India - Vietnam Economic and Commercial Relations'. Retrieved January 2012 from the world wide web http://www.ficci.com/international/countries/vietnam/vietnamcommercialrelation.htm

Institute of Peace and Conflict Studies. 'India and Vietnam in changing East Asia'. Retrieved January 2012 from the world wide web http://ipcs.org/southeastasia_publications2.jsp?action=showView&kValue=2278&country=1016&status=article&mod=a.

Kuppuswamy, C.S., 'India's Look-East Policy: More aggressive, Better Dividends' (Avail. at http://www.southasiaanalysis.org)

Manmohan Singh Keynote Address (May 2005), 'Make 21st Century truly an Asian Century' special leaders dialogue of asean business advisory council (Avail. at http://newasiaforum.org/speech_pm.htm)

Nanda, Prakash. Rediscovering Asia: evolution of India's look-east policy. Lancer Publishers, 2003.

Nguyen An (2008), 'Ngoai giao van hoa An Do o Dong Nam A' (India's Exchange and Dissemination of its Culture in Southeast Asia) (Avail. at http://www.tgvn.com.vn/Item/VN/NgoaiGiao/2008/11/AA3A95129061F779/)

Prashanth Parameswaran (May 2010), Strengthening ASEAN-India Relations in the 21st Century" (Avail. at www.project2049.net)

Retrieved January 2012 from the world wide web http://online.wsj.com/article/SB10001424053111903791504576584653465899250.html

Sayantani Sen Mazumdar, 'Mekong-Ganga Cooperation – A Brief Overview' (Avail. at www.globalindiafoundation.org)

'The Asianization of Asia'. Retrieved August 2010, from the World Wide Web: http://www.foreignaffairs.com/articles/49406/yoichi-funabashi/the-asianization-of-asia

The Hindu (July 7, 2007). 'Vietnam favours FTA with India'. Retrieved in January 2012 from the world wide web http://www.hindu.com/2007/07/07/stories/2007070761171600.htm.

The Hindu Business Line. (July 7, 2007). 'Vietnam PM urges greater trade ties with India'. Retrieved January 2012 from the world wide web http://www.thehindubusinessline.com/2007/07/07/stories/2007070752021000.htm

The Spread of Chinese Civilization: Japan, Korea, Vietnam. Retrieved August 2010, from the World Wide Web http://wps.ablongman.com/long_stearns_wc_4/0,8725,1125407-,00.html

Vietnam Business Finance (May 3, 2008). 'Trade with India to reach US $2 billion in 2008'. Retrieved in January 2012 from the world wide web http://www.vnbusinessnews.com/2008/05/trade-with-india-to-reach-us2-billion.html.

Vietnam Business Forum. (December 2011). 'Vietnam - India: 40 Years of Developing Bilateral Cooperation'. Retrieved January 2012 from the world wide web http://www.vccinews.com/news_detail.asp?news_id=25074 (Vietnam Business Forum interviewed Sir Rajit Rae, Ambassador of India to Vietnam in December 2011)

Vietnam News Newspaper. (January 7, 2012). 'India is committed continued comprehensive cooperation with Vietnam'. Retrieved January 2012 from the world wide web http://www.qdnd.vn/qdndsite/en-US/75/72/183/161/202/172270/Default.aspx; (Ties with India a Priority for Vietnam)

Vietnam-India Relations (December 2009), (Avail. at http://www.mofa.gov.vn)

Yogendra Singh, Research Scholar, Jawaharlal Nehru University. 'India-Vietnam Relations: The Road Ahead'. Retrieved January 2012 from the world wide web www.ipcs.org

11

Capitalising on Cultural Connections: Indian Influences in the Philippines

JOEFE B. SANTARITA

INTRODUCTION

This paper subscribes to an idea that culture is a resource and has the capacity to aspire. Culture, according to Arjun Appadurai in his essay 'The Capacity to Aspire: Culture and the Terms of Recognition', serves as a facility to connect individual wants and needs to cultural norms about what constitutes 'the good life, health and happiness' and more broadly to belief systems about 'life and death, nature of worldly possessions, the significance of material assets over social relations, as well as the value of peace or warfare'.[1] As such, individuals and groups try to institute change by creating powerful stories that explain, persuade and address their needs and wants in terms of norms and belief systems. This capacity to aspire and the hope as well as confidence it generates are directly related to economic growth, poverty reduction, public action[1] as well as international cooperation.

Given the capacity to aspire, culture as an instrument of diplomacy better serves as prime example of 'soft power' that has the ability to persuade through culture, values, and ideas that are communicated implicitly to touch audience's emotions.[2] Hence, this paper will look at the vestiges of the Indian influences in the country particularly from the *Ramayana*, Sanskrit words, Hindu-Buddhist artefacts and others and subsequently assess how these elements can be capitalised better to aspire the advancement of the recent India-Philippine relations.

VESTIGES AND VARIANTS: INDIAN INFLUENCES IN THE PHILIPPINES

Contrary to popular perception, there is a long history of Indian contacts in the Philippines centuries before the advent of Spanish colonialism. The first Indian immigrants into Southeast Asian region, according to Henry Otley Beyer, seemed to have been chiefly of old Vedic faith mixed with primitive nature and sun worship. Beyer further opined that although Buddhist ideas became dominant in the early centuries of the Common Era, Indian traders and colonizers of these types seem to have entered the Philippines primarily through Eastern and Northern Borneo and continued to drift in from about twelfth or thirteenth century onward.[3] Similarly, the latter movements were products of indirect interaction. As such, the following waves of Indian influences, although this time of Brahmanic character, came into the Philippines from Java and Borneo during the period of Majapahit contact in the fourteenth century.[4]

This theory, however, did not settle well in the academic quarters of the Philippines and alternative views were consequently raised by scholars such as William Henry Scott and Juan Francisco. Based on the Sanskrit presence in Filipino languages, Scott believed that the influence was introduced not by actual speakers but by Southeast Asian islanders between India and the Philippines, or by Filipino travellers themselves. Sulu and Visayas probably enjoyed these contacts independently, through trade, and perhaps at different periods of history.[5]

Francisco, furthermore, provided his own alternatives. His idea about the Indians' coming to the country is good to quote here at length:

> Indian cultural elements as they are now discernible in the fabric of Philippine culture can only be explained in terms of the intermediary of the Javanese and/or Malay who first received these Indian elements. The Javanese and/or Malay sojourn of these Indian aspects of the culture underwent modifications to suit the character and nature of the host culture. These finally reached the Philippines by the process of culture drift or stimulus diffusion. Of course, the process did not take place within a few years – say one decade or one score – but more likely centuries of slow and perhaps even "painful" percolation. This rather slow drift and stimulus diffusion may have been aggravated by the fact of history that at the period of this movement, the height of Indian influence in Java and Malaya and Sumatra had already reached its peak and was on a steady decline. Even this slow process of movement was further checked by the very successful inroads of Islam, which was to become the most important single factor that finally stopped the influence of Indian elements into the Philippines.[6]

Regardless of the real story of the early Indians coming to the country, this historical experience has been consistently invoked by Indian officials when visiting countries in Southeast Asia including the Philippines in their speeches about the civilisational links of India with the region that have lasted over a millennium.[7] As Amartya Sen rightly pointed out, the influence of interaction between Indians and the Southeast Asians is well reflected in languages and vocabularies throughout Asia through Thailand and Malaya, to Indo-China, Indonesia, the Philippines, Korea and Japan.[8] In fact, the implementation of India's recent foreign and economic policy has been justified through India's centuries old links with Southeast Asia. This was reinforced by the speech of the Prime Minister, Dr. Manmohan Singh in the 3rd India-ASEAN Business Summit in New Delhi in October 2004. He said that India wished to look east because of centuries of interaction between India and Southeast Asia.[9]

A case in point: the Indian diplomatic circles prior to this pronouncement have readily orchestrated their spiritual ties with the region. In East Asia, for instance, the connection has been capitalised through the presence of Buddhism. Indian officials are hoping that the utilisation of the ancient ties between India and East Asia may generate additional weight to India's contemporary position and hence nurture a feeling of cultural proximity.[10] In the case of the Philippines, the existence of Indian diasporic communities[11] in the country promotes various partnerships between India and the Philippines.[12]

India has capitalised this ancient link with most of the countries in the region ranging from Buddhism to arts, artefacts, architecture and even language. This is usually present in most speeches of Indian officials when visiting Southeast Asia. Former President Abdul Kalam,[13] in one of his speeches in the Philippines during his state visit in 2006, said that "the countries of Southeast Asia, including the Philippines, constitute an extended neighbourhood with whom India's links go back many centuries". He further emphasised that there is a distinctive Indian impress in this part of Asia, a religious, cultural, and linguistic stamp which Indian seafarers brought via Indonesia and the Malaya peninsula before the era of European colonisation.[14] He earlier called this link during his Singapore visit as 'umbilical connectivity.'[15]

These cultural links between India and the Philippines include the presence of the *Ramayana* in multiple variances, *Darangen, Singkil*, hundreds of Sanskrit words in Filipino languages and the discoveries of various Hindu-Buddhist artefacts among others.

One of the prominent legacies of Indian early contacts in Southeast Asian region is the existence of *Ramayana*. In the Philippines, the Rama story is popularly known as *Maharadia Lawana* which Dr. Juan Francisco discovered in 1968 as a Maranaw narrative. This version is in a condensed form in comparison to the Indian *Ramayana* but still contains the major episodes of the latter such as the winning of Sita, her abduction, the search for Sita and her return. These four episodes as they are narrated in the *Maharadia Lawana* correspond to the five kanda (songs or chapters of the *Ramayana*) such as Balakanda, Aranyakanda, Kiskindhakanda, Sundarakanda and Yuddakanda.[16]

In the *Maharadia Lawana* story, Rama is Radia Mangadiri, Laksmana is Radia Mangawarna, Sita is Tuwan Potre Malano Tihaia, Kusa/Lava is Laksmana, who in the story assumes the character of Hanuman. Ravana is *Maharadia Lawana*. The story's setting is in the legendary island of Pulu Agama Niog.[17]

Aside from *Maharadia Lawana*, people of southern Philippines still observe the *Darangen* as part of their cultural milieu especially in rural areas. It is still customary to invite the *onor* (singer) during the *kalilang* or feast, whether it is for the dead or for any other occasion. The host includes *Darangen* singing as part of the activities. If the *Darangen* sung as Princess Gandingan, the audience gets a triple treat: kulintang playing, bayok (antiphonal singing by the two characters) and singkil dancing.[18] In *Darangen*, similar episodes of the abduction and subsequent recovery of Princess Lawanen are chanted only on special occasions.[19]

In particular, this pre-Islamic epic consists of 17 cycles and a total of 72,000 lines, telling the stories of heroes as well as episodes of Maranao history and tackling the immortal themes of life, death, courtship, politics and love. *Darangen* contains Maranao social values, customary law, ethics and aesthetics.[20]

Singkil, on the other hand, is an elegant, stylized performance dance usually involving performers interpreting archetype characters inspired by and interpreted from the thread of storylines found in the Indian epic *Ramayana*. They include those of a princess, her faithful assistant, friends, as well as ardent suitors who would be stepping in and out, sitting or standing on 2 sets of bamboo poles crossed, and being thumped on the floor and hit together by men to make percussive music for the dance. Native music instruments like the *agung* (gong) and the *kulintang* (made of 8 small gongs set on a rack) complete the ensemble of musical instruments in the dance. The Maranaw people in southern Philippines even before the arrival of the Spaniards in sixteenth century and the arrival of the Islam religion in the Philippines by the twelfth century observed these oral traditions by re-telling similar stories found in the Indian epic Ramayana into *Darangen*. This re-telling is the basis of the story being interpreted and performed whenever the singkil is danced.

The body, arms, and hand swaying and movements in this dance remind those who have studied ancient dance forms from many countries of the Hindu-style of dancing, which in the *singkil* can be explained by the extensive influences made by the Sriwijaya and Majapahit empires that reached Indonesia as well as the many islands of the Philippines. In the performance, the main dancer-Princess Gandingan interprets the movements after learning the rituals from her mother, the powerful healer in the village, while gathering medicinal plants and herbs from the forest. Movements that interpret Gandingan's sojourn in the forest, either alone or with her friends and faithful assistant that usually bear a beautiful parasol for the princess wherever she goes during the dance.[21]

Other than the performing arts, the most extensive evidences of Indian influences in the Philippines are Sanskrit elements in the languages of the country. These have persisted since their introduction in the Philippines between the tenth and fifteenth centuries and have been fully assimilated into these speech systems. There appear to be about 336 words in Philippine languages that are recognizably Sanskrit in origin and 50 per cent of these have definitive provenance in Sanskrit.[22] William Henry Scott even gave actual statistical count of Sanskrit words in Philippine languages. He found out that some 150 separate Sanskrit words are identified as the origin of Philippine terms are in Tagalog and the rest in Bisaya, Ilocano and Sulu[23] (Tausog). Some of these are included in Figure 1.

FIGURE 1. SELECTED SANSKRIT TERMS IN FILIPINO LANGUAGES

Filipino	Meaning	Sanskrit	Meaning
Bakti (T)	gift, token, devotion	Bhakti	homage, love, worship
Guro (Tag)	teacher	Guru	teacher
Bangsa (T)	people, race, nation	Vamsa	lineage, race
Bichara (T,M)	speak, talk	Vicara	deliberation, reflection
Dukka (T)	poverty, misery	Duhkha	grief
Dukha (Tag)	poor		
Guna (T, I)	usefulness, profit	Guna	good quality, merit
Hina (Tag)	weak, reduced	Hina	fatigue, weak, defective
Pana (Tag)	arrow	Bana	arrow
Saksi (Tag, I, B)	witness, testimony	Saksi	witness
Suchi (T,P)	clean, pure, neat	Suci	pure, neat, innocent

Origins: T- Tausug B- Bikolano M- Maranao
Tag- Tagalog P- Pampango I- Ilokano

Source: Francisco, 1988.

In terms of concrete manifestations of Indian presence in the Philippines, Francisco identified some artefacts that are housed either in the National Museum of the Philippines or abroad.[24] These include the Buddhist Tara of Agusan, votive stamp of Calatagan, the Golden Garuda of Palawan and other glass beads.

In Agusan, a Golden Tara, an eight-inch tall image of a woman in pure gold at Maasin, Esperanza, was discovered in the early 1920s and a Molten Jar unearthed at Bahbah, Prosperidad in the early 1960's, marks the Agusan's pre-Hispanic cultural history which was greatly influenced by India. The icon, a 21-karat gold figurine, is presently kept at the Gem Room of the Chicago Field Museum of National History, Chicago, United States of America. The said Buddhist image of the Sailendra Period during the Sri-Vijaya History (900-50 CE) is the earliest known image of Indian origin, depicting early Indian-Philippine relations.

In Calatagan, Batangas, a clay medallion or votive stamp on whose obverse face is an image of the Avalokitesvara Padmapani in bas-relief was discovered. The image stands in the classic Indian pose known as 'tribhanga', three bends and appears to hold a padma, lotus in his right hand. This object was associated with fourteenth-fifteenth centuries and is now stored in National Museum of the Philippines.

Furthermore, the Golden Garuda pendant was found in Brookes point Palawan. This image is now stored in the National Museum of the Philippines and is believed to be the vehicle of the Hindu God, Vishnu at the height of power of the Hindi-inspired Majapahit Empire. This image along with other artefacts such as glass beads of various colours and the Filipino words of Sanskrit origin are testaments of Hindu influence in pre-colonial Philippine society.[25]

CAPITALIZING ON INDIAN INFLUENCES

After knowing these cultural influences in the Philippines, how do the government and other stakeholders capitalize on these to further the relations of the Philippines and India? The following are simple and doable suggestions that can maximize the potentials of these influences to advance the recent ties between India, the Philippines and other partners.

First, build sustainable cultural cooperation through multi-annual programs to promote mobility of cultural practitioners and exchange of people as well as ideas. This can be done by designing a cultural scholarship that will group together youths from ten ASEAN countries and other observers for two to three months as part of the cultural program of the India-ASEAN Dialogue similar to the successful program of the Indonesian sponsored Southwest Pacific Dialogue. This will include the study of Hindi, Sanskrit or Urdu, Arts, learning how to play an Indian musical instrument and also familiarization with the Indian version of the *Ramayana* in the form of dance or theatrical performance. The newly launched Nalanda University, Indian Council for Cultural Relations together with other cultural-centred institutions should serve as the base of this program.

Second, promote creative/cultural industries by providing support 'upstream' on capacities and methods of production and 'downstream' on promotion and sales, assist creative/cultural industries through participation in trade fairs and expositions, showcase the artistic and creative talents and encourage networking and collaboration.

Third, promote expertise in cultural heritage by developing/extending assistance programs to provide expertise to various agencies in either India or Philippines that are having difficulties in sustaining cultural heritage. This is enhanced better by arranging several interactive educational workshops and culturally driven partnership events. Furthermore, developing initiatives with the cultural sector that exploits the potential of social networking to engage with the public will ensure successful collaboration in the field of culture.

Fourth, invite Indian artists to perform in the Philippines, particularly the staging of the *Ramayana* in various parts of the archipelago. The office of Cultural Attache of the Indian Embassy in Manila has successfully initiated the first move and it is up to the stakeholders on how to sustain such effort. The Philippine government should also send *Singkil* performing group in India to participate in November 2012 Arts Festival.

Fifth, a gradual introduction of Bollywood films into the Filipino culture, by sponsoring various film showing activities in numerous universities such as the University of Philippines. Moreover, encourage the joint film production in India and the Philippines and making of each country as setting of the film. A case in point is the Filipino movie entitled 'Tum: My Pledge of Love' that was entirely shot in India in 2010. In addition to joint collaboration between India and the Philippines, the same can be done with other partner countries, to work on computer-animated film on the *Ramayana* in Filipino language in educating the children and youth. The Philippines in the past has successfully produced computer-animated movie 'Princess Urduja' in 2008 and was accepted well by the Filipinos, primarily by children. The subtitling in Filipino or preferably dubbing in Filipino of the '*Ramayana*: The Epic' produced in 2010 by Maya Digital Media and released by Warner Bros., India can be a good start. Alternately, the work of Nina Paley in 2008 entitled 'Sita Sings the Blues' can be another option.

Furthermore, attract students to pursue graduate courses in Indian Studies in the University of the Philippines and strengthen the Hindi class offerings in the university. The Indian embassy in Manila has a major role to play in encouraging potential donors from generous individuals and Indian enterprises based in the Philippines to contribute in offering scholarships (include tuition, book allowance and minimal monthly stipend) to students interested in pursuing a postgraduate degree with their thesis focusing on Indian culture.

Lastly, maximize the presence of Indian diaspora as an umbilical connections of India in the Philippines to strengthen and/or promote Hindu-Buddhist influences, for proliferation and maintenance of *Ramayana* and other cultural elements. Capitalizing on Kalam's idea of "umbilical connections" will move at least a majority of those 50,000 People of Indian Origin (PIO) who are currently residing in the Philippines, to take their part in the enhancement of Indian influences in the archipelago.[26] They are good economic and cultural gatekeepers.

CONCLUSION

To ensure the success of the dialogue as well as promote amity and cooperation among peoples of South and Southeast Asia, culture as a resource should be maximised well. In the case of the Philippines, the various influences such as the *Ramayana*, *singkil*, and *darangen* should be capitalised well by the government and private stakeholders to advance cultural diplomacy. Given the continuous rise of India, the Philippine government through its several cultural related agencies should carefully consider these cultural elements for policy formulations and subsequently in the enhancement of international relations. It should be noted that these intangible elements related to the artefacts involve emotions and sentiments when appropriately utilized serve as the best weapon in winning once more the hearts of not just those people from southern Philippines but the entire archipelago that have been historically linked to India for centuries.

NOTES

1. Carole Rosenstein. 'Cultural Policy and the Political Nature of Culture', in *International Cultural Policies and Power*, ed. J.P. Singh. New York: Palgrave Macmillan, 2010: 23.
2. Cynthia Schneider. 'Cultural Diplomacy: The Humanizing Factor', in *International Cultural Policies and Power*, ed. J.P. Singh. New York: Palgrave Macmillan, 2010: 101-2.
3. H. Otley Beyer. *Early History of Philippine Relations with Foreign Countries, Especially China: Historical Introduction to E. Arsenio Manuel's Chinese Elements in the Tagalog Language*, Manila: Filipiniana Publications, 1948: 8; also Juan Francisco. *Selected Essays on Mindanao Art and Culture.* Marawi City: Mindanao State University, 1988: 25.
4. Beyer, 25.
5. William Henry Scott. *Prehispanic Source Materials for the Study of Philippine History.* Philippines: University of Santo Tomas, 1969: 54.
6. Francisco, 1988: 35.
7. Joefe Santarita. 'The India-Philippine Relations in the Context of India's 'Look East' Policy', dissertation. National University of Singapore, 2011. Selected speeches of former Prime Ministers Narasimha Rao, and Atal Behari Vajpayee, former President Abdul Kalam and current Prime Minister Manmohan Singh mentioned partly these civilizational links. Narasimha Rao. 'India and the Asia-Pacific: A New Relationship.' *P.V. Narasimha Rao Selected Speeches*, vol. IV, July 1994-June 1995, New Delhi: Ministry of Information and Broadcasting, 1995: 390; also Atal Behari Vajpayee. India's Perspectives on ASEAN and the Asia Pacific Region, Singapore: Institute of Southeast Asian Studies, 2002: 6; also Abdul Kalam, Address at the Joint Session of the Congress of the Philippines, 6 February 2006. External Publicity Division. Visit of Dr. A.P.J. Abdul Kalam to Singapore, Philippines and Republic of Korea, 1-8 February 2006, New Delhi: Ministry of External Affairs, 2006: 127; also Manmohan Singh, 'PM Statement at the 7th India-ASEAN Summit in Thailand,' n.d., 24 October 2009. http://pmindia.nic.in/speech/content.asp?id=833.
8. Amartya Sen. *The Argumentative Indian: Writings on Indian Culture, History and Identity*. New Delhi: Penguin Books, 2005: 85.
9. Sudhir Devare. *India and Southeast Asia: Towards Security Convergence*. Singapore: Institute of Southeast Asian Studies, 2006, 28.
10. Isabelle Saint-Mezard. *Eastward Bound: India's New Positioning in Asia.* New Delhi: Manohar and Centre de Sciences Humaines, 2006. 251.
11. The 50,000 people of Indian origins (PIO) as well as descendants of sepoys (Indian soldiers serving the British colonizers) in the country are one of the 'umbilical connections' of India and the Philippines, Joefe Santarita, 'Beyond Bombay: Indians in the Philippines,' Conference in Commemoration of the 60th Anniversary of Philippines and India Ties, University of the Philippines, September 2009, unpublished conference paper.
12. Santarita, 2011.
13. Avul Pakir Jainulabdeen Abdul Kalam is the 11th president of the Republic of India

from 2002 to 2007. 'Dr. A.P.J. Abdul Kalam.' Abdul Kalam.nic.in. n.d. 7 June 2010. <http://www.abdulkalam.nic.in/profile.html>.

14. xiv) External Publicity Division. Visit of Dr. A.P.J. Abdul Kalam to Singapore, Philippines and Republic of Korea, 1 to 8 February 2006, New Delhi: Ministry of External Affairs, 2006: 120. Umbilical connectivity means the generational ties of migrants in the host country and their relatives in the country of origin which is India.
15. Ibid., 113.
16. Juan Francisco. *Sarimanok and the Torogan & Other Essays*. Marawi City: Mindanao State University, 1994: 117.
17. Pulu means island, Agama for village and Niog for coconut. Hence, Pulu Agama Niog simply means coconut grove village. Juan Francisco, *From Ayodhya to Pulu Agamaniog*, Quezon City: Asian Center, 1994: 68.
18. Ma. Delia Coronel, ICM, Introduction, *Darangen*, vol. 1. Marawi City: Mindanao State University, 1986: 6.
19. Juan Francisco. *Maharadia Lawana*. Quezon City: University of the Philippines, 1969. 4.
20. Roel Manipon. 'Dancing Darangen: The Way to the Maranao Epic'. National Commission for Culture and the Arts. 2008. http://www.ncca.gov.ph/about-culture-and-arts/articles-on-c-n-a/article.php?i=293&subcat=13.
21. In the story, a powerful spirit named "Makalinug" (thunder) who would represent himself like a handsome prince-like creature, would be waiting for Gandingan in the forest, and would try to entrap her with his charms and magic. Depending on the choreography design, the storyline would then be followed by having Makalinug creating havoc and confusion to Gandingan and her company. She then danced, jumped, swayed, ran, stepping in and out of the performance area as the audience continues to hear percussive music from the bamboo poles, the agung and the kulintang. She is supposed to be exquisitely able to overcome the challenges of the vines and other natural traps found in the forest, which are represented by the bamboo poles. Using shawls, scarves and the apir (the large pair of fans on the dancers' hands) or just bare hands, Gandingan and her company would be shown performing elaborate body movements all throughout the performance. They would also create chime-like music from the anklets and bracelets that they usually don for the performance, and which served as the basis why this dance is called singkil (or how the anklets are called in Maranao). Jerome E. Baladad, 'Singkil: The Maranao native dance', http://www.helium.com/items/2293684-singkil-the-maranao-native-dance. February 2012.
22. Francisco, 1988: 31.
23. Scott, 1968: 52-3 as cited by Francisco, 1988.
24. Francisco, 1988: 31-2.
25. www.philippine-trivia.com.
26. Joefe Santarita. 'Contemporary Indian Communities in Western Visayas', in *Rising India and Indian Communities in East Asia*, ed. K. Kesavapany, A. Mani and P. Ramasamy. Singapore: Institute of Southeast Asian Studies, 2008: 522

12

Buddhism and the *Rāmāyaṇa*: Their Strong and Lasting Impact on the Minds of the People of Southeast Asia with Special Reference to Thailand

CHIRAPAT PRAPANDVIDYA

THE EARLY INDIAN CONTACT WITH SOUTHEAST ASIA

The epigraphic evidence, which is most likely to be the oldest found in Thailand, is the seal written probably in Prakrit Language with the Brahmī script that may date back to second century BCE. It reads "*bamhadinasa*" of "*Bamhadina*." Above the word is a figure of a turtle. The seal was found at Kuan Look Pat, Ampher Klong Thom, Krabi Province, Southern Thailand (Fig. 1).

FIGURE 1: THE SEAL FOUND AT KUAN LOOK PAT, KRABI PROVINCE, THAILAND

The Indian Contacts with Southeast Asia may have been made some few centuries before the beginning of the Common Era as indicated by literary evidence. The oldest positive evidence of the Indians' movement eastward is probably the Sanskrit inscription erected in ancient kingdom known as Funan which was found at Vo-Canh, Vietnam (Fig. 2).

FIGURE 2: THE OLDEST INSCRIPTION IN SOUTHEAST ASIA FOUND AT VO-CANH, VIETNAM

It dates back to *c.* third or second century CE. (Majumdar, 1985: 1-30). One of literary evidences shows that there were contacts between India and Southeast Asia few centuries BCE. It is narrated in *Mahājanaka Jātaka* that the Bodhisattva Mahājanaka sailed to Suvaṇṇabhūmi. His ship wrecked and he was rescued by Maṇimekhalā, goddess of the sea (Malalasekera 1960: 492-3). Suvaṇṇabhūmi or Suvarṇabhūmi is usually identified with the ancient country of Mon, though it may be a more general designation of lands in the Far East (Gonda: 74).

EPIGRAPHIC EVIDENCE: THE EARLIEST SANSKRIT INSCRIPTION IN SOUTHEAST ASIA

The earliest Sanskrit inscription found in Southeast Asia is that which was engraved on a granite block found at Vo-Canh, Vietnam and belonged to the ancient Funan kingdom. It tells us that a son (nandana) of the family of Śrīmāra, who was seated on the throne, gave away all of his belongings, be it gold and silver, movable and immovable probably to some establishment. He also requests the future kings that they should appreciate, his merit making (Majumdar 1985: 1-3). We cannot say definitely whether this inscription belongs to Buddhism or Hinduism. In its nature, the inscription seems to tell us that the king gave away his belongings in order to fulfill his Praṇidhāna (strong wish, aspiration, prayer or an inflexible determination) as a Bodhisattva (Suzuki: 307-10).

According to the archaeological evidence, Buddhism must have reached this part of Southeast Asia (Indochina) not later than fifth-sixth centuries CE, as is attested by the Buddha image (now in Vietnam National Museum) belonging to the fourth century found at Dong-Duong, Vietnam (Ancient Champa). It is probably later than the image found at Celebes. Its style is that of Amarāvatī tradition. In fact, Theravāda Buddhism that used Sanskrit Language was flourishing in Funan in the fifth and sixth centuries, during the reigns of Jayavarman and Rudravarman (Cœdès, 1968: 61-2). It was probably abolished by Bhavavarman I or Mahendravarman of Chenla kingdom (ibid.: 67-8).

EARLIEST BUDDHA IMAGES IN SOUTHEAST ASIA

The oldest Buddha image is from Celebes, now in Djakarta Museum, Indonesia. It belongs to fourth-fifth centuries CE and was probably imported from Andhra or Sri Lankan centres. The robe is not held in the left hand but simply in the bend of the arm, as in the oldest statues in the Amarāvatī tradition. The second oldest Buddha image in Southeast Asia is the one mentioned earlier from Dong-Duong, Vietnam (ibid.: 17-18).

THE KURRAM COPPER CASKET INSCRIPTION

The inscription was found in Peshāwar, Pakistan. It dates to Śaka era 21 (99 CE) and it was written in Kharoṣṭhī script using Prakrit Language. It reads as follows:

1. *saṃ 20 (+) 1 masasa avadunakasa di 20 iśe kṣanaṃmi śveḍvarma yaśaputra tanukaṃmi raṃjaṃmi navaviharaṃmi acaryana sarvastivadana parigrahaṃmi thubaṃmi bhagravatasa śakyamunisa*
2. *śarira pradiṭhavedi | yatha vuta bhagravada avijja*
   pracagra saṃkaraṃ saṃkarapracagra viñana
   viñanapracagra namaruva namaruvapracagra
   ṣaḍyadana ṣaḍyadanapracagra phaṣa phaṣapracagra
3. *Vedana vedanapracagra taṣṇa taṣṇapracagra uvadana uvadanapracagra bhava bhavapracagra*

jadi jadipracagra jaramaranaśogra parideva dukhadormanasta-upagrasa |
evaṃ asa kevalasa
Dukha kaṃdhasa saṃmupada-e bhavadi |

4. Sarva satvana puya-e aya ca praticasaṃmupate |
likhida mahiphatiena sarvasatvanapuyae ||

(Sircar: 148-9)

"In the (Śaka) year 21, in the twentieth day of the month of Avadunaka (roughly means Indian months of Pauṣa-Māgha), at this auspicious moment Śveḍvarma, son of Yaśa, installed the bodily relics of the blessed Śakyamuni in a stūpa for the acceptance of the teachers of the Sarvastivādin sect in the charming monastery belonging to him. As the Blessed One said: Conditioned by ignorance, actions exists; conditioned by actions consciousness exists; conditioned by consciousness name and form exist, conditioned by name and form six senses exist, conditioned by six senses contact exists; conditioned by contact feelings exist; conditioned by feelings, cravings exist, conditioned by craving clinging exists, conditioned by clinging existence arises, conditioned by existence birth exists, conditioned by birth there arise old-age, death, grief, lamentation, unpleasant state of mind and body and turbulence. In this way all the collections of sufferings arise.

The pratītyasamutpāda is for the worship of all beings. It has been inscribed by the king for the worship of all beings."

This is exactly the Prakrit version of the Buddha's teaching on the dependent origination (Pali-Paṭiccasamuppāda). The Pali version of the same teaching is found in the Bodhikathā of the Vinaya-Mahāvagga of the Buddhist Pali Canon. This is the earliest inscription in Prakrit bearing on the Buddhist tenet on Paṭiccasamuppāda that I have come across. It also indicates that Paṭiccasamuppāda is the principal tenet in early Buddhism and that Prakrit was also used in the Sarvāstivāda sect in which Sanskrit was normally used.
It is interesting to note that part of the Paṭiccasamuppāda tenet from the Pali Canon is inscribed on a detached spoke of a Dhammacakka (the Wheel of the Law) found at Wat (monastery) Phra Śrīratna Mahādhātu, Lopburi Province, central Thailand (Fig. 3). It dates to *c.* sixth century CE. (CNPD, Book 1: 109-10).

FIGURE 3: THE DETACHED SPOKE OF THE WHEEL OF THE LAW WITH INSCRIPTION OF PAT ICCASAMUPPĀDA

EARLY INSCRIPTIONS' BEARING ON BUDDHISM FOUND IN MYANMAR

Only some inscriptions are selected for this essay. The first one is a gold plate inscription in Pali Language on the popular verse giving the essence of the Buddha's teaching which was found at Maunggun, Prome district. The ancient name of Prome was Sirikhettara (Sanskrit-Śrīkṣetra). It was written with northern Brahmī script of the first half of the sixth century CE. The third one is the stone slab inscription of the time of Vīracandra, also found at Vesali near Mrohaung, Akyab district, Arakan. It was written with northern Brahmī script of the close of the sixth century CE. The first inscription reads as follows:

Ye dhammā hetuppabhavā tesaṃ hetuṃ tathāgato āha |
Tesañ ca yo nirodho evaṃvādī mahāsamaṇo ti ||

(The Tathāgata or the Truth-finder spoke about the cause of those things (dhamma) which come into existence from a cause. He also spoke about the cessation of those things (through the cessation of the cause). The doctrine of the Great Samaṇa (The Buddha is thus.)

This verse occurs in the Mahāvagga of the Vinaya of Pali Canon. In my opinion it is about the tenet of Paṭiccasamuppāda in a nutshell.

itipi so bhagavā arahaṃ sammāsaṃbuddho vijjācaraṇasampanno sugato lokavidu anuttaro purisadammasārathi satthā devamanussānaṃ buddho bhagavā ti |
svākhāto bhagavatā dhammo sandiṭṭhiko akāliko opanayiko paccattaṃ vedtabbo viññūhīti |

This passage occurs in the Dīghanikāya Mahāvagga of the Pali Canon.

No. 2 1. *Ye dhammā hetuppabhavā tesaṃ hetuṃ tathāgato āha* |
Tesañ ca yo nirodho evaṃvādī mahāsamaṇo ti ||
cattāro iddhipādā
2. *cattāro sammappadhā cattāro satipaṭṭhānā cattāri ariyasaccāni catuvesārajjāni pañcindriyāṇi pañca cakkhūni cha*
3. *asaddhāraṇāni satta bojjhaṅgā ariyo aṭṭhaṅgiko maggo nava lokuttarā dhammā dasa balāni cuddasa buddhayoni aṭṭhārasa buddhadhammāni* ||

The second inscription is in Sanskrit and it reads as follows:

ye dharmmā hetuprabhavā hetuṃ teṣāṃ tathāga[ta] āha |
teṣāṃ ca yo nirodho (dha) evaṃvādi (dī) [ma]hāśramaṇa[ḥ] ||
śrī[nīticandra]sya candravat parchīnāsya devī(vyāḥ) sāvītāṃ
candraśrī(śri)yā nāma pare(ra)mopāsikasya
deyyadharmmo' yaṃ sarvvasatvā(ttvā)nāṃ(nā)m anukattama

The third inscription is also in Sanskrit and it reads as follows:

satyadharmmāna(nu)rāgeṇa kṛtaṃ svārtheṇa(na) bhūbhujā |
[pa]rārthaghatanodyogena samyaṅnihitaceti(ta)sā ||
śrīvīracandradeveṇa(na) mahīmaṇḍanaṃ |
dharmmādhigatarājyeṇa(na) buddhastūpaśata(taṃ) [kṛtaṃ(tam)] ||
(Sircar: 493-6).

Judging from the language used in the inscriptions, Buddhism practiced in early Myanmar must have been Theravāda Buddhism that used Pali Language or Theravāda Buddhism that used Sanskrit Language, that is Sarvāstivāda or Mūlasarvāstivāda.

EARLY INSCRIPTION'S BEARING ON BUDDHISM FOUND IN MALAYSIA

Only one inscription on this topic is selected for this paper. It is in Sanskrit and is known as Fragmentary Stone Inscription of Buddhagupta found in Kedah State (Fig. 4), then the Northern District, Wellesley Province, Malay Peninsula.

FIGURE 4: THE OLDEST INSCRIPTION ON BUDDHISM FOND IN KEDAH STATE MALAYSIA

It is on the popular verse "ye dhammā" giving the essence of the Buddha's doctrine. It was written with Brahmī script of southern class of about fifth century CE. It reads as follows:

ye dharmmā hetuprabhavā teṣā(ṃ) hetu(ṃ) tathāgato |
teṣā(ṃ) ca yo nirodha eva(ṃ)vādī mahāśramaṇ[ḥ] ||
ajñāñāc cīyate karma janmanaḥ karma kāraṇam |
jñāñāt kriyate karma karmābhāvān na jāyate ||

(The action which is done through ignorance is the cause of rebirth. One will not be born if he does action with true knowledge.)

mahānāvika[sya] buddhaguptasya raktamṛttikāvāsa. . . .

(of Buddhagupta who was the captain of a big ship and who was residing at Raktamṛttikā?) (ibid: 497)

The second verse seems to give the interpretation of the above one which is also the central tenet of the Pratītyasamutpāda (Pali-Paṭiccasamuppāda).

EARLY INSCRIPTIONS' BEARING ON BUDDHISM FOUND IN THAILAND

The inscriptions in Pali Language that date back as early as the sixth century have been discovered extensively in the central part of Thailand where Dvāravatī kingdom used to exist. The so-called Ye Dhammā inscriptions were found in largest number. They are inscribed on various objects such as stūpas, stones, bricks, etc. There are also the extracts from the Pali Canon. The *Dhammacakkappavattanasutta*, the first sermon, is usually inscribed on the different parts of the Dhammacakka and on its supporting pillar and its base. The joyful utterance (*udāna*) of the Buddha soon after his attainment of the Enlightenment is also found inscribed on the octagonal pillar probably supporting a Dhammacakka (*CNPD*, Book 1: 59-134).

From the concentration of Pali inscriptions found in the central part of Thailand it can be suggested that the Buddhism that was practiced in the area was the Theravāda Buddhism that adhered strongly to the Pali Canon.

Some sculptures found at the excavation of the stūpa called Chula Pathon Cedi in the city of Nakhon Pathom, however, suggest that Sarvāstivāda sect and Mūlasarvāstivāda sect also existed in the area (Krairiksk: 21-4). Sanskrit inscriptions that are related to both the sects, however, have not been found so far in the central part of Thailand.

The inscription of Wat Maheyong

The inscription which is in Sanskrit and fragmented dates back to sixth century CE, judging from the script form, was discovered at Wat (monastery) Maheyong

(Mahyaṅgana) in the city of Nakhon Si Thammarat, Nakhon Si Thammarat Province, southern Thailand. From its content it is quite certain that it is related to Buddhism. It tells us about the gifts and merit makings by a certain person at a Buddhist monastery (*CNPD*, Book 1: 44-7). The inscription seems to indicate the existence of Sarvāstivāda sect in the peninsular Thailand.

Inscription of Khao Rang

The inscription of Khao (hill) Rang (Śāla tree) begins with a verse in Sanskrit and the rest is in Khmer. The script used is south Indian Brahmī and it dates back to Śaka era 561 (639 CE). It was found at Khao Rang, Tambol Aran, Aranyaprathet district, Sakaeo Province, now in the custody of the National Library, Bangkok. This is the dated oldest inscription in old Khmer that is related to Buddhism found in Thailand so far.

Line 1: īṣatrayodaśadine kṛṣṇe candrarasendriyaiḥ |
Line 2: bhukte śakapater abde hastendur vṛṣabhodayaḥ||

(In the year of the King of the Śakas which is determined by the senses (5), tastes (6) and the moon (1), on the 13th day of the dark fortnight in the month called Īṣa, when the moon is in the Hasta constellation, while the constellation Vṛṣabha is rising.)

Khmer section

Line 3: kañuṃ aṃnoy sināhv pragat āy
Line 4: ta vihar jmah ge vā sir kantai
Line 5: ku yoṅ ° kon ku lāṅ si ° vā pār
Line 6: kantai vā ku sol° kon ku lāṅ tai
Line 7: va raṅeh ku cih ° vā joṅ kantai
Line 8: vā ku mās ° ku cū ° kon ku der tai. lā
Line 9: ṅ tai . pau tai. k sralañ ° kon ku
Line 10: lāṅ tai ° pau tai ° caṃdak vā thar ° vā
Line 11: din ° eve dharmmalābha. daṃriṅ āy
Line 12: tnon ° slā ta gui 100-5°toṅ tneṃ 20 cmaṃ
Line 13: gui vā men°kantai vā ku laḥ ° kon ku lā
Line 14: ṅ sī °pau sī ° daṃriṅ āy ñiṅ vihā
Line 15: r slā ta gui tneṃ 100-20-3 toṅ tneṃ 100-20 ° cmaṃ
Line 16: gui vā kdok ° sarvvapiṇḍa savālavṛ
Line 17: ddha kñuṃ phoṅ droṅ cmaṃ daṃriṅ 20-10-2
Line 18: glaṅ vihār klas saṃrit 4 thās 2
Line 19: sagreḥ 20 ° pallaṅka ° taṅtoṅ taṃpo
Line 20: ṅ° canlek uladdha jlī yau 7 kaṃvār
Line 21: yau 7 kāpaṭa jlī yau 20-7 ° ksac

Line 22: yau 10-2 kamvār yau 10 ° pnaṅ°tridhā
Line 23: vartma pi----āy car ku sa
Line 24: nre 1 kanlaḥ ti ------ [kra]pi dneṃ
Line 25: 5 ° poñ vu --------
Line 26: kñuṃ aṃnoy sināhv añ ai ta vihā
Line 27: [r] -------kantai vā ku dhan ° kon
Line 28: -------- lāṅ sī °pau tai °thā
Line 29: ---------- daṃriṅ 1 slā tne°
Line 30: --------tneṃ gui 10°gui saṃ
Line 31: --------āy vihār ruṅ °

(Cœdès 1953: 23-4; *CNPD*, Book 1: 37-9)

The significant content of the Khmer section is as follows:

The slaves were given by the past Sināhv to the Buddhist monastery (vihāra). The list of the slaves is given. The past Sināhv also donated an orchard containing 105 areca palm trees, 20 coconut trees and the list of the persons who look after the orchard is given. He also donated the orchard which is near the monastery containing 123 areca palm trees, 120 coconut trees. The person who looks after the orchard near the monastery is Vā Kdok. The total number of slaves and the persons who look after the orchard is 32. The property of the monastery includes 4 bronze water pots, 2 plates, 20 sagreh and 1 couch, a piece of paddy field, 5 pairs of buffalos. The present Sināhv gave to the big monastery slaves whose list of names is given and an orchard containing fruit trees of which the number cannot be determined as the inscription was damaged. The inscription indicates definitely the use of Śaka era in the region as early as 639 CE. In 357 Funan was ruled by Indian King named, according to dynastic histories of the Chin and the Liang (of China), "Tien Chu Chan-tan" who may probably be a Kushana in the line of Kanishka. In the seventh century a Śaka Brahman arrived from the Dekkan and married the daughter of the king Īśānavarma I. (Cœdès 1968: 46-7)

VAJRAYĀNA BUDDHISM

The earliest epigraphic evidence that hints at the existence of Vajrayāna in Thailand is the Semamuang inscription found in Nakhon Si Thammarat Province southern Thailand. It dates back to 775 CE and was written entirely in Sanskrit. It mentions that the king of Śrīvijaya erected a triple temple made of bricks to be the residence of Māraniṣūdana (Buddha), Kajakara (One who holds a lotus = Padmapāṇi Bodhisattva) and Vajrin (Vajrapāṇi Bodhisattva). The temple is compared with kuliśa (=vajra) on the mountain of defilements. Since the temple in question has not been located so far. It can be hypothetically suggested that the temple might be similar to Chandimendut near Borobudur, Indonesia (Figs. 5, 6).

The inscriptions and sculptures found at the Temple of Phimai (Vimāya),

FIGURE 5: CHANDIMENDUT NEAR BOROBUDUR, INDONESIA

FIGURE 6: THE BUDDHA IMAGE IN VITARKAMUDRĀ INSIDE CHANDIMENDUT

indicate that it was a big centre of Vajrayāna Buddhism from tenth to thirteenth centuries (Fig. 7, 8)

The Buddha is described in an inscription as having four bodies which is unique because normally the Buddha is described in Mahayāna Buddhism as having three bodies. It is mentioned in another inscription that Trailokyavijaya (Fig. 9) was erected at the temple of Vimāya to be the Senāpati of Kamrateṅ Añ Jagat Vimāya, the central Buddha image of the temple.

The inscription in Sanskrit and Khmer found at Ban Sab Bak, Pak Thong

FIGURE 7: BUDDHA WITH FOUR BODIES?

Chai district, Nakhon Ratchasima Province, Northeastern Thailand, undoubtedly indicates the strength of Vajrayāna Buddhism in that area in 1066 CE. (Prapandvidya 1990: 10-4).

The people known as Syāṃ were among the slaves of a temple in the inscription of Jaya Parameśvaravarman, the king of Champa (1044?-60). (Cœdès 1968: 140). In the twelfth century, the bas-reliefs of Angkor Wat represent at the head of the great procession of the southern gallery a group of warriors whom two short inscriptions identify as Syāṃ (Fig. 10) (ibid: 190).

The Syāṃ were probably the Thai. Thus they appeared in Southeast Asia as early as eleventh century. King Ramagamhaeng, the third king of Sukhothai kingdom, accepted Srilankan Theravāda Buddhism from Nakhon Si Thammarat as national religion as suggested in his inscription, the first inscription in Thai Language. (CSS: 13-14; ṇa Nagara and Griswold: 261-2, 274). Thai people have professed Theravāda Buddhism ever since.

FIGURE 8: DEITY HOLDING VAJRAS AT THE DOORFRAME OF THE TEMPLE OF PHIMAI

Figure 9: Trailokyavijaya?

Figure 10: Thai Army Depicted on the Southern Gallery of Angkor Wat

THE *RĀMĀYAṆA*

The earliest record of the gift of the *Rāmāyaṇa*, the *Māhābhārata* and the *Purāṇas* exists in a temple which is situated at Veal Kantel near Stung Treng, The Kingdom of Cambodia. The inscription is in Sanskrit engraved during the reign of King Bhavavarman I (sixth-seventh centuries). It also records the daily recitation of the three sacred texts (Majumdar 1953: 18-19, Barth: 28-31). This is the earliest inscription that refers to the *Rāmāyaṇa* found in Southeast Asia.

At the Temple of Phimai (Vimāya), which was erected as early as eleventh century CE, about 60 km. to the east of the city of Nakhon Ratchasima, northeastern Thailand, are found the bas-reliefs on the *Rāmāyaṇa* based on the world famous text composed by Sage Vālmīki (Figs. 11, 12)

FIGURE 11: MONEKY ARMY BUILDING A BRIDGE TO LANKA

FIGURE 12: RĀMA AND LAKṢMAṆA BEING TIED WITH SERPENT NOOSE (NĀGAPĀŚA)

THE IMPACT OF THE *RĀMĀYAṆA* IN ASIA

The traditional author of the *Rāmāyaṇa* was the sage Vālmīki as mentioned earlier. The legend was perhaps committed to verse, excluding the first and the last books, a little before the commencement of the Christian era (Basham: 414). The story of Rāma spreads over all the cultures of the Indian Subcontinent and Southeast Asia. It appears in literatures, in music, in dance and drama, in painting and sculpture, in classical and folk traditions, in hundreds of languages, in thousands of tellings and retellings from thousands of tellers. Each of these versions has its own special flavor, ambience and distinctive style (Sattar: Intro. X). According to Singaravelu the following versions of the *Rāmāyaṇa* are mentioned: Vietnamese, Bengali, Burmese, Khmer, Chinese, Gujarati, Javanese, Kashmir, Khotanese, Laotian, Malay, Marathi, Oriya, Singhalese, Tamil, Telugu, Thai, Tibetan (Thipkesorn: Thai section, 2).

The Japanese versions of the *Rāmāyaṇa* were undoubtedly derived from the Indian *Rāmāyaṇa* but they have come to differ in details from their original in the course of their transmission through India onto China and from there to Japan (Hara: English section, 69).

RĀMĀYAṆA IN THAILAND

The Thai, according to the evidence of an inscription in Champa and bas-reliefs at Angkor Wat, as mentioned earlier, seem to have appeared in Southeast Asia as early as eleventh century CE. The first Thai kingdom was Sukhothai, established in the latter half of thirteenth century CE. The third king of Sukhothai (Skt. Sukhodaya) was named Rāmagamhaeng which attested the association of the royalty with the *Rāmāyaṇa*. His successors had part of their names' signifying that they belonged to the family of Rāma (Rāmavaṃśa) of the Sun race (Sūryavaṃśa).

Later another Thai kingdom was established in the central part of Thailand by King Uthong whose name after coronation was Rāmādhibodi (Skt-Rāmādhipati). He named his capital as Ayodhyā. Many kings of Ayodhyā attached Rāma as part of their names after coronation.

The present dynasty which is designated as Phra Rājavongchakrī (Skt-Cakrivaṃśa) has ruled Bangkok since 1782. All the kings of this dynasty are designated as Rāma. The present king is Rāma IX.

KHON OR THAI MASK DRAMA

Khon is meant only for the kind of play for which the theme is exclusively *Rāmāyaṇa* (Figs. 13, 14).

It was staged in Thailand as early as the reign of King Nārāyaṇa (1656-88) of Ayudhya period as evident from the record by de La Loubère who listed it as a kind of plays in which the characters wear masks ((Loubère: 217). In

FIGURE 13: RĀMA, ASSISTED BY HANUMĀN AND LAKṢMAṆA, FIGHTING WITH RĀVAṆA

FIGURE 14: RĀMA, IN GREEN FACED MASK AND LAKṢMAṆA IN GOLDEN MASK SITTING ON A BAMBOO RAIL IN A TYPE OF KHON CALLED KHON NANG RAO

Khon performance the performers wear masks which indicate the characters in the *Rāmāyaṇa*. The masks are of various designs. As the performers wear masks they cannot utter words properly so there must be reciters whose roles are to speak and describe the events for the performers. Nowadays human characters and female demons with few exceptions, do not wear masks. Only the demon and monkeys do. Even the performers without masks do not utter any words, they make gestures according to the description of the reciters.

MURAL PAINTINGS AND BAS-RELIEFS ON THE *RĀMĀYAṆA*

The whole story of the *Rāmāyaṇa* known in Thai as *Ramakian* (Rāmakīrti) appears in the form of wall-painting in the galleries around the temple of the Emerald Buddha, better known as Wat Phra Kaew (Fig. 15)

FIGURE 15: VIṢṆU TRANSFORMS HIMSELF INTO A CELESTIAL NYMPH AND DANCES IN ORDER TO KILL NANDAKA WHO IS RĀVAṆA IN PREVIOUS EXISTENCE

It also appears in the form of carvings on stone slabs put up around the enclosure of the Ordination Hall of Wat Phra Jetubon (Jetavana) better known as Wat Pho in Bangkok (Fig. 16). In the Temple of the Emerald Buddha, some statues of demons in the *Ramakian* are also put up as guards at gates to the temple (Fig. 17).

Figure 16: Hanumān Keeps Rāma and Lakṣmaṇa in his Mouth to Protect them from Maiyarab

Figure 17: Rāvaṇ a Stands Guarding one of the Gates to the Temple of the Emerald Buddha

CONCLUSION

From both epigrapic and archaeological evidence Buddhism must have reached Southeast Asia as early as fourth century CE whereas the epigraphic evidence indicates that the *Rāmāyaṇa* reached here as early as sixth century CE. In the early stage Mūlasarvāstivāda and Sarvāstivāda, the Theravāda sects which used Sanskrit seem to existed side by side the Theravāda Buddhism which used Pali language. Mahāyāna Buddhism, especially the Vajrayāna branch seems to appear in Southern Thailand in eighth century CE and it became stronger in the region of Phimai and Pak Thong Chai of Nakhon Ratchasima Province in eleventh century CE. Thai people professed Srilankan Theravāda Buddhism since the reign of King Ramagamhaeng of Sukhotha kingdom which was established in around 1249 CE. The earliest evidence of the *Rāmāyaṇa* in Thailand was the bas-reliefs at the Temple of Phimai, Nakhon Ratchasima, which was erected as early as eleventh century CE. Hence, the *Rāmāyaṇa* has had a strong influence on Thai literature and different forms of art since Sukhothai period.

WORKS CITED

Barth, A. *Inscription du Sanscrites. In Notices et Extraits des Manuscrits de la Bibliotheque Nationale et Autres Bibliotheques*. Paris: Imprimerie, MDCCCLXXXV.

Basham, A.L. *The Wonder that was India*. Calcutta: Fontana Books, 1982.

Cāruek Nai Pradeś Daiy (CNPD), Book 1, BE 2529. Bangkok: Krom Śilpākar, 1986.

Cāruek Samay Sukhodaya. Bangkok: Krom Śilpākar, 1983.

Cœdès, G. *The Indianized States of Southeast Asia*, ed. Walter F. Vella. Trans. Susan Brown Cowing. Honolulu: East-West Center Press, 1968.

Inscription du Cambodge, vol. V (ed and trans G. Cœdès). Paris: *École Française d'Extrême-Orient*, 1953.

Gonda, J. *Sanskrit in Indonesia* (2nd edn.). New Delhi: International Academy of Indian Culture, 1973.

Hara, Minoru. *Rama Stories in China and Japan*: A Comparison. In the English Section of Souvenir Volume Prepared on the occasion of the "2nd International Ramayana Conference" in Thailand, 8 to 11 April. Bangkok: Thai-Bharat Cultural Lodge, 1986.

Krairiksh, Piriya. *Buddhist Folk Tales Depicted* at Chula Pathon Cedi (English section). Bangkok: Prachandra Printing Press, 1974.

Loubere, de la. *Du Royaume de Siam*, Vols. I-II, trans. Sant T. Komolabutr. Amsterdam, 1691.

Majumdar, R.C. *Inscriptions of Kambuja*. Calcutta: The Asiatic Society. *Champa, History and Culture of an Indian Colonial Kingdom in the Far East*, 1953. 2nd-16th Century A.D, Book I-III. Delhi: Gian Publishing House, rpt., 1985.

Malalasekera, G.P. *Dictionary of Pali Proper Name*, vol. II. London: The Pali Text Society, 1960.

Ṇa Nagara Prasert and Griswold, A.B. *Epigraphic and Historical Studies*. Bangkok: The Historical Society under the Royal Patronage of H.R.H. Princess Maha Chakri Sirindhorn, 1992.

Prapandvidya, Chirapat. *The Sab Bak Inscription, Evidence of an Early Vajrayāna Buddhist Presence in Thailand. In Journal of the Siam Society*, Vol. 78, Part 2. Bangkok: Amarin Printing Group Co. Ltd, 1990.

Sircar, Dines Chandra, ed. *Select Inscriptions Bearing on Indian History and Civilization*, vol. I. Calcutta: University of Calcutta, 1965.

———. *Ramakian (Ramayana), Mural Painting along the Galleries of the Temple of the Emerald Buddha*, Bangkok: Government Lottery, 1982.

Sattar, Arshia, trans. *The Vālmīki Rāmāyaṇa*. New Delhi: Penguin Books, 1996.

Suzuki, D.T. *Outlines of Mahayana Buddhism*. New York: Schocken Books, 1973.

Swami Satyananda Puri. *The Ramakirti (Ramakian), the Thai Version of the Ramayana*, 3rd edn. Bangkok: India Studies Centre, Thammasat University, 1998.

Thipkesorn, Choosak, trans. *A Comparative Study of Ramayana of Different Countries by S.Singaravelu.* Translated into Thai by Choosak Thipkesorn. In the Thai Section of Souvenir Volume Prepared on the occasion of the "2nd International Ramayana Conference" in Thailand, 8 to 11 April. Bangkok: Thai-Bharat Cultural Lodge, 1986.

13

Experiences in ASEAN Cultural Relation Activities

M.R. CHAKRAROT CHITRABONGS

In 1977, a summit meeting of ASEAN countries determined that a "Permanent Committee on Social and Cultural Activities" be set up with the aim of preserving the cultural heritage and traditions of ASEAN countries as well as to promote cultural cooperation and understanding between member countries for their mutual benefits and development.

In 1980, the "ASEAN Committee on Culture and Information" (ASEAN-COCI) was set up to administer over the joint cultural and information projects of member countries. Funding for the implementation of the project, now known as the "ASEAN Cultural Fund" was a donation from the Japanese government to the amount of 5,000 billion yen, or equivalent to approx 25 million US $, with the principle aim of using 80 percent of the annual interest gained. At present, the ASEAN Cultural Fund stands at approx 40 Million US $ (30 September 2010).

ASEAN-COCI is the body responsible for the approval of project proposals by member countries both at the Intra-ASEAN level and the cooperation level with "ASEAN Dialogue Partners", namely Australia, China, India, Japan, Korea, New Zealand, Russia, Pakistan, etc., as well as the cooperation between ASEAN and other international organizations such as UNESCO and GCC (Gulf Cooperation Countries).

At the initial stages, ASEAN projects came under the scrutiny of four working groups of experts:

- Working Group on Literature and ASEAN Studies
- Working Group on Visual and Performing Arts
- Working Group on Printed Materials and Media
- Working Group on Radio/Television and Film/Video

In 2000, however, these 4 expert working groups were reorganized into two sub-committees:

- Sub-Committee on Culture
- Sub-Committee on Information

INITIAL INVOLVEMENT

I was inducted into the Thai National ASEAN-COCI in the initial stages, as soon as I joined the government service in 1974. As an art teacher with the added advantage of fluency in English, I worked for the Working Group on Visual and Performing Arts. I drafted the project proposal for the first ASEAN Painting Exhibition and Symposium as well as the detailed Terms of Reference that would become a model for other related subsequent projects. This first project called for the submission of a number of paintings from each of the member countries for exhibition in Bangkok, the host country, together with relevant materials for publication. During the exhibition, experts came to present papers at a symposium. When the exhibition came to a close, the host country was responsible for the packaging and transportation of the whole collection to the next host country in rotation so that each member country could exhibit the same collection in turn, while the last host country was responsible for the dispatch and return of the art work to the country of origin.

In subsequent developments of such projects, some artists/creators of the artwork were invited to take part in the symposium resulting in a satisfactory and vibrant networking of ASEAN artists. Workshops were initiated where not only completed works of arts were exhibited, but artists actually created new works together in common studios, encouraging further exchanges at the personal level. A new development was the Sculpture Workshop in which artists cooperated to create large scale sculptural installations as a gift and tribute to the host country. Using the well-established round-robin arrangement, each ASEAN country now permanently exhibits sculptures by ASEAN artists in public spaces. Finally the sphere of activities came to embrace the folk crafts and craftsmanship. Symposia and workshops were no longer attended by well-established or famous people, but opportunity was given to indigenous people and villagers to display their traditional skills such as weaving, basketry and dying.

In the field of Performing Arts, similar arrangements were made. Member countries would send their traditional performers to perform together at the same venue in the host country. There would also be workshops where each country performs and even studies on hand-on training in the art of other countries. There would invariably be a joint performance in which all participants performed on stage. This vibrant cultural interaction has continued to the present and the ASEAN-COCI entertains every intention to continue to do so into the far future.

ASEAN-INDIA CULTURAL RELATIONS

I have no personal experience in ASEAN-COCI and India cultural relations activity. Thailand does not regard India as merely an ASEAN Dialogue Partner, but as a major or "mother" source of Thai, indeed Southeast Asian Culture. This is the reason why Thailand has engaged in Indian-Thai cultural exchange activities throughout history. My personal involvement has been in two distinct fields: *Ramayana* presentations and in the study of ancient Tribhumi Cosmology.

RAMAKIRTI

The story of *Ramayana*, or *Ramakirti* (In honour of Rama) as known in Thai, is well known and loved throughout the country. It is manifested in all art forms from the most refined classical Thai art forms as seen in the high society to the most humble social strata. The variety of art forms that displays this story is all embracing from murals paintings to puppetry. The reason is evident because of the Thai acceptance of the principle of divine kingship in which the Thai King is believed to be an avatar of Lord Vishnu. Thais delight in using the *Ramayana* as a vehicle to exhibit this profound belief and honour our beloved sovereign king.

In 1991, I had the occasion and opportunity to organize an International Ramayana Festival in honour or Her Royal Highness Princess Maha Chakri Sirindhorn on her thirty-sixth birthday at the newly inaugurated and prestigious theatre venue in Bangkok, the Thailand Cultural Centre. This celebration was also intended as a national level display of *Ramakirti* as it exists in modern society. For seven consecutive days, performing groups from all over the country were invited to perform the story on six stages on the grounds of the cultural centre. They came in various art forms from the classical Khon masked dance-drama to shadow puppets. On the international stage, five ASEAN member countries known to entertain a *Ramayana* tradition, namely Cambodia, Indonesia, Laos, Singapore and Thailand, were given individual performance opportunities. India was also invited as the originator of the story and the Thai audience delighted in an opportunity to witness the Kathakali Dance. The highlight of this festival was an opportunity for all countries to perform together on the same stage in which each country took turns to tell the story from the beginning to the end in their own performing style.

This experience which took place some two decades ago was repeated in 2011 when Thailand celebrated another important birth anniversary, that of His Majesty the King on his eighty-fourth birthday. The Ministry of Culture produced another International Ramayana Festival. This time, it was intended to invite all ASEAN countries plus India as a special guest for the same reason as before. In the actual event some ASEAN countries declined the invitation for the reason that they do not present the *Ramayana*. One country, however, the Philippines joined the festival with a contemporary dance performance of *Ramayana*. India once more presented the Kathakali dance. In this 2011 festival, I introduced something never before attempted: the joint performance of all countries on the same stage and at the same time! This followed the tried and tested sequential telling of the story by individual countries. Thailand reserved for itself the final episode of the Triumphal Return to Ayodhya in which Rama and Sita are installed on the throne while all visiting countries appear on stage to congratulate them before Thai dancers representing angels danced in celebration. This was intended to serve as an expression of our deep seated belief that the King of Thailand was an avatar of Lord Vishnu on earth.

THE TRIBHUMI BUDDHIST COSMOLOGY

As part of same celebration of H.M. the King's eighty-fourth birthday anniversary, the Ministry of Culture is publishing a new edition of "Tribhumikatha" (The Story of the Three Planes of Existance) entitled *Tribhumikatha, the Rama IX Edition*, dedicated to two great Thai Kings: Phra Maha Dhammaraja Lithai of Sukhothai and King Bhumibol Adulyadej, Rama IX of the Chakri Dynasty.

The Thai heritage of the book of *Tribhumi Buddhist Cosmology* derives from the ancient Indian Heritage of Brahmanism, Hinduism and Theravada Buddhism. In 1345, Phya Lithai, Uparaja of Sukhothai was ordained as a Buddhist monk in accordance with tradition. He spent his monkhood deep in study of the Tipitaka and other cannons on cosmological studies. Then he wrote a thesis entitled "Tribhumikatha" in the Thai language, using the Thai script, a writing system that had been invented, based on the ancient Khmer script, by his grandfather King Ramkhamhaeng in 1283. The book survives today because it has been continuously copied from generation to generation and because it has become the principle mainstay in Thai Culture. There was also an ancient offshoot of this book, the illustrated book on *Buddhist Cosmology*, presumably created to help illiterate people understand the principles of the Buddhist teachings.

The hand copying process had ensured the survival of this book in both the textual and pictorial formats, but the printing press almost put into extinction the illustrated book format. As printers delighted to put to press the text of *Tribhumikatha*, they had no technical skill to print the illustrations during the early period. Later, as book illustration techniques became available, they resorted to printing reproductions of the available illustrated manuscripts rather than creating new pictorial illustrations. Even at present, publishers prefer to reproduce the most beautifully painted illustrated manuscripts of the seventeenth-nineteenth centuries that have survived as rare books in the National Library. The ancient tradition of creating hand painted illustrated manuscripts was in danger of being discontinued.

Bearing this in mind, the Ministry of Culture has decided to create a new painting for use as the illustrations in *Tribhumikatha, the Rama IX Edition*.

A number of artists of all ages, selected from their known abilities and interests on the *Tribhumi Cosmology*, have joined together to create a work that will surely become known as "the biggest hanging scroll in Thai traditional painting". This style of painting also embraces a visual historical account of the Thai painting development. The Aruppa Bhumi is painted in the ancient style symbolic of absolute detachment from materialism. The Ruppa Bhumi section displays the majestic classical style of the Ayutthaya Period. The Kama Bhumi section allow the most recent influences of Western Art to appear, showing three dimensionality, correct anatomy, fore shortening and light and shadows. Hell beings, for example, are shown in the most grotesque rendition ever.

The publication of *Tribhumikatha, the Rama IX Edition* is expected to come to completion in December 2012. The printed form will comprise the Thai text as revised by the Rajapandit Institute, include necessary explanatory notes, the English translation of the text (produced by ASEAN-COCI in its project on ASEAN Literature) and illustrated with the new painting by the living traditional artists of today as mentioned above. This publication is intended for worldwide distribution.

All these different elements are thus strongly indicative of the long and celebrated integration of the twin cultures of India and Thailand.

PART 4

Towards Cultural Syncretism: Texts, Performance, History

14

Bhagavad Gita: Outlines of a Secular Critique[1]

MEGHNAD DESAI

The *Bhagavad Gita* is a central text of Brahmanism.[2] The German philosopher William von Humboldt called it 'the most beautiful, perhaps the only true philosophical song existing in any known language'. When the Atom bomb was first tested in the deserts of New Mexico, J. Robert Oppenheimer who led the project recited the first line of the verse 11.32 [3] from the *Gita* to invoke the terrifying sight unfolding before him.

The *Gita* is perhaps the best known book of India and as S. Radhakrishnan puts it 'the most influential work in Indian thought'.[4] Unlike the *Vedas* and the *Upanishads*, the *Gita* is short and concise, a book of just 700 verses that one can compactly carry in one's pocket and even memorise in its entirety as many have done.

Of course what makes the *Gita* sacred is that presumably the Supreme Lord himself in his avatar as Krishna recited it for the benefit of his friend Arjun. It is because of this unique characteristic of having divine authorship that the *Gita* has become the best known and the most commented upon text over the centuries. Its status was confirmed by Shankara's commentary in the ninth century CE. While Shankara refers to commentaries before his own,[5] his is the first and most authoritative commentary. Indeed Swami Vivekananda thought Shankara may even have written the *Gita* himself. Thus, he says in his *Thoughts on the Gita* "(T)he book, *Gita*, had not been much known to the generality of people before Shankaracharya made it famous by writing his great commentary on it. . . . Some infer that Shankaracharya was the author of the, *Gita* and that it was he who foisted it in the body of the *Mahabharata*" [*Complete Works*, vol. 4: 102-3].

THE MODERN LIFE OF THE *GITA*

The modern life of the *Gita* begins with the enterprise of Warren Hastings to have it translated in English. Sir Charles Wilkins (1750-1833) who did the translation made it possible for those who could not read Sanskrit to access the message. Soon after, the fashion of translating the *Gita* into European languages grew till Max Weber was able to say that the *Gita* had been 'Translated into almost all the languages of the earth.' [Weber, 361], Wilkins opened the door to the global popularity of the *Gita*.[6]

Yet the best read version of the *Gita* was by Sir Edwin Arnold. 'The Song Celestial' published in 1885 was to influence the young Mohandas Karamchand Gandhi when he reached London three years later. The *Gita* became a weapon in the independence struggle when after the partition of Bengal in 1905, a militant movement broke out across India, most especially in Bengal, Maharashtra and Punjab. Young people formed a society called "Anushilan" which was dedicated to a violent overthrow of British Rule. Khudiram Bose who was hanged for the killing of two English ladies died with the *Gita* slung across his neck on the gallows.[7] When the offices of the Dacca (now Dhaka) Anushilan Samiti were searched, a dozen copies of the *Gita* were found. Members of secret societies dedicated to a violent overthrow swore on the *Gita*.

QUESTIONING THE *GITA*

Most people who take part in listening to lectures on the *Gita* or sometimes even read the *Gita*, do so uncritically. Just to recite or listen as many do is, by itself, supposed to give you *punya*- good marks with God. One need not question or even try to understand the contents of the work. Suffice it to know that at the beginning of the Mahabharat war, Krishna the God-charioteer told Arjun what the *Gita* now contains. The divine association is a guarantee of the truth and the sanctity of the text. As it is, it is a difficult, often confusing book which suddenly launches into new topics in the midst of other matters, has largely redundant Manichean sections attacking lower castes and non-Aryan people and at times is baffling. If you take it all as the saying of a single Divine persona, then you have to perform intellectual acrobatics to make it sound consistent. This is why commentators have disagreed among themselves and found whatever they wish to find. Tilak found in it a message for militant action while Gandhi, an apostle of nonviolence, accepted a text which is a long persuasion to go out there and kill all.

Yet, there are a few critics who differ from the majority of readers about the merits of the *Bhagavad Gita*. Kosambi and Ambedkar are two worth quoting. Kosambi in his essay 'Social and Economic Aspects of the *Gita*', fires an opening salvo:

> The *Gita* has attracted minds of bents entirely different from each other and from that of Arjuna. Each has interpreted the supposedly divine words so differently from all the others that the original seems far more suited to raise doubts and to split a personality than to heal an inner division. Any moral philosophy which managed to receive so many variant interpretations from minds in widely different types of society must be highly equivocal. No question remains of its basic validity if the meaning is so flexible (12).[8]

Ambedkar starts with the same question as Kosambi does.

One is forced to ask why there is such divergence of opinion among scholars? My answer to this question is that scholars have gone on a false errand. They have gone on a search for the message of the *Bhagvad Gita* on the assumption that it is a gospel as the *Koran*, the *Bible*, or the *Dhammapada* is. In my opinion this assumption is quite a false assumption. The *Bhagvad Gita* is not a gospel and it can therefore have no message and it is futile to search for one. (T)he *Bhagvad Gita* is neither a book of religion nor a treatise on philosophy. What the *Bhagvad Gita* does is to defend certain dogmas of religion on philosophic grounds...It uses philosophy to defend religion. (p. 193)[9]

(T)he dogmas which the *Gita* defends are the dogmas of counter-revolution as put forth in the Bible of counter-revolution, namely Jaimini's *Purva-Mimansa*. There ought to be no difficulty in accepting this proposition. If there is any it is largely due to wrong meaning attached to the word *Karma yoga*. Most writers on the *Bhagvad Gita* translate the word *Karma yoga* as 'action' and the word *Jnana yoga* as 'knowledge' and proceed to discuss the *Bhagvad Gita* as though it was engaged in comparing and contrasting knowledge versus action in a generalized form. This is quite wrong. The *Bhagvad Gita* is not concerned with any general, philosophical discussion of action versus knowledge. As a matter of fact, the *Bhagvad Gita* is concerned with the particular and not with the general. By *Karma yoga* or action, the *Gita* means the dogmas contained in Jaimini's *Karma Kanda* and by *Jnana yoga* or knowledge it means the dogmas contained in Badarayan's *Brahma Sutras*.... It is to lift the *Gita* from the position of a party pamphlet engaged in a controversy on small petty points and make it appear as though it was a general treatise on matters of high philosophy that this attempt is made to inflate the meaning of the words Karma and Jnana and make them words of general import. Mr. Tilak is largely to be blamed for this trick of patriotic Indians.

Dr Ambedkar raises several issues in this critique. Of course by counter-revolution, he means the fight waged against Buddhism by Brahmanism in which the *Bhagavad Gita* becomes a weapon. This fight was waged over more than a thousand years between the sixth century BCE and the ninth century CE when Shankara wrote his commentary. Not much has been written about this war between Buddhism and Brahmanism, and the traditional version of ancient Indian history erases all mention of Buddhism and pretends that Brahmanism was the most tolerant of all religions. There was a philosophical as well often a physical battle between the champions of Brahmanism and Buddhism.

THE PLACE OF THE *GITA* IN THE *MAHABHARAT*

The *Gita* is read as a separate, stand-alone text. But, within the *Mahabharat*, it is a part of the *Bhishma Parvan*. When reading the *Gita* on its own, we get the impression that on the first day of the *Mahabharat* war, as the armies are assembled, there is Arjun depressed and shaken. Then, in front of the waiting armies, Krishna launches into his long exposition of philosophy of the paths to attain moksha. At the end of the 700 verses, Arjun is convinced and decides to fight.

The *Bhishma Parvan* however presents a very different picture. After all attempts at preventing war fail, as described in the *Udyog Parvan*, the *Bhishma Parvan* starts on the tenth day of the War, not the first one. Sanjaya who has magical powers to see into the past, present and the future (*pratyakshadarshi sarvasya bhutabhavyabhavisyavit)* comes to Dhritarashtra the blind King to report that Bhishma is dead.

In the sixteenth *Adhyaya* of the *Bhishma Parvan*, Sanjaya begins to describe in great detail the armies arranged on either side on the morning of the first day. The eighteen armies, eleven of Duryodhana and seven of Yudhishthira are ready once again. In the seventeenth *Adhyaya*, Bhishma is reported by Sanjaya to have said

Adharmah ksatriyasyaisa yad vyadhimaranam grhe
Yad ajau nidhanam yati so'sya dharmah sanatanah. [Bhishma, 17.11]

It is a breach of the Law [*Dharma*] for a baron [*ksatriya*] to die of sickness at home, and his everlasting Law is it to find death on the battlefield. [Van Buitenen, 50-1; bracketed insertions are mine]

In the twentieth *Adhyaya* we begin again with Dhritarashtra asking as to which were the troops to greet the sunrise- his son's led by Bhishma or those led by Bhīma. Sanjaya gives a long description of the armies.

'The warriors in both armies exulted, and in both rose a fragrance of flowers and incense. The first clash of the massed, marshalled troops that slowly and proudly advanced was magnificent, and the sound of music mixed with peals of conches and drums and the noise of roaring elephants and churning troops was deafening.' [Van Buitenen, 68-9]

It is at this stage that Dhritarashtra asks once again the famous question with which the *Bhagavad Gita* proper starts

Dharmakshetre Kurukshetre samaveta yuyutsava
Mamaka pandavaschaiva kim kurvat vada Sanjaya. [Bhishma 23.1 .Bhagavad Gita 1.1.]
When in the Field of the Kurus, the Field of the Law, my troops and the Pandavas had massed belligerently, what did they do, Samjaya ? [Van Buitnen, 68-9]

There are several things to notice about this famous opening *sloka*. This is the first and the only time the expression *Dharmakshetre* is used, thus elevating a war over a fraternal property dispute into a sacred encounter. Why would Dhritarashtra call it a *dharmakshetra*, thus admitting the justness of the claim of his nephews? Then again the question that the Blind King asks has been asked by him twice in the previous *Adhyayas* already and answered by Sanjaya. Why do we now need the Blind King to ask again what Sanjaya has already told him?

The answer has to be that whatever was the original course of the narrative, someone wanted to make a stand-alone text of the eighteen *Adhyayas* which are form the *Gita*. The introductory question and Sanjaya's reply which then takes up the next twenty verses allow us to ignore all that has gone before in the *Bhishma Parva* and focus on Arjun's problem. This is no proof but a strong indication that the *Gita*, if not inserted into the *Bhishma Parva* as Vivekanand suspected, at some later stage was so rearranged that it could be extruded so as to be read separately.

Sanjaya repeats much of what he has already said to Dhritarashtra in 23.2-20 (*Bhagavad Gita* 1.2-20) but then in 23.21[*Bhagavad Gita* 1.21] Arjun requests Krishna to place his chariot in the middle of the two armies [*senayorubhayor madhye]*.

But then once the chariot is moved to the middle of the two armies, Arjun begins to have what can only be called a nervous breakdown: his body begins to shake, his mouth is parched, his limbs collapse and his favourite bow Gandiva slips from his hands as his skin burns. In short, he is in a funk. Thus he raises the fundamental issue: What is the point of war? I don't want victory, nor kingdom nor pleasures.

Krishna begins very much as one would expect any coach or mentor to do. He rebukes him and tries to shame him into action. Yet Arjun is unmoved and in distress submits to Krishna seeking instruction from him (*shadhi maam tvam prapannam)* Krishna replies to him laughing at first (*prahasan)*. Then from 2.11 onward begins the *Gita* proper as many have come to see it. This is the beginning of Krishna's exposition of his response to Arjun's grief. The response can be described as two fold to begin with. The first response is what I would call Irrelevance of Agency. This occupies 2.11 to 2 .30. Then there is a sudden change in the response and Krishna tries Humiliation of the Ego (2.31-38). This latter response is much more in line with what any good coach would do while the first is at a higher philosophical level.

When these two responses are done, I believe the *Gita* proper should have ended. What follows from 2.39 is another switch in theme. The text catches up with 2.30 and goes down philosophical byways and highways for the next sixteen more *Adhyaya*s. Why should this be so?

Radhakrishnan gets to the heart of the matter when he says, "It is possible that Arjuna might have had pointed advice from his friend Krishna which the poet (i.e. the author of the *Gita*) worked up into the poem of seven hundred verses."[10] What is implied is that there was an author other than Krishna who found the original short text and then elongated it into a 700 verse poem. We shall see later why this is a very plausible idea.

IRRELEVANCE OF AGENCY

This is the first and what may be called Vedantic response. Krishna tells Arjun that in fact he will not be the author of his actions if he does fight and kill his relatives. Life and death are delusions that Arjun suffers from. He neither kills nor is he killed. Those he thinks are going to die have had their destiny already determined independently of what Arjun might or might not do. He has to wise up since the Wise know what is not what.

This is then a 'get-out-of-jail free' card from the Lord himself. You don't kill and are not killed. The body is transient and the soul cannot kill or be killed. So there are no consequences of human action. One can regard this as a deep doctrine as many do or as a fantastic escapism. Dr Ambedkar, being a lawyer, was unconvinced:

> To say that killing is no killing because what is killed is the body and not the soul is an unheard of defence of murder. This is one of the doctrines which make some people say that the doctrines make one's hair stand on their end. If Krishna were to appear as a lawyer acting for a client who is being tried for murder and pleaded the defence set out by him in the *Bhagvad Gita* there is not the slightest doubt that he would be sent to the lunatic asylum. [Ambedkar, p. 197]

HUMILIATION OF THE EGO

But starting with 2.31, Krishna changes tack. The next argument is what I label Humiliation of the Ego. This is a conventional argument in which Krishna uses the logic that Bhishma has already been quoted above as using. Arjun had objected that killing and destruction of the kin group could be *adharma* (1.39). This could lead to sin (1.36). Krishna now changes tack and talks of *svadharma* which overrides any general concern for *dharma*. Svadharma for a Kshatriya is to fight and not brood over consequences of killing.

I reckon this short passage of eight verses 2.31-38 is much more likely to appeal to Arjun's own sentiments. He has been brought up as a Kshatriya, aware of his duties and his obligations. In the earlier *Adhyaya*s of *Bhishma Parvan* the discourse of the Blind King and of the Grand Sire Bhishma, is very much embedded in the culture of the family in *Kshatradharma*, a trap out of which Dhritarashtra knows neither his sons nor his nephews can escape. This is Arjun's duty explained in terms of the here and now rather than from the point of view of higher philosophy of the nature of the soul.

It is quite likely that the 'pointed advice' that Radhakrishnan thought Krishna may have given to Arjun is contained in 2.31-38. Nothing more would be needed to make Arjun fight. To be told that if he does not fight, his rivals would not credit him with higher wisdom but cowardice would be enough to rouse him. To be told even more pointedly that he could not lose either way would reinforce the message. To be told that it was sinful not to fight and no sin to fight clinches the moral argument as far as a Kshatriya like Arjun is concerned.

I would therefore suggest that Arjun's *Gita* is 1.21-46 and 2.1-10 and 2.31-38; forty four slokas in all. It would make a perfect 23rd *Adhyaya* in Bhishma Parva. It is my argument that the *Gita* as it finally came to us is a result of many additions to what could have been a small original fragment, if there was one at all.

GITA AS A MULTI-AUTHORED TEXT

The idea that the *Gita* may be a multiple authored book is not new. Indeed it began with the first translation of Charles Wilkins' *Gita.* [11] Von Humboldt in reviewing Schlegel's Latin translation was "aware of the possibility that the text had been composed by more than one author over a considerable period of time. . . . (H)e regards the first eleven chapters as the 'original' ones" [Malinar, p.16]. Deussen another distinguished Sankritist divided the text into three thematic units, (1) ethics (Chs 1-6) (2) metaphysics (7-12) and (3) psychology (13-18). The French scholar Charpentier believed that what follows 2.38 "can in no wise have belonged to the original epic text" (23-25).

The most cogent argument for multiple authorship was made by the Maharashtrian scholar Dr Gajanan Shripat Khair. His book *Quest for the Original Gita* was published in 1969 and a revised edition was issued in 1997.[12] Khair does not seem to be aware of any of the literature from which I cited earlier. He has arrived at his contention entirely on his own analysis which makes the coincidence of his ideas with those of previous scholars all the more remarkable.[13]

He divides the *Bhagavad Gita* into three parts –*Trikala Gita* as he calls it. According to him:

The First Author wrote most of *Adhyaya*s 1 to 6. The period of writing was of the Older Upanishads and pre-Buddhist, around 600 BCE. The principal philosophical issue is Sannyasa and the solution is *Karma yoga* (126 verses or 18 %).

The Second Author wrote portions of *Adhyaya* 8, *Adhyaya*s 13 to 15, 17 and portions of 18. The period was contemporaneous with the Buddha and the philosophical authority is Old Upanishads as before. The problem is karma –choice (as Khair describes it) and the solution is *sattvikatva.* (119 verses or 17 %).

The Third Author is the editor and the final arbiter of the document. He wrote the entire *Adhyaya*s 7, 9-12, 16 plus interpolated in the *Adhyaya*s the two others wrote. The problem is 'diverse creeds' and the answer is bhakti. His authority is the New Upanishads and his period is 300 to 200 BCE. (455 verses or 65 %). Note that while Khair has a tripartite division of the *Bhagvad Gita,* his analysis is more subtle than that of Deussen as he argues that the third author mixed up the different parts which disguises the divisions.

If we are to take this classification as a working hypothesis, it would seem that the *Gita* gets settled into its final shape at the time when the battle between the Buddhists and the Brahmanists is at its most ferocious. Of course, Kosambi puts the final rendition of the *Gita* much later to the Gupta period rather than the highpoint of the Buddhist period as Khair does. The ideas common to Kosambi and Khair are that (a) there are multiple authors and (b) that the text evolves over time as it responds to different circumstances prevailing as per the struggle between Buddhism and Brahmanism while Khair alone contributes the idea that (c) the Third Author adds to and edits the text to give it a sort of unity.

This makes sense if we see that the First Author is not joining a battle against Buddhism but expounding the Upanshadic doctrine in a concise way. It is like a catechism for young students. Once we are beyond 2.38 Arjun becomes only a vehicle for expounding what has to be taught. Hence, we begin with a mention of Sankhya in 2.39 and other philosophical issues follow.

The Second Author is a contemporary of Buddha if we are to take Khair's dating seriously. He is also a didactic writer expositing what has to be learnt. His style is dispassionate. He uses words such as *jnanin, munih, yatih, yogin* but sparsely. This is also a teaching text, meant for select audiences.

It is the Third Author who addresses the ordinary people who have little time and inclination for philosophical subtleties. As Khair says, "His main audience is the common people and the neglected persons, who were deprived of opportunities of spiritual and moral salvation. Traders, merchants, atheists, worshippers of ancestral and popular gods- this was his audience" (51) since by this time the need to spread Brahmanism as widely as possible to counter Buddhism's popularity is urgent. The second or third century BCE which Khair gives as likely date is the high point of spread of Buddhism with Ashoka having given royal patronage to Buddhism. The champions of Brahmanism had to fight back. The *Gita* with a popularised section moulded along with the earlier parts was to be the weapon. The date suggested by Kosambi of 150-350 CE would be even more suitable because under the Guptas, the Brahminical fightback had Royal patronage.

Khair's virtue is that he proposes a plausible hypothesis of how the different layers were integrated into a seamless whole which gives the impression of an integral text which most readers of the *Bhagavad Gita* take it to be. The idea that there was an author who was also the last one in and who edited the entire text by his interpolations to weave the separate texts into one is the missing link in the discussions of the experts who wrestled with the problem before he came along. Above all, his virtue is that he arrives at his conclusion unprompted and uninfluenced by the previous literature. He is a home-spun amateur reader of the *Bhagavad Gita* who stumbles upon his discovery all by himself and proceeds to construct a theory of why the *Bhagavad Gita* should be as it is- choppy and seamless at the same time.

We can conclude, however, that apart from Arjun's *Gita*, there may have been three other *Gitas*. Ignoring the interpolation attributed by Khair to the Third Author, we can say that the three *Gitas* were:

1. The Veda-Vedanta *Gita* or *Karma Yoga Gita* of the First Author mainly across *Adhyayas* 2 to 6
2. The Samkhya *Gita* or *Jnana Yoga Gita* of the Second Author *Adhyayas* 8 (part), 13, 14, 15, 17, 18 (part)
3. The *Bhakti Yoga Gita* of the Third Author *Adhyayas* 7, 9-12.

Indeed, the role of the *Bhagavad Gita* as a weapon in battle between Brahmanism and Buddhism is well explained by Pande (1994):

'The *Bhagavad Gita* is an evolving response which deals with the conflicts between Veda and Vedanta and then with the challenge posed to Vedanta by Buddhism. Its shift to Bhakti is thus the climax of the battle between Brahmanism and Buddhism. Indeed as Pande has observed "The *Bhagvad Gita* represents a progressive adaptation of the Vedanta to the challenges of the *Mahajanapada* Age."

CONCLUSION

What seems to be a cautious conclusion from the discussion above is that:

(a) There are probably multiple authors of the *Bhagavad Gita* as shown by stylistic changes and the frequent shift of subject matter.

(b) There was probably an original short sharp lesson for Arjun by Krishna assuming that these were historical characters as described in the *Mahabharat.*

(c) The periodisation of the three other segments follows the pattern of pre-Buddhist, contemporary with Buddhism's early days and lastly in the period when Brahmanism was reviving.

The purpose of essaying such a secular or humanist critique of the *Gita* is not to delve into the religious ideas of Buddhism as against Brahmanism. The important point is that the battle between the two was waged on the social terrain as much as the religious one. Buddhism rejected *varna* distinctions, challenged the hegemony of Brahmins and the necessity of ritual performance. It doubted the existence of a God and of the soul. Its challenge to the Brahmanical social order was the most profound revolutionary challenge to the old order. Urban groups mainly Vaishyas and Shudras joined Buddhism in large numbers. For around five hundred years between the death of Buddha and the advent of the Common Era Buddhism shaped the social order in parts of India north and south.

The recapture of the initiative by Brahmanism which took place during the first seven hundred years of the Common Era, was achieved as much by the religious and philosophical debates as by the contest for patronage from one or the other King.[Verardi op.cit.]

When Buddhism was defeated and left India for other Asian regions, the caste society was re-established firmly in India. Buddhism was wiped out from the historical memory of India till James Prinsep inaugurated the rediscovery of Budddhism by his decipherment of the Brahmi script. We now know much more about Buddhism and its place in Indian history but that is no thanks to Brahmanism which suppressed all memory of the challenge. When Ambedkar chose to reject Brahmanism for himself and his followers he chose Buddhism. This as much as anything else demonstrates the radical challenge of Buddhism.

The *Bhagavad Gita* was the most effective instrument in this struggle. It offered a simple, easy to read or recite, source of philosophical ideas of Brahmanism. It lent authority to these verses by attributing them to Krishna whose *bhakti* became a powerful instrument for winning over the masses to the cause of Brahmanism.

All this happened over a thousand years and more. We still lack a proper history of the rise and fall of Buddhism and the decline and renaissance of Brahmanism. Further analysis of the *Bhagvad Gita* may yet help in this task.

NOTES

1. Based on the forthcoming book *Who Wrote The Bhagavad Gita?*
2. I use the word Brahmanism rather than Hinduism because I think it better represents the nature of the religion both because of the centrality of the notion of Brahman and the apex position of the Brahmins. Max Weber the famous German Sociologist in his book *The Religion of India* says "Only in recent literature have the Indians themselves begun to designate their religious affiliation as Hinduism. It is the official designation of the English census for the religious complex also described in Germany as 'Brahmanism'". [Weber, *The Religion of India*, p. 4]
3. *Kalo'smi lokakshayakrut'pravruddho lokan samahartumihah pravruttah* The Blessed Lord said: I am the Time-Spirit, destroyer of the world, arisen huge-statured for the destruction of the nations. Aurobindo's translation of verse 32 first line of the 11th *Adhyaya* of the *Gita*.
4. S. Radhakrishnan. *Indian Philosophy*, vol. 1 (Oxford India), p. 510. Humboldt quote is also on the same page.
5. Shankara mentions critics as Vrittika but not by name. Baudhayan is often cited as a possible earlier commentator but his manuscript has not been recovered as yet.
6. Malinar, op. cit gives a detailed account of the many translations in German and the debates which followed.
7. This and other details on the use of the *Gita* by 'terrorists' is from Bhiku Parekh (1989/99) *Colonialism, Tradition and Reform: An Analysis of Gandhi's Political Discourse* (Sage Publications, Delhi).
8. D.D. Kosambi (1962) 'Social and Economic Aspects of the *Bhagavad-Gita*', in *Myth and Reality: Studies in the Formation of Indian Culture* (Popular Prakashan, Bombay), 'Myth' hereafter.

9. 'Krishna and His *Gita*', in Valerian Rodrigues (ed.), *The Essential Writings of B.R. Ambedkar* (Oxford India, 2002), 193-204.
10. S. Radhakrishnan (1923/1999), *Indian Philosophy*, vol. 1, (Oxford India), 523.
11. Malinar, op. cit is a good source of the debates about the text of the *Bhagavad Gita* in Germany.
12. G.S. Khair (1969/97), *Quest for the Original Gita* (Somaiya Publications, Mumbai).
13. Malinar does mention Khair but does not give his ideas any more room than she does those of the others [27-28].

WORKS CITED

Rodrigues, Valerian ed. 'Krishna and His *Gita*', *The Essential Writings of B.R. Ambedkar*, (Oxford India, 2002), 193-204 (2010)

Khair, G.S. *Quest for the Original Gita*. 2nd edn. Mumbai: Somaiya Publications, 1997.

Kosambi, D.D. *Myth and Reality: Studies in the Formation of Indian Culture*. 2nd edn. Mumbai: Popular Prakashan, 2005.

Malinar, A. *The Bhagavad Gita: Doctrines and Context*. Cambridge: Cambridge University Press, 2007.

Minor, Robert. *Modern Indian Interpreters of Bhagavad Gita*. Albany, New York: State University of New York Press, 1986.

Pande, G.C. *Life and Thought of Sankaracharya*. Delhi: Motilal Banarasidass, 1994.

Radhakrishnan, S. *Indian Philosophy*, 2nd edn. New Delhi: Oxford, 1999.

——. *The Bhagavad Gita*. New Delhi: Harper Collins Publishers, 2010.

Verardi, Giovanni. *Hardships and Downfall of Buddhism in India*. New Delhi: Manohar, 2011.

Vivekananda, Swami. *The Complete Works of Swami Vivekanada*. 29th impression. Kolkata: Advaita Ashrama, 2009.

Gerth, Hans and Don Martindale trans. Max Weber. *The Religion of India: The Sociology of Hinduism and Buddhism*, 2nd edn. New Delhi: Munshiram Manoharlal, 2007.

15

The Old Javanese *Ramayana*

VINOD C. KHANNA

The precise nature of the cultural encounter of India with Indonesia in ancient times has been often been misunderstood. Early Western and Indian scholars tended to have an exaggerated perception of Indian influence; some later scholars swung to the other extreme, arguing that the cultural impact of the Indian subcontinent on the archipelago was marginal.[1] More recently a more balanced consensus is emerging which believes that Indian cultural elements arrived in a society which was already fairly sophisticated and sufficiently mature to absorb seminal inputs in such crucial areas as language, writing, religion, the arts and political concepts. Most importantly, this acculturation process was characterized by increasingly creative and assertive localization. Indonesia accepted such Indian cultural elements as appealed to it and creatively transformed them into integral parts of its own very rich culture.[2] The *Ramayana* was a very important partner in this amazingly productive civilizational phenomenon. It did not come to Indonesia in the form of a religious text or a holy book carried by proselytizers or conquering armies. It came as an important ingredient of a cultural movement of great intellectual power which was, amazingly, almost entirely peaceful.

In the course of history, Indonesia – like India – saw the birth of many *Ramayanas*. The work with the greatest claim to be Indonesia's *Adikavya* is the *Ramayana* written in Central Java some thousand years ago, during the reign of Balitung. . . 898-910 CE, according to the most famous Indonesian authorities on the subject, Poerbatjaraka[3] It is written in Old Javanese, a language rich in Sanskrit vocabulary but which is a distinct language belonging to the Austronesian linguistic group. There is no credible evidence about the name of the author though the Balinese, on the basis of a verse towards the end of the work, believe his name was Yogiswara.

This work belongs to the genre of Old Javanese poetry known as *kakawin* written in various metres largely borrowed from classical Sanskrit literature. It is the oldest and lengthiest *kakawin*. And according to many authorities it is also the finest work written in ancient Java, where the art of poetry was given the name *kalangwan,* 'beauty.' P.J. Zoetmulder in fact entitles his masterly survey of Old Javanese literature "Kalangawn", for to quote him: "it was the creation and enjoyment of the products of literary art which conveyed the ecstasy of losing oneself in the experience of beauty." (Preface)

The research by H.B. Sarkar, Manmohan Ghosh, Camille Bulcke and finally the detailed analysis by C. Hooykaas, has established beyond doubt that the main source to which the Old Javanese poet turned was not Valimiki's epic but another much later classical Sanskrit work *Ravanavadha,* more popularly known as *Bhattikavyam* after its author Bhatti [sixth-seventh centuries]. Bhatti narrates the story of Rama basically along Valmikian lines. However, he concludes his work with the triumphant return of Rama to Ayodhya and drops the Uttarakanda altogether. So does the Old Javanese *Ramayana Kakawin* [OJRK].

It was argued by Hooykaas that after following *Bhattikavyam* more or less closely for the first two-thirds of his work, the old Javanese poet abandoned it and went his own way borrowing from the "flotsam and jetsam of general knowledge concerning the *Ramayana* that was current in those days in Southeast Asia" (34). But as my co-author Malini Saran and myself have shown first in an article in *Bijdragen* in 1993 and later in our book *The Ramayana in Indonesia*, the Old Javanese poet, who knew not only Bhatti, but indeed Valmiki as well, went to the latter for many of the parts of the book where he feels that Bhatti has either missed out on an important episode or has been too laconic in its treatment. In fact the Old Javanese poet was also well-versed in many other Sanskrit texts ranging from *Manusmriti* to *Bhagwad-Gita* to Kalidasa's *Meghaduta* and used them with brilliant effect to enrich his narrative.

As Sanskrit scholars know, and as Bhatti himself declares boldly, his is a relatively difficult text. He uses the epic tale as vehicle to illustrate some of the more complicated elements of Sanskrit grammar. The latter half of the work is also devoted to Sanskrit poetics, [illustrating *alamkaras* so dear to Sanskrit poets]. *Bhattikavyam* is certainly an impressive work but many critics have found it lacking in literary beauty. S.K. De in his *History of Sanskrit Literature* speaks of Bhatti's "consciously labored language" and regrets that he makes "all thought, feeling, idea or expression" a slave to his didactic purpose (183-5). This judgment may be unduly harsh but it certainly contrasts sharply with the near unanimous praise showered on the literary qualities of OJRK. The eminent Dutch scholar Ulhenbeck ranks it as the most beautiful work in the entire history of Indonesian literature.

It is striking that, while Bhatti claims no religious, spiritual or even ethical aspirations in writing his Rama story, the Old Javanese poet, like Valmiki and a great number of his Indian followers, asserts the sacred, redemptive and ethical character of the tale. Though *Bhattikavyam* is indeed its main prototype, there are many features of the OJRK which make it a superb independent literary triumph.

For one thing, it is a lively work, full of drama and colour. A number of the most exciting and moving episodes of the great Valmiki *Ramayana* have become rather matter-of-fact in Bhatti. OJRK, on the other hand, is full of drama, tension, confrontations adroitly managed, racy dialogue, with characters vibrantly alive. Dasharatha's anguish when faced with the sage Vishvamitra's demand to let young Rama go with him to take on the murderous *rakshasas*, Rama's near dementia at the abduction of Sita, the electrifying debates between Ravana and Rama's envoys Hanuman and Angada and with his own brothers Vibhishana and Kumbhakarna, the touching leave-taking by the demon soldiers as they bid goodbye to their families before marching into battle--episode after episode acquires a life and intensity, colour and feeling, which is missing in Bhatti.

Thus, for instance, the Old Javanese poet describes the leave-taking between a rakshasha soldier and his pregnant wife thus:

> Her look was languid and frail, arousing affection and pity. Her hair undone, black and gleaming, hung down her beautiful cheeks. She beckoned her husband and wanted to walk with him, but her knees trembled and her legs lost their strength. 'My husband, look at me. Much too obviously you do not love me. Yet I do not want to stay behind. I want to go along with you to battle. I do not want to be separated from you. I want to die together with you. . . .

Shattered was the mind of the hero because of his deep love. . . .

> 'My love, do not be so attached, return home, and stay there and wait. You are very weary because you are pregnant and your legs are weak and feeble. Besides fighting is very dangerous, like living in the mouth of Death . . . Look after yourself and your child very carefully, my dear.
>
> 'And I will not be killed, my love. The enemy, Raghava, will clearly be defeated, because your king is powerful . . . Therefore, wait for me, my love . . . Kiss your husband, my dear. I bid you farewell.' Thus spake the hero and went away, but his heart was broken forever [XIX, 22-27].

As far as characterization is concerned, many leading characters of the epic have become rather two-dimensional in *Bhattikavyam*. By contrast, in the Old Javanese *Ramayana Kakawin* they come vibrantly alive. Particularly memorable is the Old Javanese poet's depiction of Sita, Hanuman and Kumbhakarna but his most impressive innovation is the character of Trijata, Sita's sole comfort during her captivity in Lanka. Unlike the Trijata in the Valmiki *Ramayana*, she is not an old demoness but a spirited young daughter of Vibhishana. Trijata also figures in several other Indian *Ramayana*s. But OJR's Trijata surpasses them all. She shows much courage, intelligence and initiative in enabling Sita to retain her sanity in the face of the intense psychological pressures to which she is subjected by Ravana. Most memorable is her frontal assault on Rama when he repudiates Sita after triumphing over Ravana:

My lord, you go too far. You are like a blind man, though adept in all the teachings of religion. The princess has no equal in the world, concerning faithfulness and devotion to my lord. . . .

And her conduct was exceedingly pure! Alas! How distressed I am by her fate. You come and seem to have no feelings of love, as if you are bereft of all emotion. . . .

I say that as the protector of the world, it is but meet that you should know what is good and what is not, to become the refuge of the pitiful and the sinful looking for shelter. In fact, you are the elixir of immortality, the cure for [the sufferings] of the world.

However, if your heart is wicked and cruel, impure, irrational, then I doubt very much that you can protect the world because then you become sinful, corrupted by impurities...

Due to the sorrow which has overwhelmed my heart on observing the distress experienced by princess Janakatmaja (Sita, the daughter of Janaka) I feel neither fear nor veneration towards Your Majesty. I do not care if I be sentenced to death, I do not mind at all. . .'

(XXIV, 169-77)

This passage also illustrates another striking feature of OJRK which distinguishes it from *Bhattikavyam*. Bhatti, having an entirely different objective, skirts around the multiple ethical issues involved in the epic tale. Old Javanese poet on the other hand is profoundly interested in analysing the moral issues underlying the behavior of the concerned characters or at stake in the situations confronting them. He views with sympathy the moral ambivalence inherent in some situations: the debate between the dying Bali and Rama, Kumbhakarna choosing to fight unto death in defence of his king despite being repelled by his moral folly. But the poet is quite unequivocal in projecting Sita as the faithful wife, Lakshmana as devoted younger brother and Hanuman as the paragon of loyalty, courage, and diplomatic wisdom. It is almost as if the poet had set out to prepare a compendium of ethics.

In Javanese cultural history OJRK was to acquire even greater significance for its passages on political philosophy and good governance of which the most famous is the advice Rama gives to Vibhishana after consecrating him as king of Lanka. Clearly drawing his inspiration from Chapters V and IX of *Manusmriti* which speak of eight divinities embodied in the king, who should be his role models, the poet articulates through Rama the *Ashtabrata* in an extensive discourse on *nitishastra:*

, , , he [the king] is supposed to be respected, because deities are in him. There are eight deities in the body of a king, which gives him power without equal.

These eight gods are Indra, Yama, Suryya, Candra, Anila, Kuwera, Baruna and Agni.

They are embodied in the king. {That is why he should have cherished the Asta-brata [the eightfold meritorious acts].

Then he goes on to list the characteristic feature of each of them which the king must emulate. For instance he says of Indra,

He gives rain to the satisfaction of the world. You should take Indra as an example and carry out his acts. Generosity is your rain overflowing the world.

Or of the Sun

Rawi [the Sun-god] always absorbs the water, slowly not forcefully. If you have to take [from the people] to obtain [something], you should do it the way the sun does, in a gentle way.

And so on.

Whether or not the OJRK was designed to honour a specific king, it certainly celebrates the institution of kingship. Among the major attractions of Indian cultural elements for the Javanese ruling elite were the political concepts which exalted the monarchical system. If the poet (or his royal master), wished to borrow from Indian literature a work which elevated the status of the king among his subjects, then the Rama story was an incomparable choice. If he further wished to play the role of the royal priestly counsellor, presenting in a manner both pleasing and persuasive the norms which should permeate an ideal polity, what better vehicle than the *Ramayana* story?

Another striking feature of this Old Javanese masterpiece is its depiction of the *sringara rasa* – the erotic sentiment – several notches above its Indian proto-type, rendering with equal felicity, both categories; the *Sambhoga* or Enjoyment and *Vipralambha* or separation. In many ways, OJRK is a moving and vivid narration of the Rama-Sita love story.

The most touching expression of Sita's love comes in the message she sends Rama through Hanuman. In the *Bhattikavya*, as in Valmiki, Sita sends her crest-jewel to Rama. So does the Sita of the OJRK, but to this the Indonesian poet adds a letter. She describes her letter as an expression of her longing and her crest-jewel as herself coming to pay homage to him. To Sita the ring which her husband sends is like his embraces and its sight fills her with 'pangs of love and longing'. She writes:

11.30 If it happens that you reach me, my lord, what is it you might expect to find,
My state is pitiful here among the enemy, driven to distraction from not knowing what the outcome will be,
My only guest-offerings will be my longing and the distress in my heart,
Along with the tears that I have stored up as a sign of my desire for you.
11.31 "What adds to my affliction is that this worthless slave was the cause of such torturous pain,
It was at my request that we separated, and you did so out of your affection for me,
If I meet with you again, my lord, it will never be thus again,
I will take on the behaviour of a slave, holding fast to the vow of servitude.

Many of the thematic innovations reflect Javanese cultural mores of the day. Take for instance this letter of Sita to Rama. Writing letters appeared to have been a favourite mode of communicating feelings to one's beloved. The very special relationship which Sita has with Trijata, as Professor Haryati Soebadio told us,[4] mirrored a well-known phenomenon in Javanese courts: of queens and princesses being attended by intelligent and loyal companions.

In subsequent centuries the OJRK went on to occupy a place of unusual importance in the cultural history of Java and Bali. It has been a major influence through the centuries on literature, political and moral philosophy, and the performing and plastic arts.

Beginning around the thirteenth century a great majority of Javanese gradually adopted Islam as their religion while Bali remained Hindu-Buddhist. The *Ramayana* and *Mahabharata* stories continued to flourish in the new religious context and even appeared in new manifestations. Indeed this was one of the most striking features of the cosmopolitan spirit of Southeast Asian Islam. The new religion blended into local culture in which these stories were deeply embedded. Those in charge of the Islamization process in Indonesia were keenly aware that a people's mythology cannot be erased from their shared memory, and that any effort at conversion would be better served by building on the familiar and loved.

We come across passages such as this:

> In fact, however, the essence of kawi works
> Such as the Bima Suci and the Wiwaha
> Is expressed in many metaphors
> From which the quintessence of mystical knowledge can be mastered
> If the interpreter is penetrating and exact.
> And these just as the books of Rama in kawi
> Are books on Sufism. (VIII, 6)

As historian Ricklefs points out, what is stated above is not that *Bima Suci, Arjunawiwaha* and *Ramayana* are as good as Islamic works, or better than Islamic works, but that they *are* Islamic works. This is how Javanese Sufism blended the intellectual heritage of international Sufism with that of pre-Islamic Java. "There is no question of a choice between religious traditions here: the religions between which a modern scholar draws a distinction are asserted to be one." (150-1).

From our point of view a very significant fact is that the most famous *Ramayana* produced in mid-eighteenth century Islamic Java, *Serat Rama,* by the renowned modern Javanese poet, Yasadipura drew its inspiration from OJRK.

The *Serat Rama* opens with the poet declaring that he has been ordered (presumably by his royal patron):

> . . . To retell
> An enjoyable tale,
> The story of Lord Rama, in Kawi,
> Rendered in [new] Javanese.

So it is made clear at the outset that of all the multiple *Ramayanas*, Indian and Indonesian, it is the OJR which the *Serat Rama* is "retelling". Not only the story and characterization but the frequent appearance of more or less identical phrases, indicate that the author was familiar with either the Old Javanese text or of some very competent Modern Javanese rendering of it. One thing is clear: he was very consciously using the ancient classic as his prototype, in preference to any other. Of course, Yasadipura was too great a poet to merely copy the old classic. But one of the themes from his prototype which he renewed and reinforced was that of the *Ashtabrata* which continues to be cited by contemporary leaders as the source of their inspiration.

Turning to Bali, *Ramayana's* ubiquitous presence is obvious to even the most casual visitor. For our presentation on OJRK it needs to be emphasized that the Hindus of Bali continue to regard the Old Javanese classic as sacred in contrast to the Javanese for whom it has become a secular phenomenon. The Balinese preserved the ancient *Kakawin* in the original language by copying and re-copying it in palm-leaf manuscripts known as *lontars*. It has been kept alive in oral performance rather than by silent reading.

It might be fanciful to uphold that when Valmiki quoted *Brahma* as saying that, as long as mountains stand and rivers flow on earth the *Ramayana* tale would continue to flourish in the world, he expected his prophecy to come so literally true. The multiplicity of *Ramayanas* in India, Indonesia and many other lands is history's tribute to the genius of the original composer as much as it is a monument to the talents of the countless known and anonymous participants in this amazing transnational process in which the author of OJRK most certainly deserves a very honoured place.

NOTES

1. The 'Greater India' framework originates from earlier European scholarship, but was taken up uncritically by Indian scholars writing in the first half of twentieth century. [For a well-known example see R.C. Majumdar, *Ancient Indian Colonies in the Far East*, Dacca, 1937-38]. Some later scholars swung to the other extreme. Thus for instance the Dutch scholar J.C. van Leur dismissed Indian influence as a mere 'thin and flaking gaze'.
2. Among the most impressive and balanced are the writings of another Dutch scholar J.G.de Casparis. He summarized his views lucidly in his 'Third Sri Lanka Endowment Fund Lecture' delivered at the University of Kuala Lumpur, 1983.
3. The original reference is in Dutch. Cited in P.J. Zoetmulder, *Kalangwan: A Survey of Old Javanese Literature*, p. 231 [The Hague, 1974].
4. In private conversation with the author and Malini Saran.

WORKS CITED

Casparis, J.G. de. 'India and Maritime Trade in Southeast Asia: A Lasting Relationship'. Kuala Lumpur, Third Sri Lanka Endowment Fund Lecture, 1983.

De, S.K. *History of Sanskrit Literature: I.* Calcutta: University of Calcutta, 1947.

Hooykaas, C. *The Old Javanese Ramayana Kakawin, With Special Reference to The Problem of Interpolation In Kakawins.* Netherlands: The Hague, 1955.

Khanna, Vinod and Malini Saran. 'The *Ramayana Kakawin*; A Product of Sanskrit Scholarship and Independent Literary Genius'. *Bijdragen totde Taal-, Land- en olkenkunde* 149 (1993), no. 2, Leiden, 226-49.

Leur, Jacob Cornelis. *Indonesian Trade And Society: Essays In Asian Social And Economic History.* Netherlands: W. Van Hoeve, 1955.

Ricklefs, M.C. *The Seen and the Unseen Worlds in Java.* Honolulu: University of Hawaii Press, 1998.

Saran, Malini and Vinod Khanna. *The Ramayana in Indonesia.* Delhi: Ravi Dayal Publisher, 2004.

Zoetmulder, P.J. *Kalangwan: A Survey of Old Javanese Literature.*Netherlands: Martinus Nijhoff, 1981.

16

Civilizational Dialogue between India and Myanmar

KHIN MAUNG NYUNT

Geopolitically speaking, India and the entire Southeast Asian region have been as immediate and proximate just as China and Southeast Asia have been. Southeast Asia, both peninsular and insular, sandwiched between two big countries, the Indian subcontinent and Cina, Cathay or China, has always been a vacuum into which the spills-over of both countries' population have found their ways since time immemorial. This connection is age-old. Today, we talk so much about the process of globalization and its consequences since we are so conscious of the impact of the superhighways of information and communication technology (ICT). However we should also be aware of the similar process from our remote past that had taken place, leaving many cultural and civilizational footprints, both tangible and intangible, upon the sands of time. Therefore, the theme of this paper is nothing but the revival of old historical context with the added reflection on past concepts.

The ASEAN ten member States have gathered to present the commonalities in the cultural and civilizational impacts from our interactions with India. There can be some diversities in the stories among five peninsular Southeast Asian countries (Myanmar, Laos, Cambodia, Thailand and Vietnam) and five insular Southeast Asian countries (Indonesia, Malaysia, the Philippines, Brunei and Singapore) depending upon their location and the land or the sea routes by which they had interacted and have been interacting with these two big neighbours, India and China. But such diversities are not differences; they are individual features and characteristics of their national identities. The surplus population spills over from these two big neighbours, bringing in their cultures and civilizations which interact and intermingle with those of their indigenous counterparts resulting in a new breed of culture and civilization.

India, a subcontinent with its boundless capacity of imbibing and absorbing, is the birth place of almost all belief systems and the main fount of spreading them beyond its borders. China too has her own credit in history to claim. That India has an earlier and wider hold on Southeast Asia has been proven by history. Even to China, India had exported Buddhism and other religions at the early date of civilization. Therefore, it is not a sweeping statement to say that most Southeast Asian countries are more Indianized in terms of culture and civilization. But China does have a role in colonizing Southeast Asia both materially and spiritually and its claim and credit are equally important.

Myanmar which is an immediate neighbor to both India and China, has many stories of interactions with them. A coastal country comprising one geographic entity, Myanmar has both land and sea routes by which her interactions with the big neighbours have been affected. Hindu Brahmanism, which Indian colonizers brought with them, is the most far reaching of all pre Buddhist belief systems. Buddhism provides volumes of evidences of Indian impact upon Myanmar. Archaeological sites like Beithano (Vishnu), Sre Kestra, Hanlin, Tagaung and Maing Maw in Central and Upper Myanmar are the store houses of artifacts of different genres, tools, weapons, ritual, religious, funerary and artistic objects, coins and seals and epigraphs indicating the existence and influence of Hindu-Brahmanic culture. Statues of Brahma, Siva, Vishnu, Ganesha and others were unearthed at the excavations there. Moreover, in town planning and architecture of all buildings and monuments, the fundamentals of Vedic culture are noticed. The Mandala system of Hindu Buddhist cosmography was faithfully followed, while planet-worship still persists, with Hindu priests being revered and respected as Gurus by the society from the monarchy to the grass roots.

The legend of Tagaung which was believed to be the earliest dynastic kingdom in the country says that it was founded by an exiled king from India. King Abhiraja of Sakya race of Gautama Buddha was defeated in the tribal war and he was exiled or fled to escape. He founded a new kingdom at the place now called Tagaung and set up his dynasty. Hence a Myanmar traditional couplet states:

> Tradition says Myanmar dynasty originates in Tagaung. He was king Abhiraja of Sakya race who escaped to that ground.

The history of the arrival of Buddhism to Myanmar tells the stories of interaction between India and Myanmar. The first arrival which took place in the Maha sakarit year of 103 (Buddhist Era) was the legend of the Shwedagon Pagoda. The two merchant brothers Taphusa and Balika who brought home the Dhamma (Buddha's Teachings) and eight strands of sacred hair relics of Gautama Buddha at Bodhgaya vividly tell us of the overseas trade and cultural relations between the two countries. A regular exchange of Myanmar agricultural productions with Indian textiles and luxuries took place by the sea routes in every monsoon, bringing to Myanmar Hindu culture and religions, including Buddhism.

Two new arrivals that followed in 111 and 123 BCE were led by the living Buddha himself, through land route, establishing his Dhamma as well as leaving his sacred hair relics and foot prints that are enshrined in the Dhatu zedia and Pada zedis in lower and middle Myanmar hill ranges. The fourth arrival was by two Buddhist missionary monks *Asin* Sona and *Ashin* Uttara sent by the great Buddhist Emperor Asoka of India. But the most important of all arrivals was the fifth arrival not from India but from Lanka Dwipa (Sri Lanka). After Asoka's son and daughter Beikhu Mahendra and Beikhuni Sangamitre took Buddhism and established it in that island kingdom, Sri Lanka became the centre and the sole distributor of the Buddha's teachings. It was from this island that we received for the first time the canonical texts of the Dhamma in writing on plant leaf. That was the beginning of Theravada Buddhism that embraced the entire Southeast Asia.

Even then, though Sri Lanka began to take the place of Buddhistic learning after this religion began to decline in the country of its birth, India, Bodhgaya and other places sacred to the Buddha, continue to be places of pilgrimage. Evidences of earliest and later Buddhism of India are noticed in the pre-Bagan, Bagan and post-Bagan dynastic kingdoms of Myanmar. There was conspicuous absence of Buddha statues and images at the excavations of Beithano (Vishnu) city site, though there are other evidences of Buddhism there. Scholarly consensus was that the earliest Buddhism that flourished in Amaravati and Nagarjunaconda of central India were Aparaseliya and Mahinsasaka sects which must have their branches in Myanmar. These sects of Buddhism allowed no icon worship. Only learning and practice of the Dhamma was emphasized. But later Buddhisms that arrived in Myanmar faithfully represented their places of origin. Archaeologists, both local and foreign have classified pagodas, monuments and religious buildings at Bagan into four categories on the criteria of their design, size and decorative arts. The categories are the North India type, Mid India type, South India type and Sri Lankan type. Though these buildings have undergone local adaptations and innovations, their architectural fundamentals are still visibly maintained. Besides Myanmar, kings sent out to India and Sri Lanka monks and laymen to bring home exact designs and copies of prominent sacred monuments such as Sanchi stūpa (Raja Manisula dome-shaped Pagoda or Kaung Hmu Taw Pagoda at Sagaing), the Maha Bodhi Temple of Bodhgaya (the temple with the same name at Bagan), seven places at which Gautama Buddha stayed after his enlightenment (Thatha Thana) Mahazedi, Maha Vihara and Lalyani Sima in Sri Lanka (their replicas as Pegu), and Maha Bodhi trees-planted across the country. The legend of Ananda Temple at Bagan says that king Kyinzittha got the design of this Temple from eight saint monks of Himalayan Caves. Now the Government of India has agreed to send Indian experts to repair and renovate this temple.

As the original place of Buddhist learning, India still retains the pride of place for Myanmar. Through Buddha's *Jataka* stories, we have the knowledge of Taxila, the most reputed university of Buddha's time. Later Myanmar history and literature have accounts of Myanmar Buddhist monks spending long years of their life in pursuit of Tipitakas, commentaries and sub-commentaries at the Nalanda University and other Buddhist centres at Varanasi, Rajasthan, Kusinagara, etc. There learned monks not only translated Buddhist literature but also secular literature in Pali, Sanskrit, Hindi and Bengali into Myanmar language thus enriching the culture of Myanmar. This process of interaction between the two countries in the fields of trade, religion and culture has been consistent regardless of the ups and downs of political and international relations.

This influence is also visible in Myanmar Visual Arts traditionally classified in following ten genres: (1) The arts and crafts of Black Smithy, (2) The arts and crafts of Gold and Silver Smithy, (3) the arts and crafts of alloy (bronze, brass, copper) or *pancha lawha* smithy, (4) the arts and crafts of stucco or plaster (5) the arts and crafts of mason (masonry), (6) the arts and crafts of the carver, (7) the arts and crafts of stone sculptor, (8) the arts and crafts of turner (turnery) (9) the arts and crafts of painting and (10) the arts and crafts of lacquer-wear making and other appertaining genres such as weaving, embroidery, lapidary, papier mâché works. Their concepts, fundamental principles and technical terms have Pali, Sanskrit, and Hindu Brahmanic characterstics and origins. For example, we have four basic methods of our traditional visual arts namely (1) *Knote* for drawing lotus flower and all delicate and intricate objects in its extended meaning, (2) *Kapi* for drawing monkey or ape and all agile and action objects in its extended meaning, (3) *Gaza* for drawing elephant and all massive, heavy objects in extended meaning.

Most early mural paintings in the temples and buildings in Myanmar reveal the influence of Indian paintings in the Ajanta caves, until Myanmar features were gradually assumed in later centuries. Art historians can easily identify the Ghandara, the Gupta, the Mauryan, the Asokan and the Sri Lankan styles of Myanmar visual arts of early history. There is no need to stretch one's imagination to say for sure that either Myanmar artisans of those days went to India to learn their trade or Indian artists and artisans were brought to Myanmar for royal or public services. In the history of post Bagan dynastic kingdoms we find accounts of the dispatches of Myanmar artists and craftsmen sent by Myanmar kings to do repair and renovation works on the sacred Buddhist buildings in India, especially Bodhgaya, and instructions to bring home the replicas, designs for use in the home country. King Dhammazedi (1472-92 CE), Hamsavedi (1782-1819 CE), and King Mindon of Konbaung dynasty (1752-1885 CE), were well known patrons of arts, crafts, architecture and literature and enthusiasts of Buddhist culture from the country of its birth. They sent Myanmar scholars to India for further studies.

Apart from this, *Jataka* or Buddha's birth stories were also dramatized and performed to impart moral and religious lessons also teach the appeal of nine *rasas*. So we call drama "zat", shortened form of *Jataka*. Nevertheless, in this context *Mahabharat* and *Ramayana* come first and foremost, though they are not *Jatakas*. These two ancient Hindu epic dramas are as great in the oriental world as two ancient Greek epics the *Illiad* and the *Odyssey* of Homer are in the Western world. We received these two epic dramas by two ways. First, they were brought directly from India by Indian settlers and in their original form they still exist among Hindu Brahmin settlers in Mandalay and at other major towns. Secondly, indirectly from Thailand, Java and Sumatra, through our frequent contacts with them. In the seventeenth, eighteenth and nineteenth centuries Myanmar's contacts and relations with her eastern and south eastern neighbours had resulted a great deal in the enrichment of Myanmar performing arts amongst which music song and dance drama were prominent.

Furthermore, the Thai *Ramayana* drama had profound influence upon Myanmar drama so much so that though the original *Ramayana* from India in concept, theme and plots is still maintained, the presentation, performance, music and theme songs of the Thai *Ramayana* had been adapted and well blended into Myanmar. In spite of the impact of the Western culture through colonization and globalization the *Ramayana* drama still remains deep in Myanmar's heart in all ages and all generations. The *Ramayana* is sung and performed as pop and hip hop too. One pop writer Chit Oo Nyo daringly changed the character roles of Rama and Ravana, thus Rama becoming the villain and Ravan the hero, who unjustly and unfairly has lost his love Sita and his kingdom Lankadwipa. Regarding the *Mahabharata*, Myanmar playwrights were reluctant to dramatize it for theatrical performance simply because it is full of fighting and battles and it is not as romantic, exciting and appealing as *Ramayana*. So they adopted a Javanese drama called "E-naung".

However there is one dramatic performance we call "Dwe Mei Naw" which is very common not only in Southeast Asian countries but also in Yunan, China, Korea and also in Russia. The well known Swan Lake Ballet of Russia and the Peacock Princess Ballet have been adapted and tell the tragic love story of a human Prince (Sudanu) and a fairy Princess (Manawhari) who after many encounters have to end up separated because they belong to two different planes of life. The Princess dies of a broken heart and the Prince forever remained forlorn. In the Myanmar version of this drama, names of the characters, places and surroundings are all Indian. So, I wonder if it originated in India and travelled wide to Russia, Korea, China and Southeast Asia? But I have not tried to trace its footprints as yet.

Our dance gestures, mudras and acting definitely bespeak Indian influence. The *Natyashastra* was the textbook for learning our classical dances and drama. Myanmar performing artists of the classical age were quite familiar with Indian classical dance-drama forms. Typical Hindu dance posture "Tribhanga" or three curves of the dancer's body, is adopted in our basic dance lesson. The formula of head-hip-hands-legs movements and later facial expressions to indicate inner feelings caused by the nine *rasas* are also followed.

Historically and politically, our common background of British colonialism provided the two countries many avenues of cultural and civilizational interactions. Till 1937, Myanmar was ruled and administered as a province of the British Indian Empire. So the British colonial administration of our country was an extension of its Indian origin. With the blind assumption that Myanmar was a part of Further India, the British Raj introduced all its Anglo Indian systems into Myanmar. The first Yangon College was modeled on the typical English University of the Victorian Age. Therefore, both India and Myanmar shared the Anglicanization by the British rulers, inculcating into the natives the British Imperial Ideals. The so called liberal education of the British had illustrated the importance and the benefits of the rule of law and the principles and practice of democracy. This education acted as an eye opener for us to start our national freedom movements. In political awakenings and freedom fights, Myanmar and India cooperated and outstanding Indian leaders (Gandhi, Nehru, Bose, and Indian intellectuals like Rabindranath Tagore and others) supported Myanmar's national cause. Even on the eve of regaining our respective freedoms from the British Colonial yoke, the late Bogyoke Aung San and Pandit Nehru pulled their heads together to chart their countries foreign policies in the post Second World War period. Again, Nehru and U Nu were the leading movers torn apart by the cold war and the still vibrant Non-aligned movement (NAM) was the happy and enduring corollary of it.

Similarly in our modern education, English and Anglo Indian influence was strong since its inception. Even a decade after teachers were hired from India. In 1948, Myanmar Universities and colleges had hired Indian teachers from India. I still recall my memories of Indian Professors of Modern History, Political Science, Economics, Logic and Philosophy. There were also Indian teachers in Science and Applied Science departments. The names Das, Guha, Soni, Moonie, Desai, Dutt, Subramanian, Sundaram, Chakravarty were of well known professors of our times and some of whom even chose Myanmar as their home after retirement.

Additionally, India and Myanmar also retain their traditional interactions. Myanmar's surplus of agricultural products have permanent market in India regardless of the changes across time. So also are Indian textiles and industrial products and luxuries in popular demand in Myanmar. When the British introduced modern facilities and amenities like rails, navigation, roads and other infrastructure they simply extended what they had established in Indian over centuries earlier. So what remained in Myanmar of these facilities is basically Anglo Indian. To up-date, up-grade and modernize them we need India's cooperation and assistance, as we are historically used to Anglo-Indian methods and system.

In the early colonial days, the first bankers in our country were Chettiars, the moneylender class from India, who came to Southeast Asia. Although, they earned the ill reputation of "black jews" who sucked the life blood of Myanmar peasants, following the Great Economic Depression of 1929, they had to their credit in colonial days of funding Myanmar peasants who were in urgent need of money to till their soils. Some of their descendants settled in the country and threw their lot with Myanmar through thick and thin. Enclaves of these law-abiding Myanmar Chettiars are still found across the country. In big cities like Yangon, Mandalay, Mawlamyine, Pathein, Sittway, Dawei, Taungyi, Kalaw and Pyin Oo Lwin (May Myo), Indian merchants from Bombay, Gujarat, Madras, Calcutta and Karachi, formed the leading wealthy classes who prospered in gold, diamond, textile, rice and bean trades till the nationalization by Ne Win Government of 1962. Though many of them have left, some of their relatives and descendants still live here as Myanmar citizens. Recently, the Prime Minister of India, Dr. Manmohan Singh visited Myanmar and made very encouraging and inspiring speeches at Naypyitaw and Yangon Sedona Hotel (29 May 2012) on "India and Myanmar: A Partnership for progress and Regional development". The Myanmar and Indian communities were pleased and are looking forward to the realization of that partnership in the near future.

Today, after a long lethargy of past decades, the new Myanmar government with the new constitution and a new leadership is kicking off a new place in the international arena. The process of reforms and modernization under multiparty democracy cannot be stopped anymore. In the fast changing world of today's globalized age, the geopolitical locations of Myanmar and India have huge significance. Myanmar with her wartime backgrounds of the Burma Road in the north east and the Ledo Road in the north west and her current tripod position of the bridge between East, West and Southeast Asia is assuming a major role in the regional and international affairs. Her traditional spiritual and cultural leader, India is now reviving its age old policy towards Myanmar, and with her Look East stand, a new Indo-Myanmar cultural and civilizational interaction age has dawned in this new century.

WORKS CITED

The Archaeological Survey of Burma, Annual Reports. Rangoon: Government Press, 1927-65.

Annual Reports of the Archaeological Survey of India. Delhi: Government Press, 1902-37.

Aung, Thaw. *Historical Sites in Burma.* Yangon: The Ministry of Union Culture, Sarpay Beikman Press, 1972.

Bulletin of the Burma Historical Commission. Rangoon, 1960.

Harvey, G.E. *History of Burma.* London, 1967.

Hamannan, Yazawin. *The Glass Palace Chronicles*, 3 vols. Mandalay, 1908.

Htin Aung, Maung. *A History of Burma.* New York: Columbia University Press, 1968.

Khin Maung Nyunt. 'The British Imperial Idea and the Mandalay Palace'. *The Guardian,* vol. 39, no. 5, May 1992.

———, *Pilgrim's Guide to Yangon.* Bagan, Mandalay and Bago, 1991.
O'Connor, Scott. *The Silken East,* 2 vols. London, 1902.
———, *Mandalay and other Cities of the Past in Burma*. London, 1907.
Pictorial Guide to Rangoon. Reprint 1971.
Yule, Henry. *A Narrative of the Mission Sent as the Governor General of India to Court of Ava in 1858*. London, 1858.

17

The Changing Faces of *Ramayana* in the Performing Arts of Java and Bali

MALINI SARAN

A prominent feature in the transmission of India's knowledge systems to Southeast Asia, particularly on the islands of Java and Bali in Indonesia, was the hold of Hindu and Buddhist narrative traditions on popular imagination. Among the wealth of stories we find recorded in Java for over a thousand years, those from *Ramayana* and *Mahabharata* were accorded a unique status.[1] From the ninth to the fifteenth centuries, i.e. for the duration of the Hindu Buddhist period in Java, *Ramayana* and *Mahabharata*[2] lent their presence in the sanctity of temple compounds to validate the rule of the king at one level, and on another, to entertain and educate people on a desired code of ethics embodied by the characters and situations in this vast reservoir of stories. In this period, while the Rama story was recreated in beautiful poetic works in the language of Old Javanese and illustrated on stone reliefs of sacred temples, the stories and characters of the *Ramayana* were assimilated into the popular mythology of Java and Bali primarily through the agency of a thriving, sophisticated and diverse tradition of the performing arts such as recitation and singing, the puppet theatre and dance. With the active patronage of the ruling powers as documented by inscriptions from the ninth and tenth centuries,[3] the worlds of the *Ramayana* and *Mahabharata* were experienced collectively in the public enactment of textual and oral tellings.

When the courts of Java adopted Islam in the sixteenth century, the pace of change in *Ramayana* was accelerated by the requirements of the new religion. *Ramayana* was consciously tailored to suit Islamic norms in newly written texts in several languages, skilfully and peacefully transforming sacred Hindu gods into the cultural heroes of Java with elevated secular status who continued to be role models in a largely Muslim society. In a parallel reconfiguration of the Javanese performing arts that conformed to the tenets of Islam, *Ramayana* retained its popularity in the shadow puppet theatre, *wayang kulit* and its off shoots *wayang wong* (played by human figures imitating the form of puppets in dance movements), *wayang topeng* (three dimensional figures in wood manipulated by rods in the hands of the dalang), and in more recent times *wayang wong sendratari*, the dance drama by humans that combines music and song. Through the agency of the poet in literature and the *dalang* or puppeteer in *wayang* theatre, innovative sub-plots were created and most characters, the well-known and the newly invented, evolved in startling ways. With each telling, the dramatic material changed to suit the occasion, to amuse or explain, interpret or enlarge the meaning of words and actions in poetry and on stage. Even today, the adventures of Rama and Sita, Hanuman and Ravana continue to be relevant in this way. *Ramayana* characters are cherished, their values and their conduct held in high esteem as ideals of political and ethical conduct.

The island of Bali, in noticeable contrast to Java, resisted the tide of Islam. It preserved the sanctity of its *Ramayana* culture in an unbroken tradition, clinging to it's uniquely Hinduized way of life tied to rituals and rice growing. Even today, the Old Javanese *Ramayana Kakawin* lives on in Bali through its arts that are considered sacred and organically integrated with daily life, yet have acquired a modern character. For example, the recitation of *Ramayana* (known as *Kawi* in Bali) is perfected through competition in clubs. The singing of *Kawi* lies at the heart of Bali's robust and vivacious performing arts, in its a unique shadow puppet theatre known as *wayang kulit Ramayana* and its renowned dances particularly the ritual masked dance dramas of *wayang wong*. In Bali's contemporary version of *sendratari*, lavish productions of dance drama and music, now supported by its flourishing tourist trade, have familiarized *Ramayana* to international audiences.

The *Ramayana*'s continuous adaptations through the centuries and the evolving cultural ethos of Java and Bali in its performing and literary arts, is an intriguing phenomenon. This essay attempts to highlight this process of change by which *Ramayana* remained integrated with the evolving cultural ethos of Indonesia.

Inscriptions from the ninth and tenth centuries in Java suggest that religious ceremonies and rituals were closely connected with recitation, theatre, dance and music of which *Ramayana* was a part.[3] The recitation of *Ramayana (macarita Ramayana)* along with singing, play acting and clowning, and other types of entertainment are mentioned.[4] We also see the portrayal of dancers in the reliefs of Borobudur- and in the reliefs of the Prambanan *Ramayana*-where musicians and dancers celebrate state rituals.

Hence it is not a surprise that the first *Ramayana* works known in Java, sponsored by the Kings of the Sanjay dynasty and rooted in the Hinduised culture of the Central Javanese court, seem to derive from a mature dramatic tradition based on the principles of the Indian *Natyashastra*. Located in the Prambanan complex of Central Java, a series of 72 reliefs etched into the stone balustrades of the Shiva and Brahma temple can claim to be most comprehensive performance of a sculpted Rama story seen anywhere in the world in that period. The language of gesture it employs, as codified by the *Natyashastra*, establishes that Rama, the perfect king, is the hero of the story.

FIGURE 1: SHIVA TEMPLE PRAMBANAN: THE ABDUCTION OF SITA

In kingly attire even in the forest, Rama displays his physical valour as he vanquishes a variety of opponents such as demons in the forest, the bird who disturbs his wife, the golden deer she covets, and Ravana the *rakshash* who dared to abduct her. Salience is given to episodes involving the characters of Sita, Kumbhakarna, and Hanuman. The sculptors of Prambanan combined Valmikian episodes with several non-Valmikian incidents originating in the oral and folk tradition (Fig. 1).

The exercise of such freedom bore the hallmark of Javanese creativity indicating that *Ramayana* has moved beyond its Indian origins. This placement of extensive *Ramayana* reliefs around the *pradakshinapath* of a Shaivite temple, and the inclusion of the *Uttarakanda* is unlike anything we see in India or elsewhere in this period. Java left a discernible stamp on the final product. This was the first and last time that a complete *Ramayana* would be illustrated in the temple sculpture of Java. The nature of Javanese tradition dictated that in the centuries that followed only selected episodes would be chosen for depiction even in the performing arts tradition.

In the same period, the first full length literary *Ramayana* appeared in Java – the *Ramayana Kakawin* – a classical work of poetry composed in the language of Old Javanese. The structure of this work and the choice of its metres noticeably heighten the dramatic content, suggesting a symbiotic relationship with the *wayang kulit* theatre. While *Kakawin* and the sculptural telling are born in the same cultural ethos, however, one does not seem to have been based on the other. In their choice and portrayal of episodes there are marked differences, the most obvious being the depiction in temple sculpture of the concluding canto of the epic, the *Uttarakanda*, whereas *Kakawin* ends with the coronation of Rama and Sita. What unifies them, however, is the aesthetic style that in both works is intrinsically Javanese.

The next milestone of far reaching consequences for the history of *Ramayana* in Java occurred in the tenth century. In 996 CE in the newly established court of East Java, a visionary king inaugurated an ambitious project of translation of the *parwas* of *Mahabharata* from Sanskrit into Old Javanese prose. The *Uttarakanda* – the seventh and concluding canto of the *Ramayana* – was included in this exercise. The distinction between the two epics begins to blur as the *Uttarakanda parwa* came to be viewed as part of the body of the *Mahabharata parwas*. The *parwas* in Java are simple, direct and lucid translations of Sanskrit into Old Javanese prose and adapted so as to be comprehensible to ordinary people. They were often shortened in length and snatches of Sanskrit *slokas* have been embedded throughout to enhance its magical and sacred character adding to its prestige and authenticity. Although its stories were already well known in Central Java as seen by their illustrations in the Brahma temple in Prambanan, perhaps it was felt necessary to give the stories a literary form which together with the Old Javanese *Ramayana* provided a rich reservoir of stories for poets, sculptors and performance artists for generations to come.

The *Uttarakanda* with its past histories and genealogies of leading characters became the source of several later *Kakawins*. The most important was *Arjunawijaya*, an enlarged poem about a short encounter between Arjunasasrabahu and Ravana, which later transformed this into a classic work that introduced new characters into the *Ramayana*'s lexicon such as the minister Suwandha and Arjuna's spouse Chitrawati, who later became iconic emblems of loyalty and fidelity The inclusion of *Uttarakanda* into the realm of the *parwas* of Mahabharata paved the way for the linkage of *Ramayana* with *Mahabharata* in the *wayang purwa* of Islamic times. By the fifteenth century we have clear evidence of *Ramayana* blending the worlds of sculpture, literature and theatre into the sacral and artistic traditions of Java.

In East Java, in the state temple of Panataran visited regularly by fourteenth century Majapahit king Hayam Wuruk, a series of reliefs portray selected episodes of *Ramayana* on the terraced walls of one shrine.

Almost like a Javanese *lakon* (the play in a *wayang kulit* performance comprising extracts selected from a larger story), the episodes illustrated here relate to Sita's captivity in Lanka, and Hanuman's attempt to rescue her (Fig. 2). This telling closely follows a few cantos on this theme in the Old Javanese *Ramayana* .[5] Of equal interest is the stylized form of the sculpted figures that bear a strong resemblance to the shape of *wayang* puppets of Bali (Fig. 3).

This effect is enhanced by the dwarf like characters in attendance that resemble the *panakawans* or servants in *wayang kulit* theatre (Fig. 4). Royal patronage played a key role in the development of *wayang* culture of Majapahit times as King Hayam Wuruk himself was a dancer of the *wayang* style.[6]

The spread of Javanese Islam in the sixteenth century hardly altered *Ramayana*'s privileged status in the culture of a people, now largely Muslim. In the changing cultural landscape, *Ramayana* was perceived not as a product of Hindu civilization or inimical to Islam, but viewed as an integral part of

FIGURE 2: PANATARAN TEMPLE, HANUMAN IN ACTION, LANKA. *WAYANG* STYLE

FIGURE 3: *WAYANG* PUPPETS

Javanese traditions. The Sufi or mystical brand of Islam that entered Java did not forbid music, dance or the portrayal of the human figure in art. Sufi practice permitted greater latitude in the individual's inward exploration of the truth and favours both within the courts and among the people outside. In fact, the Javanese mythology credits the spreading of the religion of Islam to the *walis sembilan* or the nine saints of Java, principally Sunan Kalijaga, who is said to have authored a large number of books including the *Ramayana*. Legend has it that he was the first *dalang* or puppeteer and it was he who created the stylized shape of the Javanese puppets in keeping with Islamic tenet that forbade the depiction of the human form.

FIGURE 4: SITA AND THE GOLDEN DEER, *WAYANG KULIT*, SURAKARTA STYLE

Barring references in past literary works, we have no details of actual performances of *wayang kulit* and *wayang wong in* Java and how the plays were organized until we come to the eighteenth and nineteenth centuries. Modern *dalangs*, however, provide an insight into its past. They dip into the cycle of plays that has its roots in the Islamic *Ramayanas* of the sixteenth century. One such *Ramayana* is *Hikayat Seri Rama* written in Malay, the language of the traders, in Arabic script. It broadly follows the oral and folk tales of Rama familiar to the Malay trading world and casts them in the historical mould of a *hikayat.*[7] More familiar to the Javanese and central to the repertoire of the *wayang kulit* is *Serat Kanda ningringgit parwa* or 'Book of Tales' written in the language of modern Javanese into which stories outside the Valmikian tradition were incorporated. This work was structured like a universal history that attempted to unite all known myths, legends and histories in a single frame into which the *Ramayana* and *Mahabharata* episodes were fitted as consecutively occurring historical cycles. They acted as a link in a genealogy from Nabi Adam to historical Javanese rulers through a mixture of Islamic (Old Testament) and Hindu mythical figures. Hindu gods merged into an Islamic genealogy. Siwa Guru for instance became the great grandson of Nabi Adam. The birth of Wisnu and Basuki after the Great Flood provided the bridge to the genealogy of the mythical Javanese rulers. The mythological succession leads us to the ancestors of Rama and Ravana. The *dalang* today also dips into the eighteenth century classic, *Serat Rama*, a literary work in *macapat* verse that is based on Old Javanese *Ramayana Kakawin*, esteemed and loved by Javanese today, thus injecting Valmikian element into these oral

FIGURE 5: IN THE CIREBON PALACE, A *WAYANG KULIT* PERFORMANCE WITHOUT A SCREEN

tales. The encounter of Arjunasasra and Ravana is a great *wayang* favourite. These varying streams can be seen in the distinctive *wayang* traditions of West Java and in Yogyakarta and Solo (Central Java).

The concept of a harmonious continuity of rulers from one dynasty to the next was of great importance to Javanese tradition. The genealogy that was constructed in literature to link both the Arab prophets and Hindu mythological figures as ancestors of Javanese kings was also adopted in the *wayang kulit*. To underline this continuity in *wayang* without offending the requirements of Islam, the status of Hindu gods was transformed into that of historical heroes, albeit extraordinary ones, who were seen as ancestors of the Javanese kings. They mingle comfortably with others from local history or indigenous myth and together form a popular way to explain the origin of Javanese civilization. This secularization of *Ramayana* allowed local *dalangs* great latitude in the creation of fresh episodes and the behavior of old and new characters.

In the time frame of two cycles, several characters from *Ramayana* are linked together in one way or another in narratives relating to their birth or lineage, reminiscent of the technique of *Uttarakanda*. Sita is the daughter of Ravana born to Mandodari. Mandodari is born from a clump of bamboo. Rama is the father of Hanuman. Several unusual sub-plots have been woven into this cycle of plays: Devi Sita's birth in Ravana's palace – to a clone of one of Dasaratha's wives; Hanuman is son of Rama; the notion of the gift of eternal life – *aji panchasona* – which Bali bestows on Ravana. Towards the end of the *Serat Kanda*, there is an unusual motif, unknown in India as far as we know, in which Hanuman is given the unusual task of watching over the grave of a half-dead Ravana, whose head is still lying at the foot of the mountain *Kundali Sade*, eternally alive owing to Subali's gift to him of the *aji pancasona* formula. On account of his excessive old age, Hanuman occasionally falls asleep on his watch, at which time Ravana swiftly comes to disturb the tranquility of the Pandavas. This is a brilliant metaphor for the never ending struggle between good and evil. However this *lakon* known as The Fall of Alengka and The Fall of Dashamukha is rarely performed on account of its inherent power.

There are characters in the *Ramayana* that continue to live in the age of the *Mahabharata*. King Duryodhana is looking for the glory of Rama's crown that has descended on earth as are Prince Arjuna helped by Wibisana and Kumbhakarna. The crown is nothing but the wisdom of Astabrata, or guidance for people living in the physical world to better serve mankind.[8] In another story, the unhappy souls of Rama, Lakshamana, followed by Sita, look for a place to be re-incarnated. They discover the ideal characters for the purpose. Rama reincarnates in the form of Krisna, Lakshamana into Arjuna. While the re-incarnation of Devi Sri/Wedawati/Devi Sita is manifested in the form of Devi Subhadra, the sister of Krisna. A *lakon* then occurs in which Prabu Rama and his faithful companions Sita and Lakshmana put an end to their lives by burning themselves, to enable all of them to find a new place of reincarnation.

Descendants of other characters from the *Ramayana* age continue to play a part in the age of the Pandavas, a metaphor for the continuity of the rule of truth and justice. Interestingly, while the Hindu attributes of *wayang* were given an Islamic interpretation, its spiritual and mystical content was re-enforced. The structure of the performance symbolizes the stages of an individual's development from infancy to youth and the growth of awareness, the attempt to learn from a wise man, the struggle to overcome obstacles in the path of spiritual development, the success in the battle of good against evil with the help of faith and ideology. The final scene ends with thanksgiving to the supreme and advice from elders regarding the significance of life. The spiritual quality of *wayang* rendered it suitable as a powerful medium for the explanation of mysticism and morality. It is not surprising that in the *Serat Rama*, by the eithteenth century, Rama turns into an expert on meditation. As *wayang* puppets were thought to have spiritual personalities which released supernatural energies, they were used with potent psychological effects. The *dalang* fits his *lakon* into this formulaic structure and invents the dialogue and events as he proceeds. It is easy to see how the *Ramayana* is perfectly suited to this narrative – good versus evil, the loss of virtue and the search for it by the hero, a war to fight evil and finally the victory. With the clever use of *pasemon* or allegory, the *dalang* is free to discuss or criticize any issue of political, moral, or social import in the veiled language of metaphor that the audience quickly understands. Folded into this entertainment is the strong didactic intent to instruct, educate and edify. The wise and funny clowns, Semar in particular, provides the mouthpiece for social and political comment. When in the mid-eighteenth century the divided Islamic kingdoms of Surakarta and Yogyakarta, deprived of any real power by the Dutch, concentrated on making each of their courts as competing cultural centres, the art of *wayang kulit* and the newly re-invented *wayang wong* dances reached new heights evolving into a high status art forms. This is the period when the virtues of loyalty, fidelity and political allegiances of Kumbhakarna and Wibhishana were debated at length in the medium of *wayang*. *Ramayana* performances became grandiose spectacles, increasingly elaborate and ritualistic.

Ramayana remains an effective ideological tool even today and most recently played an effective part in the struggle to overthrow President Soharto in the 'velvet revolution' in which Ravana, Sita, Hanuman and Rama were metaphors for the dictator Soharto, abducting the state which could only be saved by the Indonesian people with a new leader.

In the case of the island of Bali as mentioned earlier, it clung to its Hindu heritage. The pervasive Indian influence found in Balinese culture had its roots in the direct contact with the subcontinent 2,000 years ago. However, there is no evidence of the *Ramayana* until the eleventh century when Balinese tradition believes that *Ramayana Kakawin* came to Bali as a consequence of Java's political and cultural expansion. Whereas the knowledge of Old Javanese steadily declined in Java, after the advent of Islam, the people of Bali preserved the classical *Kakawin* literature in written and spoken form. They inscribed it on palm-leaf manuscripts or *lontars* generation after generation in carefully prescribed rituals. The sacred *akshara* sprung to life by the activity of small groups who met regularly, and this continues even today in organized groups, or reading clubs. *Mbebasan* is the Balinese term used to describe the activity of reading and discussing the grammar, content and meaning of classical texts. A part of the text is carefully chosen and it is recited by an expert and translated into Balinese by another expert. This is followed by a general explanation through discussion. Once known as *sekaa pepaosan*, they are now popularly referred to as *pesantian*, because they give *santi'* or peace.

With respect to a good performance, the following aspects are critical: the musicality of the voice (which becomes critical without musical accompaniment), mastery of a metrical rhythm *(wirama)*, the personal performance *(wiraga)* and the expression which is brought to the meaning of the text, its accuracy of delivery and interpretation (*wirasa).* The Old Javanese classics form the heart of the *Ramayana* performing arts tradition in Bali. Ordinary people in Bali can recite the Old Javanese *Ramayana* because the *dalang* of *Wayang kulit Ramayana* goes directly to the source material provided by *Kakawin* and *parwas*. All the *suluks* or mood songs come from *lontar* manuscripts of the

Ramayana. He sings extracts from the *Kakawin* to bring extra power and authenticity to the performance. The *Ramayana Kakawin* is believed to contain *wayah* or spiritual force and therefore its chanting in any form is of great ethical and instructional value.

A better-educated *dalang* is more than just a puppeteer who entertains by the artful manipulation of leather puppets. He conscientiously reads his *lontar* like a holy book. In fact, he is often called upon by the village community to officiate at religious functions. The preparations for a performance are similar to those of a priest performing a ritual involving fasting, meditation, yogic breathing and the ritual eating of betel-nut. The Balinese *wayang kulit Ramayana* is markedly different from its Javanese counterpart in many ways. Firstly the Balinese puppets preserve the shapes that were depicted in the Panataran temple reliefs of the Majapahit period. A *Ramayana* performance in Bali generally lasts for about four hours in contrast to its nightlong rendition in Java and is a fun-filled, action packed evening without the long philosophical passages so dear to the Javanese. The *dalang* enjoys great flexibility in the interpretation of the plot. He uses the bare skeleton of the story on which he builds his extensive improvisations, sometimes even borrowing material from pop culture to garnish his oeuvre. Every *dalang* has his own style from the rollicking slapstick rendition of the experienced village *dalang* of Amlapura, to the more measured pace of a better known one. In both performances, the *dalang* praised Kumbhakarna as a patriot who sacrificed his life for his country through loyalty to his brother even though he denounced as immoral Ravana's abduction of Sita.

The prominent role given to the monkey characters is a defining feature of *Wayang Kulit Ramayana.* The number and quality of monkey figures in the puppet collection often increases its popularity, coupled with the special vocal effects provided by the *dalang* to accompany their antics. Most have prominent features by which they are recognized, colour being one example – Hanuman is white, Sugriva red and Anila blue. Each character has an exclusive, recognizable voice. All the characters in a *wayang kulit* performance that derive from the classical literature speak *Basa Kawi,* the language of the texts, with the exception of the clowns who interpret the meaning of *Basa Kawi* into Balinese for ordinary people whom they represent. Purely a creation of Balinese imagination, the clowns, known as *penasar* or base figures, are given a highly significant role to play in the *Ramayana* and they voice the opinions of the common man.

The Old Javanese *Ramayana* is also dramatized in a ritual masked dance known as *Wayang Wong* in which the masks endowed with sacred power are worshipped. In Tejakula, a performance of "The Death of Kumbhakarna" lasting 2 hours is based on 100 lines of the *Kakawin* recited through the performance.[9] Dancers too become familiar with the *Kakawin,* hearing it sung during their performances.

Indonesia's flourishing tourist industry in modern times is built on the cornerstone of *Ramayana*s of both Java and Bali. The Prambanan temples in the vicinity of Yogyakarta in Central Java are heavily advertised and even today tourists to the island of Java are drawn to visit its extended series of *Ramayana* reliefs. On the nights of the full moon in the month of August, these temples come alive with dance and drama as the reliefs are enacted in the *wayang sendratari* (Fig. 6).

FIGURE 6: PRAMBANAN TEMPLE: *WAYANG SENDRATARI*

In the town Yogyakarta, regular performances of *wayang topeng* and *wayang wong* are advertised and in Taman Mini Indonesia, weekend performances of *wayang sendratari* are well attended by tourists and students alike. We can thank Indonesia for popularizing *Ramayana* through International dance festivals seen all over the world.

While the *Ramayana* traditions in Bali and Java diverged widely in certain ways after the fifteenth century, many reasons account for its continuing popularity in modern times. This had as much to do with the inherent nature of this capacious story telling tradition to instruct, edify and entertain as much as its capacity for flexible interpretation by each teller of the tale to meet the societal need of the time. The *Ramayana* discourse continues to have a potent role in the political imagination of Indonesia and provides a popular forum for debates on the ethics and morality of public and personal conduct. Absorbed into the local culture through the filter of performance, people identified with the stories aided by the insight and proficiency of its mediators whether it was the king as patron or the local interpreter be it poet, sculptor, dancer or *dalang* (puppeteer) who enriched the layers and textures of the narrative with his own responses to the environment and audience. His additional commentaries enlarged, explained and situated the narrative in a specific time. These adaptations gave an unmistakable Javanese or Balinese emphasis to what was recognizably Indian in origin and subject matter.

In this way, the perennial reinterpretation of *Ramayana* has kept the tradition alive and relevant until today. The *Ramayana* remains an integral part of the visual and performing arts. To retain its freshness and appeal, each generation preserved the older forms but revitalized them with fresh ideas and new techniques so that the old and new in both the performing and visual arts coexist in dynamic yet harmonious interaction. Few countries in the world can boast of an uninterrupted artistic tradition of the range and diversity found in Java and Bali that dates back to a thousand years. Fewer still can speak of such a tradition being used as an efficient vehicle of its literary heritage.

NOTES

* All photo credits to late Ajit Saran.

1. Java's familiarity with India's story telling traditions is witnessed in stories from the Panchatantra, the Buddhist Jatakas and Buddhist scriptures and the epics of *Ramayana* and *Mahabharata* that were sculpted in stone reliefs in Hindu and Buddhist temples starting from the ninth century. See Marijke Klokke, *Tantri Reliefs on Ancient Javanese Candi*, Leiden: KITLV Press, 1993; and Malini Saran, 'A System of Knowledge Transmission: The Narrative in Indonesia (c. AD 700-900)', in *Sacred Landscapes in Asia*, ed. Himanshu Prabha Ray. India International Centre and Manohar, 2007.
2. The two worlds of *Mahabharata* and *Ramayana* are often mentioned together in the earliest inscriptions of Java; they are etched into stone reliefs in different shrines of the same Hindu temples; they share the title of *parwa* literature from the eleventh century onwards; and their unique association is later cemented in the *wayang kulit* plays of Islamic Java.
3. A mid-ninth century inscription mentions the Javanese word *arringit* which is an Old Javanese synonym for *mawayang* or puppetry. An inscription written in Old Javanese issued by King Balitung in 907 CE confirms the granting of freehold land to the monastery of Dalinan (Sarkar 1972: 85-9). A variety of performances marked the celebration of this event that may have been the most important for the whole region. The performances include singing (*mamidu*); play acting (*mamirus*); clowning (*mabanol*); a spectacle with songs in which a certain Nalu recited the story of Bhimakumara and danced as Kicaka, a recitation of *Ramayana* by Jaluk (*macarita Ramayana*) and a wayang performance by Galigi with the story of Bhimakumara .
4. Supomo, the noted Old Javanese scholar compares it to the Indian institution of *harikatha* or public reading of the epics and the Puranas by trained masters of the art,

in which a priest reads and explains a religious story in the common language to his audience. This was possibly the method that allowed ordinary to access classical literature. Supomo S. *Bharatayuddha*: *An Old Javanese Poem and its Indian Source.* Sata Pitika Series, Indo-Asian Literatures, vol. 373, International Academy of Indian Culture and Aditya Prakashan, New Delhi, 1993.

5. A comparison of the Panataran reliefs with the *Ramayana Kakawin* can be found in chapter 5 of The *Ramayana* in Indonesia (Saran and Khanna, 2004)
6. Mentioned by the poet Prapanca in *Negarakratagama.*
7. In Malay literature, the *hikayat* came to stand for a prose tale probably meant to be read aloud to gatherings, whose subject was generally concerned with myths or legendary history as well as with historical chronicles. It seems probable that popular literature of an earlier period was inserted into the genre of the *hikayat* to legitimize its links with Malay society's pre-Islamic past as well as to ensure its continuity in the Javanese present. In its mode of narration and arrangement of material, Hikayat Seri Rama differs from all Indian *Ramayanas*.
8. Soewito Santoso, narrates the story of the lakon, Wahyu Makutha Rama in The Glory of Rama's crown in *Asian Variations of Ramayana*, Sahitya Akademi, New Delhi, 1983.
9. A ritual performance witnessed in Bali by the authors in the course of their research.

WORKS CITED

Klokke, Marijke. *Tantri Reliefs on Ancient Javanese Candi.* Leiden: KITLV Press, 1993.

Saran, Malini. 'A System of Knowledge Transmission: The Narrative in Indonesia (*c.* AD 700-900)', in *Sacred Landscapes in Asia*, ed. Himanshu Prabha Ray. New Delhi: India International Centre and Monohar, 2007.

S. Supomo. *Bharatayuddha*: *An Old Javanese Poem and its Indian Source.* Sata Pitika Series, Indo-Asian Literatures, vol. 373. New Delhi: International Academy of Indian Culture and Aditya Prakashan, 1993.

Santoso, Soewito. *Asian Variations of Ramayana.* New Delhi: Sahitya Akademi, 1983.

PART 5

Ancient Material Culture and Shared Histories

18

'Indianization' and the Religious Sites of Southeast Asia

MARIKA VICZIANY

In 1933, Paul Mus gave a lecture in Paris that was published in the same year as *'L'Inde vue de l'Est: Cultes Indiens et Indigenes au Champa'* in the *Bulletin de l'ecole Francaise d'Extreme-Orient*, XXXIII, no. 1: 367-410. Monash University published the first English translation by Ian Mabbett in 1975. In 2011/12 the Monash Asia Institute republished the English translation as a 2nd edition with a revised introduction by Ian Mabbett and David Chandler. This time we included the original illustrations used by Mus and also a complete bibliography of his work. In this essay I begin with a review of the Paul Mus paper, reflecting on its ongoing importance and what we can learn from it. In the second half of this essay I consider new work on the religious sites of Southeast Asia, specifically the chapters in a new publication by the Monash Asia Institute in 2012 titled: *Old Myths and New Approaches: Interpreting Ancient Religious Sites in Southeast Asia* edited by Alexandra Haendel. This work is sympathetic to Mus' insights some 80 years ago and takes us further into even bigger questions about the nature of the cultural interactions between India and Southeast Asian cultures and traditions.

The ongoing debates about these interactions are intrinsically very important and will, I hope, be able to avoid the dangers of becoming harnessed to any notions of 'soft power' and regional influence by any nation or group of nations in the newly emerging power structures of the Asian region. In their introduction to the Paul Mus essay, Mabbett and Chandler summarise the key debates and terms used in the discussions about India's cultural history and its interactions with the Kingdom of Champa, in territory that is now part of modern Vietnam. In their review of the literature they go beyond Champa and more broadly address issues about the so-called 'Indianization' of Southeast Asia. They note that the term 'Indianization' was a post Second World War idea that belonged to the early postcolonial period when nation-building exercises were of primary importance throughout the region as former European and Japanese colonies sought to consolidate their new-found independence. For some decades, however, the term 'Indianization' has lost currency because new scholarship has emerged in the Asian region that recognizes the complexities of the historical and cultural interactions between India and Southeast Asia. As we will see, the Mus paper from 1933 foreshadowed much of the new scholarly maturity that now defines cultural studies in India and Southeast Asia.

THE ENDURING SIGNIFICANCE OF PAUL MUS' WORK

Mus used the term the 'Indianised Kingdoms of Funan, Cambodia, Champa' because of the existence in these locations of statues featuring recognizable Indian gods such as Vishnu and Shiva, Buddhist images and Hindu and Buddhist religious artefacts. But these representations all had Cham features. Mus argued that they displayed adapted ideas that had become integrated into local 'lived lives' and traditions. He went on to ask: what is this 'India' that has influenced the Cham? Mus argued that the syncretic nature of religious representations in Champa were a reflection of the 'cultural continuity' of Asia, a continuity promoted by communications via sea lanes. More deeply, Mus suggested that there was a cultural continuity between India and Champa and that both countries belonged to 'monsoon Asia' and shared a common religion that was 'a religion of the monsoon zone'. This religion was animism. Mus insists that animism is not merely about spirit worship but more inclusively the recognition of sacred places and spaces where god is not symbolized by anything but is the living essence of the place itself. So Mus' definition of animism can be expressed as a relationship, for instance in the case of stones, where they were the essence of the earth and the earth was the essence of god. These common beliefs in the soil or sacred sites were shared across India, China, Champa and many other localities. It was this pre-existing belief system that allowed Indian influences to be 'influential' or naturally compatible with local beliefs in Champa. In the words of Mus (2012, p. 52):

> Thus it came about that when Hinduism...reached the Far East, what we witness is above all a diffusion of the old Asiatic ideas; ideas that were instantly recognised, understood and endorsed by peoples who perhaps were not always aware of wholly changing their religion in adopting those of India.

Even more dramatically Mus wrote that the Cham:

> ...no more abandoned their Hindu Gods in the 15th-19th centuries than they really believed themselves to be adopting entirely new ones from the 2nd-5th centuries.

Mus lived in Vietnam for many years and was a keen observer of people. He puzzled at how the old connection between local people and the ancient sites of kingdoms such as Champa had been lost. How and why was this possible? His conclusion was perfectly logical: if Indian and Chinese ideas and forms had been grafted onto local ones, then a reversion to indigenous inspirations was not entirely surprising. But he also warned us against making simplistic assumptions about the neglect suffered by royal and religious monuments. If the jungles had overtaken the royally sponsored high cultural and artistic achievements of the old elites, this did not mean that folk beliefs had also lost their old connection to previously mixed beliefs and practices. Indeed, Mus stressed that many folk beliefs and practices endured and continued to reflect syncretic histories in which local and outside ideas were mixed in living traditions.

The important achievement of Mus was that he broke down divisions that had previously made it impossible to understand what the Champa kingdom really stood for: he removed the separation between what was Indian and what was indigenous and he compelled us to see Champa culture not exclusively as an elite creation but as a shared tradition between elites and ordinary people. By implication, he helped us to break down these same dichotomies in our understanding of Southeast Asian, or Indian or Chinese culture.

Mus' approach, moreover, is equally relevant to cultural changes that have taken place inside India or elsewhere. For example when Buddhism moved beyond its original home in present-day Bihar to western India, similar processes of acculturation must have taken place. Here transmission occurred via land routes taken by monks, priests, traders and pilgrims rather than the sea lanes that Mus talked of. My new research with Jayant Bapat and Sanjay Ranade on the Ekvira Temple outside the Buddhist Karla rock-cut temple at Lonavla (near Mumbai) shows the multilayered nature of these transmissions in western India. Moreover, acculturation continues today amongst the Koli people who have made Ekvira their clan goddess and who in the process have converted this sacred Buddhist hill into a shared religious space (Vicziany et al., 2013 forthcoming). Regardless of how transmission occurs, the distances between localities, and the era in which the streams of cultural influences meet, the processes are the same – namely a mixing between local belief systems and traditions and imported ones. So if we persist in speaking of the 'Indianization' of Southeast Asia we had also better start talking about the 'Indianization' of India itself.

I find the concept of the 'Indianization' of India very odd. I suggest here the value of abandoning this terminology for other words that better reflect the nature of cultural flows and the interactions between local and imported ideas. Another example of that interaction is particularly well demonstrated in the work of George Michell and his team on the kingdom of Vijayanagara in Hampi, western India. Pampa was the goddess attached to the Tungabhadra River and an important part of the belief system of the people who lived in the Hampi region. When the Sangama brothers became politically ambitious in the early fourteenth century they sponsored a cultural process by which Pampa 'married' Shiva, whose local name is Virupaksha. This marriage elevated Pampa into a major goddess (Michell, 1991, 24). The Sangama family's ongoing sponsorship of Pampa and Shiva, in turn, helped to legitimate their expanding power across the region. The surviving temples at Vijiayanagara are testimony to the importance of this new cult, while the ongoing worship of Pampa, the Tungabhadra River, and the annual spring festival that celebrates the marriage of Pampa and Shiva (Michell, 1991, 49-50), tell us about the enduring importance of local beliefs and traditions. The story of Vijayanagara is almost a mirror image of the processes that Mus speaks of in the case of Champa.

NEW RESEARCH ON THE RELIGIOUS SITES OF SOUTHEAST ASIA

In 2012 the Monash Asia Series of Monash University Publishing brought to the attention of an international audience significant new work on the ancient religious sites of Southeast Asia. Haendel's title, *Old Myths and New Approaches: Interpreting Ancient Religious Sites in Southeast Asia,* stresses the innovative nature of the work that is the subject of her collection of sixteen papers. It is noteworthy that the term 'Indianization' appears only once in the 300 pages (Degroot, 121), bearing out Mabbett and Chandler's statement that the term has long since been abandoned as useful. In what follows I will discuss a section from each of the three main parts of this collection to illustrate the kind of new questions that are driving research on Southeast Asian archaeological sites today. Much of this work talks directly to the issues that Paul Mus raised in 1933, even though Mus has not directly influenced the works in this volume.

PART 1: NATURE AND HUMANS: ADAPTING TO THE ENVIRONMENT

Haendel's introduction leads into seven chapters by Heng Sophady, Christophe Pottier, Bob Acker, Roland Fletcher & Damian Evans, William A. Southworth, Mitch Hendrickson and Peter Worsley.

I have selected Christophe Pottier's chapter 'Beyond the Temples: Angkor and its Territory' because he reminds us that despite the extensive romanticism associated with the history, excavations and renovations of Angkor, until 1990 our knowledge of this kingdom was piecemeal and narrowly focused on its temples and royal sites. Moreover, the geographical boundaries of what was thought to constitute 'Angkor' have literally exploded with the application of new methodologies that have revealed hundreds of secondary temple sites and thousands of non-royal structures including tanks, ponds, canals, roads, land bundles, and houses for the pre-Angkor, proto-Angkor and Angkor periods. In moving away from the earlier obsession with temples and royal and religious texts, our conceptualization of what constituted Angkor has changed dramatically. New work by Pottier and others uses multidisciplinary approaches and multiple technologies to generate a complete and holistic perspective on what Angkor was and meant. Environmental, spatial, palaeological and new archaeological data have all been used to generate complex pictures of human settlement, land use and water management. As Pottier notes, the analysis of 'secondary sites', including lower-order temples which used 'humble materials', tells us about the nature of social hierarchy in Angkor. Most important of all, the shift away from vast monuments and courtly religious cults throws the emphasis of our understanding of Angkor civilization onto non-religious factors. In the words of Pottier: ". . . a comprehensive spatial approach can identify and stress the evolution of secular elements that characterise settlements and land use" (2012, 27).

The seminal findings of Roland Fletcher and Damian Evans, which also appear in the first section, complement the work of Pottier. The opening sentence of their chapter describes Angkor not as a bounded site of temples and palaces, but as a "low density urban complex [of]... about 1,000 square kilometres" (Fletcher and Evans, 2012, 42). Nothing could throw the focus off courtly culture more effectively than this realignment of the actual boundaries of Angkor. Using the kind of new techniques and methodologies Pottier referred to, Fletcher and Evans describe the extensive agricultural system that dominated Angkor. They argue that the 20-km-long canals put massive pressure on the environment which, together with vast building projects, led to soil degradation, siltation and the destruction of forests. Our admiration for the enormous buildings of Angkor begins to diminish as we remember that the ecological collapse that awaited this civilization was partly caused by the lack of agricultural innovations which could have taken Angkorians in the direction of high-yielding, intensive farming practices. But the collapse of the Angkorian system was not sudden or dramatic – rather it probably died of 'inertia' and 'redundancy'. Yet the residents were not inevitably doomed – they were able to adjust their lifestyles to more simple ways by abandoning the main sites, moving away and adopting more flexible living places. This change may have been facilitated because the servants and slaves of the Angkor elite already lived in small spaces often beneath the houses of the nobility. In the words of Fletcher and Evans (2012, 61 and Fig. 4.4):

> If it is the case that Angkor's physical structure became unworkable and rigid and the inhabitants had a sufficiently flexible social life that they were able to move away from it, then Angkor became a redundant mode of practice. The populace chose to move away to a new and different way of life. In this view, Angkor became redundant – no longer needed as the Khmer freed themselves from it.

Fletcher and Evans's conclusion has tremendous significance for the long-term peace and stability of mainland Southeast Asia today. If Angkor collapsed under its own cultural-cum-environmental weight, then neighbouring peoples and states, particularly Thailand, were not to blame. Fletcher and Evans continue (2012, 61):

FIGURE 1: DOMESTIC SPACE- FROM THE BAYON BAS-RELIEFS (LATE TWELFTH CENTURY) PHOTOGRAPH: CATHERINE WU REPRODUCED FROM FLETCHER AND EVANS, 2012, 51 WITH THE KIND PERMISSION OF MONASH UNIVERSITY PUBLISHING.)

By contrast what is explicit in the story of the Thai sack is that Angkor was lost, stolen from the Khmer, and is a tragic loss to be mourned and regretted. The potent alternative implications of these two perspectives for contemporary Cambodian society suggest that the issues and the debate deserve intense attention, analysis and discussion.

PART 2: SITES AND GROUPS OF BUILDINGS

Part 2 is a smaller section of the book, containing only four chapters introduced by David Chandler, the eminent historian of Cambodia. The authors are Veronique Degroot, Jo Grimmond, John Miksic and Heng Piphal. Here we consider the work of John Miksic because it speaks directly to the old theme of the 'Indianization' of Southeast Asia.

'Indianization' is not a term that Miksic uses; in fact, his chapter explains why Trowulan, the capital of the Majapahit empire on Java, which used to house rulers, Hindu priests and Buddhist monks, was not spatially arranged in the manner that one might have expected in an 'Indianized' capital, in particular as suggested by the *Arthaśāstra,* an Indian text that provided advice on many aspects of rule including urban planning. Trowulan was not organized around a central palace but around an elegant and ritually-powerful crossroad (Miksic, 2012, 164). The general spatial arrangement within the four sections of Trowulan also diverged from the *Arthaśāstra* template. The temples and religious sites were located outside the city in the surrounding rural areas. The location of the royal court in the southwest corner was "consistent with Balinese cosmology" (Miksic, 2012, 166). The economic centre of Trowulan was not driven by religious or political considerations but by the economic activities of merchants, artisans and foreign traders and settlers. The rulers, of course, patronized the temples and other structures but the local people seemed to have greater faith in the power of hermits. Most interesting of all, the people of Trowulan had a pragmatic response to the practical needs of their capital: the temples were built in areas with low water tables so that the high water-table regions could support denser human settlement.

Miksic's analysis of Trowulan shows that pragmatic considerations dominated the urban configuration of the capital of Majapahit and that religious interests were less important. The secular nature of the factors analysed by Miksic confirm the emphasis that Pottier, Fletcher and Evans place on the non-religious issues that had to be taken into account by local residents in order to establish their livelihoods. Miksic also reminds us, as do the other authors that we are really at the beginning of understanding the archaeology of the religious sites of Southeast Asia and the daily lives of the peoples who lived there:

> According to Veth (1896-1907), writing in the second half of the 19th century, a study of the remains of Majapahit that conforms to the demands of archaeology was lacking. Sadly, Veth's lament is still relevant today (Miksic, 2012, 179).

PART 3: LIVING THE SITES – THE COMMUNITIES AROUND

The last section of this book begins with an introduction by Stuart Robson, a prominent language and cultural expert. Five chapters follow by Alexandra Haendel, Tom Chandler and Martin Polkinghorne, Angelo Andrea Di Castro, Stuart Robson and Tran Ky Phu'o'ng and Rie Nakamura. I look at the work of Di Castro because he asks a general question of importance for the whole volume: what continues to drive this obsession with temples and kings in our understanding of the lives and religions of the people of Southeast Asia? Alexandra Haendel has a partial answer: the task of reclaiming these vast monuments from the jungle was heroic. And acts of heroism attract attention and obsessions.

In his chapter titled 'Graves, trees and powerful spirits as archaeological indicators of sacred spaces', Di Castro has a more fundamental purpose when he asks why are we compartmentalizing the many religions of Asia? Why must we differentiate between Hindu, Muslim, Buddhist, Shaman, animist and so on when there are compelling fundamental similarities in the day-to-day worship of followers of all religions? By implication, we can ask why a whole generation of historians of India spoke about the 'Indianization' of Southeast Asia? And later the 'Islamization' of Southeast Asia? Why did it take until the 1970s to refocus on inter-religious and inter-cultural dialogue and the syncretic nature of cultural interactions?

In his discussion of what different worshippers have in common, Di Castro talks about holy graves, shrines, saints, spirits, dreams, sacrifices, rags, footprints, sacred groves and spaces, guardian spirits and sacred trees. He undertakes an intellectual journey across Asia to show that similar practices can be found across geographical, cultural and political boundaries. He emphasises that cross-regional references need not stop at the boundaries of Asia: perhaps the oldest reference to a sacred footprint is in Herodotus (the Greek historian of the fifth century BCE) (Di Castro, 2012, 249).

As Di Castro notes, studying the archaeology of religion requires us to understand the broader environment and the sacred spaces that typically surround religious monuments, holy graves, temples and so on. Often these sacred spaces reveal a much deeper history and more complex cultural practices than the official religious teachers, textbooks or inscriptions allow. In Xinjiang province in western China at the site of the tomb of Mahmud of Kashgari, the great Turkic scholar of the early eleventh century, there is a lovely garden surrounding an enormous desert poplar festooned with ribbons. This site forms part of a research project by the Monash Asia Institute in Kashgar, and Di Castro is a member of that team. The ribbons are tied by visitors who come to pray at the tree for good luck – perhaps another child, a new job, sacred intervention for a sick family member or assistance with exams or business deals. Behind the shrine in which the tomb is located, there is a vast

FIGURE 2: THE SACRED DESERT POPLAR TREE NEAR THE TOMB OF MAHMUD OF KASHGARI, AT KASHGARIA (UPAL VILLAGE). PHOTOGRAPH BY JOHN GOLLINGS IN MICHELL, TSUI AND VICZIANY, *KASHGAR, OASIS CITY ON CHINA'S OLD SILK ROAD,* FRANCES LINCOLN, LONDON, 2008.

mazar (grave) which also reveals evidence of religious beliefs and practices that predate the current Islamic beliefs of the Uygur people who continue to bury their dead in this sacred landscape. For example, chickens continue to be sacrificed today and the sacred blood is strewn across the ground as a way of providing extra support to help the departed in the new life that awaits them.

In our work on the archaeological sites of Kashgar and the current cultural and religious practices which continue to be performed around them, we found no incompatibilities between Islamic and pre-Islamic belief systems. But had we only focused on a study of the funerary monuments themselves, we might have been misled into thinking that the tolerant form of Sufi Islam that is practiced so widely in Kashgar today is the complete story. In fact, the cultural interactions between Islam and pre-Islamic thought, practice and representations, are very intricate and again remind me of the cultural adaptations that Mus addressed in 1933.

CONCLUSION

In his contribution to this volume Miksic writes:

> The nature of cultural evolution in Southeast Asia will only be clarified if each part of the region is viewed in its own terms rather than as an example of a larger regional identity (Miksic, 2012, 179).

This call to focus on the particular details of micro regions or localities can be more generally applied to Asia, whether we work on India, China or Central Asia. Avoiding generalizations is a first step towards preventing the homogenization of the nature of cultural interactions and taking seriously Mus' suggestion that we study the interactions between local peoples and imported ideas. And local peoples are just that – they belong to specific localities. At the same time, focusing on the particularities of cultural synthesis should not prevent us from noticing what is also universal about human behaviour- this is the point made by Di Castro. Moreover, this universal factor includes the challenge that all peoples faced in handling the environment in which they lived. The natural environment imposed conditions and opportunities that had to be factored into human settlement patterns in a way that was totally pragmatic and not determined by religious priorities.

In summary, we have travelled a great distance from the early generalizations about the 'Indianization' of Southeast Asia to a more humble position of admitting that the details of many of the cultural interactions between India, China, Central Asia and Southeast Asia in the pre-modern era still elude us. We have much more work to do to understand exactly how local peoples interacted with newly imported ideas, irrespective of whether those ideas arrived by sea lanes, on the backs of horses or camels, or by foot in the wanderings of traders, monks, priests and pilgrims. In understanding these movements, there is no reason (and indeed it is dangerous) to give any special place to the modern political boundaries that separate us today. With the rise of Asia, we hope that research on the archaeology of Asia and inter-religious dialogue will receive increased impetus.

WORKS CITED

Degroot, Véronique. 'Temples and landscape in South Central Java', ed. Alexandra Haendel. *Old Myths and New Approaches: Interpreting Ancient Religious Sites in Southeast Asia.* Monash Asia Series, Monash University Publishing, 2012: 121-34.

Di Castro, Angelo Andrea. 'Graves, trees and powerful spirits as archaeological indicators of sacred spaces', ed. Alexandra Haendel. *Old Myths and New Approaches: Interpreting Ancient Religious Sites in Southeast Asia,* Monash Asia Series. Monash University Publishing, 2012: 237-51.

Fletcher, Roland and Evans, Damian. 'The Dynamics of Angkor and its Landscape', in Alexandra Haendel, ed., *Old Myths and New Approaches: Interpreting Ancient Religious Sites in Southeast Asia.* Monash Asia Series, Monash University Publishing, 2012: 42-62.

Haendel, Alexandra. *Old Myths and New Approaches: Interpreting Ancient Religious Sites in Southeast Asia.* Monash Asia Series, Monash University Publishing, 2012.

Michell, George. 'Reflections on Vijayanagara'. *South Asia: Journal of South Asian Studies.* 1993: 15-32.

Michell, George and John Fritz with photographs by John Gollings. *City of Victory: Vijayanagara, the Medieval Hindu Capital of Southern India.* New York: Aperture, 1991.

Michell, George, Yen Hu Tsui and Marika Vicziany. *Kashgar, Ancient City on China's Old Silk Road.* London: Frances Lincoln, 2008. Photographs by John Gollings.

Miksic, John. 'Life among the Ruins- Habitation sites of Trowulan', in Alexandra Haendel, ed., *Old Myths and New Approaches: Interpreting Ancient Religious Sites in Southeast Asia.* Monash Asia Series, Monash University Publishing, 2012: 159-79.

Mus, Paul. *India seen from the East: Indian and indigenous cults in Champa.* Trans. Ian Mabbett. Monash Asia Series, Monash University Publishing, 2012.

Pottier, Christophe. 'Beyond the Temples: Angkor and its Territory', in Alexandra Haendel, ed., *Old Myths and New Approaches: Interpreting Ancient Religious Sites in Southeast Asia.* Monash Asia Series, Monash University Publishing, 2012: 12-27.

Vicziany, Marika, Jayant Bapat and Sanjay Ranade. 'Ekvira, the Karla temple and the Koli of Bombay City: Cultural Transformations of the 20th Century'. Jayant Bapat and Ian Mabbett, *The Devi in India and Tibet,* forthcoming.

19

Banteay Srei, the Cambodian Citadel of Women: A Look at the Scenes from the Ancient Indian Epics and the *Purāṇas*

K.T.S. SARAO

The famous Khmer temple, Banteay Srei, was built by Yajñavarāha, a Brāhmaṇa priest, who served during the reigns of Khmer kings Rajendravarman and Jayavarman V. According to stele inscription of Banteay Srei, work on its construction began in 967 CE and Yajñavarāha's brother, Viṣṇukumāra, is also mentioned as a co-patron. Banteay Srei was the only major temple at Angkor not built for the king. This temple lies near the hill of Phnom Dei located 25 km to the northeast of the main group of temples, where Yaśodharapura, the Khmer capital of that time, was located. It consists of three shrines, laid out in a row from north to south: the north shrine (dedicated to Viṣṇu), and the central and south shrines (both dedicated to Śiva). The original name of this temple was *Śrī Tribhuvanamaheśvara* (Great Lord of the Threefold World), an appellation of Lord Śiva. The temple's modern name, Banteay Srei – citadel of women or citadel of beauty – is most probably related to the intricate bas-relief carvings that can be found on the walls as well as the tiny dimensions of the structures themselves (Freeman and Jacques, 1999: 206). The other explanation is that the temple has got its name from the fact that it has many *devatās* (female deities of fertility) carved into the walls of the structures (Jessup, 2004: 101). A typical *devatā*, embellishing each of the corners of the various shrines, is shown standing with a lamp hung over her head and swans adorning the base. These *devatās*, with naked torsos and playing with flowers, are known for being the most voluptuous of the Angkor *devatās*.

Due to the miniature size of the structures, the uniqueness of the tiny details, and the exceptional refinement of the sculptures, the Banteay Srei temple has become extremely popular with tourists and is popularly admired as a "*Precious Gem*," or the "*Jewel of Khmer Art*." "Through refinement it takes the best of all that had preceded. . . and submits it to new creation in a dynamic form of high art. . . the work relates more closely to the art of the goldsmith. . . or to carving in wood than to sculpture in stone. The very nature of the material used – a hard red sandstone that can be worked like wood – has inspired the artist not to carve in volume, but rather, in the reduced scale of the composition and the proximity of the buildings" (Glaize, 2003: 183).

According to an inscription of the early twelfth century, at some point, the temple came under the control of the king and its original dedication was changed but was again rededicated to Śiva (Higham, 2001: 114). The temple was functional at least until the fourteenth century (Apsara Authority, *Banteay Srei*). The temple was rediscovered in 1914 and immediately became the target of art thieves: André Malraux who stole four *devatās* in 1923, being one such high profile looter (Freeman and Jacques, 1999: 207). The temple was restored in the 1930s, using the technique of anastylosis involving analysis and rebuilding of the temple using as much of the original material as possible. As the temple continued to be attacked by vandals repeatedly, towards the end of the twentieth century some of the original statues were shifted and replaced with concrete replicas. But vandals did not even spare the replicas. So much so, a statue of Śiva and his śakti Umā that was shifted to the National Museum (Phnom Penh) for safekeeping was vandalized on the premises of the museum itself (Jessup, 2004: 104).

At this temple, for the first time pediments, lintels, and colonettes appear with stories from the *Mahābhārata,* the *Rāmāyaṇa,* and the *Purāṇas* relating to themes associated with Śaivism and Vaiṣṇavism:

1. THE KIRĀTĀRJUNĪYA (*VAṆA PARVA, MAHĀBHĀRATA*)

When the Pāṇḍavas were getting ready for war with the Kauravas, Arjuna, propitiates Lord Śiva in the forest. Happy with Arjuna's penances, Śiva takes a decision to reward him. When Muka, the demon, in the form of a wild boar, charges toward Arjuna, Śiva makes his appearance as a Kirāta. Arjuna and the Kirāta simultaneously shoot arrows at the boar and put it to death.

Both get into an argument as to who shot first. This results in a protracted battle between the two. Overconfident Arjuna is astounded that he is not able to defeat his adversary. In the end, Arjuna realizes that the Kirāta is actually Lord Śiva himself, and submits to him in all humility. Śiva is pleased with his devotee and awards him with the powerful weapon, the *Paśupatastra*, which later proved very useful in the Mahābhārata war. The *Kirāta* is a generic term in Sanskrit literature for people who lived in the mountains, particularly in the Himalayas and Northeastern India and are considered to have been of Mongoloid origin (Mukharji 1998: 132). It has been mentioned in the *Mahābhārata* that Bhīma had met the Kirātas to the east of Videha, where his son Ghaṭotkacha was born and on this basis it has been suggested that the Kirātas were dwellers of the Eastern Himalayas (Chatterji 1974: 30). The texts mention them along with Cīnas as people of "gold-like" skin in sharp contrast to the Niṣādas or the Dāsas who were of dark complexion (26).

2. MADANA-BHASMA (*MATSYA PURĀṆA, ŚIVA PURĀṆA*)

This episode, which is depicted on the west-facing pediment on southern library, is mentioned in the *Matsya Purāṇa* (vv 227-55) repeated with variants in the *Śiva Purāṇa,* relates to Kāma's incineration by Śiva. Śiva is shown as

seated on the summit of Mount Kailāśa and is looking to his left at Kāma (Madana), the god of desire, who in turn is aiming an arrow at him. Goddess Pārvatī is seated to Śiva's right and Śiva is handing her a bead necklace. Beings of different categories are shown in a hierarchical order on the slopes of Mt Kailāśa. In the top tier and immediately below Śiva are seated a group of bearded wise men and ascetics. Below them are the mythological beings with animal-heads and human-bodies.

Common people occupying the lowest tier are shown as mingling with a bull and a deer. It has been told in the legend that *asura* Tāraka was harassing Indra and the other gods. However, Tāraka could only be defeated by Śiva's offspring. Brahmā suggests that Pārvatī should woo Śiva and consequently, Indra assigned the task of breaking Śiva's meditation to Kāmadeva. Kāmadeva creates an untimely spring (*akālavasanta*) and enters Śiva's abode with his two wives Rati and Prīti. Though Madana succeeds in awakening Śiva with a flower arrow, Śiva is furious and incinerates Madana instantaneously turning him into ashes. Later Pārvatī prevails over Śiva to resuscitate Madana. Though Śiva brought Madana back to life but only in a disembodied form. As a result, Kāmadeva is also called '*Anaṅga*'= *an* (without) + *aṅga* (body) = bodiless or '*Atanu*'= *a* (without) + *tan* (body). Later, Śiva's son Kārtikeya succeeded in defeating Tāraka.

3. BURNING OF THE KHĀṆḌAVA FOREST AND INDRA'S RAIN (*MAHĀBHĀRATA* AND *HARIVAṂSA*)

This east-facing pediment on the northern library relates an incident from the *Mahābhārata* and *Harivaṃsa*. Agni, the god of fire, has started fire to the

Khāṇḍava forest to kill the nāga king Takṣaka who lived in this forest. Indra who is riding Airāvata, his three-headed elephant and is surrounded by imploring devotees, produces rain to extinguish the fire to save his friend Takṣaka. Kṛṣṇa and Arjuna, standing in their chariots on the bottom right and left, are helping Agni by firing a dense barrage of arrows to block the rain produced by Indra. The arrows move so close together that they almost turn into a roof, buttressed by a line of swans, in the midst of the falling water and the forest below. At the centre of the scene, nāgas are trying to get away by climbing the roof of arrows whereas the forest animals, including elephants, lions, monkeys, and deer who attempt to escape are driven back by Kṛṣṇa and Arjuna. With a few exceptions, all these animals perish in the fire.

4. BATTLE BETWEEN VĀLI AND SUGRĪVA (*RĀMĀYAṆA*)

At two places, the western *gopura* of the second enclosure as well as the eastern lintel of the northern shrine, show the episode from the *Rāmāyaṇa*. Two monkey-chiefs, Vāli and his younger brother Sugrīva, fight against each other for kingship of Kiśkindha. Rāma, standing on the right, shoots an arrow at Vāli from behind piercing his heart and causing his death. Consequently, Sugrīva is declared the victor.

5. RĀVAṆA SHAKING MOUNT KAILĀŚA (*RĀMĀYAṆA*)

This pediment depicts one of the stories from the *Rāmāyaṇa* in which Rāvaṇa, the king of Laṅkā, is shown shaking Mt Kailāśa. The background to

the incident is that following his conquest of Lanka, Rāvaṇa went to see Śiva. But Nandi, the vehicle of Śiva, refused to let him in. This annoyed Rāvaṇa greatly and he began to tease Nandi who in turn got annoyed with Rāvaṇa and cursed that his Laṅkā would be destroyed by a monkey. However, to demonstrate before Nandi his love for Śiva, Rāvaṇa tried to lift Kailāśa on a whim. In the pediment Śiva is shown seated on the summit of Mt Kailāśa, his heavenly abode. His consort Umā is sitting in his lap and is holding him nervously. Various kinds of beings are shown in a hierarchical order on the slopes of Mt Kailāśa. In the top tier and around Śiva are seated bearded wise men and ascetics. Below them are the mythological beings with animal-heads and human-bodies. Animals occupy the lowest tier. In the middle of the scene stands the ten-headed Rāvaṇa. He is shaking the mountain in its very foundations as the animals flee in terror and as the wise men pray. Śiva, annoyed by Rāvaṇa's arrogance, is using his toe to press down on the mountain to trap Rāvaṇa underneath.

6. KṚṢṆA SLAYING KAṂSA (*BHĀGAVAT PURĀṆA AND HARIVAṂŚA*)

This pediment depicts various episodes inspired by the *Bhāgavata Purāṇa* and the *Harivaṃśa* that culminate in Kṛṣṇa slaying his wicked uncle Kaṃsa. Kṛṣṇa and Balarāma are shown as making their way to the wrestling arena where they respectively defeat and kill the wrestlers Canura and Muṣṭika followed by the decapitation of Kaṃsa by Kṛṣṇa.

7. NARASIṂHA SLAYING HIRAṆYAKAŚIPU
(*MAHĀBHĀRATA AND PURĀṆAS*)

According to the *Mahābhārata* and some of the *Purāṇas*, Hiraṇyakaśipu, the king of the asuras, had obtained a boon from Śiva that neither a human nor

a non-human can kill him. However, when he began to persecute his own son Prahlāda for worshipping Viṣṇu, the latter decided to put an end to his cruelties. In this pediment, Viṣṇu in his reincarnation as Narasiṃha half-man and half-lion) is shown as slaying Hiraṇyakaśipu, whom he is holding upside-down below him while clawing at his chest.

8. ŚIVA NAṬARĀJA

In this lintel, Śiva Naṭarāja is shown as the cosmic dancer who performs his divine dance to destroy a weary universe so that Brahmā may start the process of creation. At the lower edges are a drummer providing the music and Kareikkal Ammeyar, Śiva's disciple.

9. DURGĀ MAHIṢĀSURAMARDINĪ (*MĀRKAṆḌEYA PURĀṆA*)

According to the story given in the *Devī Mahātmya* of the *Mārkaṇḍeya Purāṇa*, Mahiṣā, the Buffalo Demon, undertook severe austerities and acquired such powers that he unleashed a reign of terror in the three worlds (earth, heaven and the nether world) and he could not be defeated anywhere by any man or god. Consequently, the entire Cosmic Order was thrown into disarray. To sort this problem out, all the gods together offered their own individual powers back to their common source and as they did so, Durgā, the warrior goddess, was born. She with eight arms, assisted by her lion, grappled with Mahiṣā whom a snake entangles in his coils. Finally, she slayed him and restored the

Cosmic Order, thereby earning the title of Mahiṣāsuramardinī, the Slayer of Mahiṣā. Her victory is celebrated each year during the Navarātri (the Festival of Nine Nights) or Durgā Pūjā.

10. ABDUCTION OF SĪTĀ (*RĀMĀYAṆA*)

This carving depicts a story from the *Āraṇya Kāṇḍa* of the *Rāmāyaṇa* in which Rāma's wife Sītā was abducted by a *rakṣasa* called Virādha. Virādha who lived

in Daṇḍaka forest had a boon from Brahmā which made him invincible to weapons. In order to kill him, Rāma and Lakṣmaṇa first broke his arms, then buried him alive in a grave.

11. SUNDA AND ASUNDA FIGHTING OVER TILOTTAMĀ (*MAHĀBHĀRATA*)

In this pediment, now at the *Musée National des Arts Asiatiques*, Guimet (Paris), is shown the story of the *apsarā* Tilottamā, causing a discord between the two brothers, Sunda and Upasunda, leading to their mutual destruction. According to the story mentioned in the *Ādi Parva* (Book 1) of the *Mahābhārata*, sage Nārada warns the Pāṇḍava brothers that their common wife Draupadi could be the cause of dispute between them. To substantiate his argument, he relates the story of the death of Sunda and Upsunda due to Tilottamā. Sunda and Upsunda were inseparable siblings who shared everything between them including bed, food and the kingdom. As a reward for severe austerities, they had received a boon from Brahmā that nothing but they themselves could hurt each other. After receiving the boon, the demons conquered the entire universe and put it in complete disarray. Consequently, Brahmā then ordered the divine architect Viśvakarma to create Tilottamā, a woman with unrivaled beauty. She was directed to seduce the demon brothers to the extent that she would become an issue of contention between them. Enchanted by her irresistible charms and voluptuous figure and drunk with power and liquor, Sunda and Upasunda took hold of Tilottamā in right and left hands respectively. As they argued that Tilottamā should be his own wife, they took hold of clubs and clubbed each other to death.

12. WRESTLING BETWEEN BHĪMA AND DURYODHANA (*MAHĀBHĀRATA*)

This pediment depicts the episode from the *Mahābhārata* in which Paṇḍava, Bhīma, and the Kaurava Duryodhana wrestle each other in the presence of the four-armed Kṛṣṇa and his brother, Balarāma who is armed with a ploughshare. In the battle, Bhīma strikes a foul blow below the waist of Duryodhana and fatally wounds him. At this, Balarāma is enraged and criticises Bhīma. But Kṛṣna calms him down.

13. HAYAGRĪVA KILLING MADHU AND KAIṬABHA (*MAHĀBHĀRATA*)

This pediment describes the story from the *Mahābhārata* of two *asuras,* Madhu and Kaiṭabha. They had snatched the Vedas from Brahmā and deposited them

in the nether world. Brahmā was very unhappy over this and approached Viṣṇu for help in the matter. Viṣṇu, in his manifestation as *Hayagrīva* (Horse-headed avatāra of Viṣṇu) waged a war against them, killed them, and retrieved the Vedas. Consequently, Viṣṇu became known as Madhusūdana (the killer of Madhu).

The formation of the material milieu which inspired the creation of temples such as Banteay Srei appears to have taken place from the middle of the first millennium onwards as a consequence of the widespread assimilation and acculturation in the Khmer territory of the religious and political traditions whose roots lay in the Indian subcontinent. The driving force behind such a development was the coming into prominence in the latter half of the first millennium of the priest-peasant alliance and its support to the political élites. This Bhakti-influenced temple-based alliance grew into a dynamic and progressive force through the mushrooming of temples of Śaiva and Vaiṣṇava deities under the Khmer kings. The cult of the Devarāja (god-king), a 'descent' of god Śiva and a form of the Cosmic Overlord, became the basis of royal authority. In the consecration ceremony (*abhiṣeka*) the king was transformed into a this-worldly god Śiva. Being a member of this kind of socio-political system, whether one was a king or an ordinary peasant, ensured a special status through proximity to both the heavenly gods (Śiva and Viṣṇū) and the Devarāja, the earthly god. It worked in promoting simultaneously the power of kings and priests and also acted as a unifying force by bringing together kings, brāhmaṇa priests, and the common masses at religious gatherings, ceremonies, and festivals. In it can clearly be seen the all-pervasive influence of the Bhakti movement which during its first phase in the Indian subcontinent had already successfully taken Brāhmaṇical-Hinduism away from its orthodox philosophy by rejecting abstract metaphysics and caste regulations. Thus, it is not surprising that the agrarianized popular form of Brāhmaṇical-Hinduism which inspired sites such as Banteay Srei was devoid of not only caste but also of metaphysics and philosophy rooted in the Vedas and the Upaniṣads.

But who were the conduits of this cultural transfer? The "Indianized" Khmer civilization was, firstly shaped by "underlying ideas associated with the older Megalithic cults of Earth and Ancestor" (Wales, 1967: 2). As suggested by N.J. Krom, Indian traders impressed indigenous people with their artefacts and cultural achievements, intermarried with them, and transferred their culture to an Indianized élite (see Mabbett, 1977: 144). This Indianized élite adopted customs of Indian origin as a means not only to increase their dominance over local groups and to improve their contacts with other cultures but also to legitimize their political control (Mabbett, 1977). The credit for the cultural grafting should clearly go to the traders though some renegade brāhmaṇas, who may have accompanied the initial waves of traders, could have contributed indirectly (see Larus, 1979: 181-2). Like the brāhmaṇas, many of the adventurers and fortune-seekers of aristocratic background who were well-qualified to act as priests may have also made some contribution. Besides, adventurers and traders too might have lent a helping hand to each other. Hence, it may be said that the "Indianized" culture of Southeast Asia was "scholastic" in nature which was sustained by the locals through the learning of Sanskrit and importation of texts that dealt with matters relating to religion, rituals, and art and architecture (Stutterheim, 1929: 4ff).

WORKS CITED

Chatterji, S.K. *Kirāta-Jana-Kṛti: The Indo-Mongoloids, Their Contribution to the History and Culture of India*, 2nd rev. edn. Calcutta: The Asiatic Society, 1974.

Coe, Michael D. *Angkor and the Khmer Civilization*. London: Thames & Hudson, 2003.

Cohen, Joan L. *Angkor: The Monuments of the God Kings*. New York: Harry N. Abrams, 1975.

Freeman, M. and C. Jacques. *Ancient Angkor*, Bangkok: River Books Co. Ltd., 1999.

Freeman, Michael and Roger Warner. *Angkor: The Hidden Glories*, Boston: Houghton Mifflin Company, 1990.

Glaize, Maurice. *The Monuments of the Angkor Group*, Eng. trans. of the 1993 4th French edn, http://www.theangkorguide.com/images/download/Angkor.pdf., 2003.

Higham, Charles. *The Civilization of Angkor*. London: Phoenix, 2001.

Jacques, Claude. *Angkor: Cities and Temples*. Bangkok: River Books Co. Ltd., 1997.

Jessup, Helen Ibbetson. *Art & Architecture of Cambodia*. London: Thames & Hudson, 2004.

Larus, Joel. *Culture and Political-Military Behavior: The Hindus in Pre-Modern India*. Calcutta: Minerva, 1979.

Laur, Jean. *Angkor: An Illustrated Guide to the Monuments*. Flammarion: Airphoto International Ltd., 2002.

Mabbett, I.W. 1977. 'The "Indianization" of Southeast Asia: Reflections on the Prehistoric Sources,' *Journal of Southeast Asian Studies*, vol. 8, no. 2: 143-61, 1977.

Mukharji. R.K. *Hindu Sabhyatā*, in Hindi, 7th edn. New Delhi: Rajkamal Prakashan, 1998.

Polkinghorne, Martin. 'Cosmology and Khmer Architecture at Banteay Srei,' *TAASA Review, The Asiatic Art Society of Australia Review*, 10: 12-15, 2001.

Rovedo, Vittorio. *Khmer Mythology: Secrets of Angkor*. New York: Weatherhill, 1997.

Russel, J and R. Cohn. *Banteay Srei*. Bookvika Publishing, 2012.

Smith, Monica L. '"Indianization" from the Indian Point of View: Trade and Cultural Contacts with Southeast Asia in the Early First Millennium CE,' *Journal of the Economic and Social History of the Orient*, vol. 42, no. 1: 1-26, 1999.

Stutterheim, W.F. *Indian Influences in the Lands of the Pacific*. Weltevreden: G. Kolff & Co., 1929.

Wales, H.G.Q. *The Indianization of China and of South-East Asia*. London: Bernard Quaritch, 1967.

20

Meditational Symbolism of the Borobudur

NIRMALA SHARMA

Born from silence and unfolding into the serenity of the yonder shore, Borobudur expresses the glory of Indonesia's awareness and contemplation, the smile of her plastic forms over the centuries, as well as her journeying along the horizons of *dhyāna*, in the moments of transcendent experience of an unknown Shailendra monarch who envisioned this wonder of the Tathagata.

Contemplation needs a visual symbol. In the words of Professor Lessing (1942: 101) "the paintings serve as support (*ālambana*), a starting point in meditation, as a means of mental self-identification with the deity in the process of *sādhanā*

'realization'". "Besides paintings, the sacred edifices themselves are symbols and catalysts for contemplation. The word 'contemplate' itself is derived from *con* and *templum* 'sanctuary, temple'." The Chinese Buddhist master Shandao (613-82 CE) pointed out that paintings and architectural structures enhance meditation. There are two methods of cultivation (i) recitation and (ii) visualization. As a master of the Pureland School, he promoted the use of Pureland illustrations of *the Amitāyur-dhyāna-sūtra*, as meditating agents. The role of architectural elements is one of mediation between the heavenly and the earthly experience.

This paper deals with the meditational symbolism of the Borobudur as follows:

I. Structures for meditation.
II. The symbolism of the architectural elements.
III. The symbolism of the reliefs on the walls and balustrades.
IV. The symbolism according to Abhidharma.

I. STRUCTURES FOR MEDITATION

First I will take up the characteristics and types of meditation.

Characteristics of Structures for Meditation are

i. Elaborate and vast complexes.
ii. Multi-storeyed edifices as indicative of the several planes of spiritual ascension or *dhyana-bhumis*.
iii. They illustrate a number of texts in ascending order of evolution. They coordinate multiple-level teachings. They are based on the principles of *p'an-chiao* 'classification of doctrines'. It means that one particular scripture contains the highest Dharma and other scriptures belong to a sequence of evolving stages of Dharma.
iv. These complexes encode the cosmology and theophany of several doctrines leading to the summum of meditation.
v. As such they illustrate several paradises, with illustrations of thousands of deities, and are significantly termed *sku.ḥbum* 'myriads of deities' in Tibetan, and *ming-oi* in Turkish with the same meaning. They are known as *ch'ien fo t'ung* 'caves with thousands of Buddhist images' or *wang fo t'ung* 'caves with myriads of Buddhist images.'

There are three types of structures: namely:

(i) Guhā, (ii) *Satadvāra*, and (iii) *Sumeru*.

(i) The first types are complexes of cave (*guhā*), excavated in a mountain. Some of their examples are Bamiyan, Ming-oi at Kizil, Tun-huang and Yun-kang. The cave has been a syllogism of soul in India from ancient times. The (Atharvavada (11.05.10) says that the treasures of the sacred lore of brāhmaṇa are hidden in a cave. *Śatapatha-brāhamaṇa* equates the *guhā* with the heart (*tasmād idam guheva hṛdayam*).

(ii) The second type of edifices are *śatadvāra* with 'hundreds of doors', called *sgo.maṅ* in Tibetan. They are tapering pyramidal structures with several chapels. The chapels have hundreds of icons and their walls were covered with murals all over. The walls outside are bare and simply plastered. The term *śatadvāra* occurs in Pāṇini 4.1.123. The Gyantse Kumbum is an outstanding example of this type of meditational architecture. It can be studied in the detailed descriptions by Franco Ricca and Erberto Lo Bue. They have indicated the scriptures followed in each chapel.

(iii) The third type of edifices are the stepped pyramidal montane structures known as the Sumeru. They are solid inside. The icons and bas-reliefs are sculpted on the visible exterior walls. The sanctification of the outer walls and the balustrades exposed to the fury of elements is the symbolism of open space as Brahma. In the *Chāndogya-upaniṣad* the open firmament is worshipped as Brahma (*sa yaḥ ākāśaṁ Brahmeti upāsate*). The sky provides a comparison with the highest state in the *Bodhicaryāvatāra*.

The Borobudur immortalises the meditation of its architect Guṇadharma who retired in Mount Menoreh to contemplate. According to tradition he is integrated into this mountain range where the silhouette of his chin, mouth and nose can be seen. It is a Sumeru or base for the deities of the maṇḍala. A miniature Sumeru (Japanese Sumi) is placed on the altar under the mandala to this day in Japan to integrate the cosmos and the maṇḍala.

II. THE SYMBOLISM OF THE ARCHITECTURAL ELEMENTS

Now I come to the meditational symbolism of the architectural elements of the Borobudur. Buddhaguhya's commentary on the *Sarva-durgati-pariśodhana* gives the symbolism of the structures of four-sided Sumeru and its decorative elements *in extenso*. For instance, the four corners are the four knowledges (*catur-jñāna*); the four gates in the four directions are the four marvellous actions (*prātihārya*) and so on. They are:

Four corners	four knowledges
Four gates	four kinds of marvellous action (Mkhas grub rje, 232)
Four arches	four boundless states
Four staircases	four means of conversion

Arches adorned with	
garlands	infinite compassion
Eight posts	eight liberations
Lions	one with great compassion of means is not frightened of samsara
Bulls	infinite marks of right powers
Gates adorned with	
Silk, five-coloured (*pañcarāga*)	five kinds of knowledge
Tassels, three-coloured (*trirāga*)	pure nature of body, speech and mind
Pendant necklace of pearls	Bodhisattva's joy
Garland of pearls	set of requirements for samādhi
Bells, combined with necklaces	purity of speech, to teach Dharma to living beings
Yak tails	no shifting of the mind of enlightenment
Adorned with mudras of	
Round fence of diamonds	wisdom-knowledge (*vidyā-jñāna*)
Garland of jewels	all sorts of merits
Lotus	great compassion of skill in the means while being unattached
Svastika	union of means (*upāya*) and insight (*prajñā*)

Lines i.e. threads	contemplation of the mind of enlightenment
Eight lines	four directional threads and four inner threads
Eight kinds	eight auspicious symbols on the body
Outer gate projections	means of entering by Samādhi comprehension

The commentary of Buddhaguhya explicitly states that adornment is for the perception of inner symbols.

III. THE SYMBOLISM OF THE RELIEFS

Borobudur is the visual symbol for dhyāna or meditation. Its reliefs are the physical seeing, while dhyāna accompanying them is spiritual visualization. The reliefs of the Borobudur are supports for four systems of meditation: Karma-vibhaṅga, Pāramitās in the Jātakas, Gaṇḍavyūha, and the STTS. The four systems are represented as follows:

Genre	reliefs	text	walls
1. Karma	160	Karma-vibhaṅga	hidden base
2. Pāramitās	120	Lalitavistara	I a
,,	120	Jātakamālā	I b
,,	600	Avadanas	IBa-b, IIB
3. Avataṁsaka	388	Gaṇḍavyūha	II, III, IIIB, IVB
,,	72	Bhadracāri	IV
4. Mantrayāna	504	Buddhas STTS	all around

1. The Karma-vibhaṅga illustrated in the hidden base of the Borobudur forms the substratum of transcending the Six Lower Worlds or *durgati*, to commence the four initial stages of meditation.
2. The second system is the Jātakamālā and Lalitavistara reliefs on the inner wall of the first gallery represent the practice of Pāramitās.
3. The third system of the Gaṇḍavyūha represents 54 stages of meditation on 110 panels.

The 54 stages of meditation are

(i)	The ten degrees of faith/*śraddhā*	Gv.1
(ii)	The ten abodes/*vihāra*	Gv.2-11
(iii)	The ten degrees of action/*caryā*	Gv.12-21
(iv)	The ten degrees of diversion/*pariṇāmanā*	Gv.22.31
(v)	The ten stages/*bhūmi*	Gv.32-41
(vi)	The ten *vimokṣa*	Gv.42-52
(vii)	Mañjuśrī, Samantabhadra	Gv.53, 54.

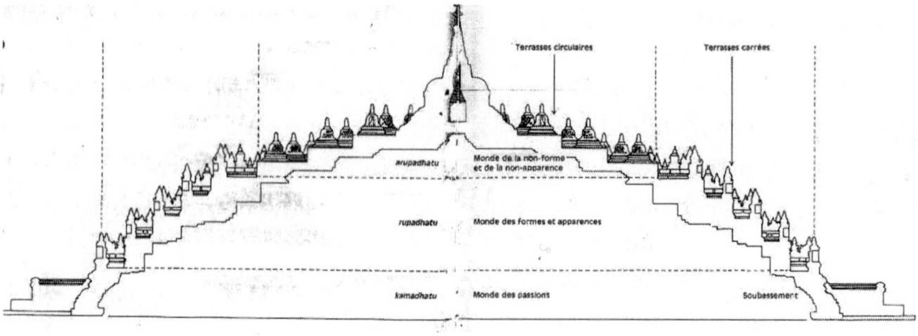

4. The fourth system is the large images of 504 Buddhas in six mudrās representing the Vajradhātu system of Mantrayāna. The Vajradhātu-mandala was highly sacred and must have been installed in the topmost stūpa when rituals were conducted at the Borobudur.

IV. SYMBOLISM ACCORDING TO ABHIDHARMA

According to Abhidharma the architectonics of the Borobudur can represent the three realms of Abhidharma. The correlation of these realms of dhyāna to the Borobudur has been tabulated. The three realms are Kāmadhātu, Rūpadhātu and Ārūpyadhātu.

Kāmadhātu		
1-4	four unhappy states (*durgati*)	hidden base
5	world of humans	,,
6-11	six deva-lokas	Ia (life of Lord Buddha)
	,,	Ib, IBab, IIb (avadānas)
Rūpadhātu		
12-27	four dhyānas	II, III, IIIB, IIb (avadānas)
28	culmination: akaniṣṭha	vairocana
Ārūpyadhātu		
29-32	beyond depiction	open sky

The last Realm of Non-form, the *ārūpyadhātu*, being beyond form, cannot and is not configured. It culminates on the summit of existence as the open space (*ākāśa*) on top of the Borobudur.

The four dhyānas of the *rūpadhātu* are the planes of meditation and hence formless. The seventeen states (12-28) of these dhyānas represent meditative planes of impersonal immensity (*brahman*), radiance (*ābhā*), aura (*śubha*), and beyond them all to the most subtle. They are immaculate (*an-abhraka*), outdo immensity (*a-bṛha*), excel austerities (*a-tapa*) and go beyond (a) the subtlest (*Kaniṣṭha*). They are betokened by depictions of the Gaṇḍavyūha on the second and third walls as well as on the third and the fourth balustrades of the Borobudur. The last state of Akaniṣṭha, the 28th, is the culmination of rūpadhātu, the realm of subtle form. Akaniṣṭha means the most subtle (*kaniṣṭha*) state, ultimate subtlety that cannot be surpassed. Vairocana dwells in the Akaniṣṭha heaven. He is the culmination of the Yoga-Tantras. As the Yogācārins say: "the threefold world is only mind". Residing in one realm, the consciousness has potentialities to move forward or backward to other realms. Dhyāna is a process of transmuting the lower states of consciousness to higher states. It is ascension from the world of sense-desires to the realms of finer forms and finally to the formless, to the Absolute Sublime.

WORKS CITED

Hikata, Ryusho. 'The wall reliefs of the hidden base – 160 panels', *International Symposium on Candi Borobudur*. Kyoto, 1980: 97-100

Hurvitz, Leon. Chih-I, *Melanges chinois et bouddhiques*, vol. 12, Bruxelles, 1962.

Lessing, Ferdinand D., *Yung-ho-kung*. Stockholm, 1942.

Lessing, Ferdinand D. and Alex Wayman, *Mkhas grub rje's Fundamentals of the Buddhist Tantras*, the Hague (Mouton), 1968.

Leo M. Pruden's English translation of Louis de la Valle Poussin, *Abhidharma-Kosa-bhasyam*, vols. 1-4, Berkeley, California (Asian Humanities Press).

Wayman, Alex. *The Buddhist Tantras*, New York (Samuel Weiser), 1973.

PART 6

Indian Heritage and its Cultural Representation

21

India and the ASEAN: The Islamic Linkages of the Past

B.A. HUSSAINMIYA

India is home to a large population of Muslims constituting nearly 13.4 per cent of the country's population estimated at 160.9 million in 2009. Islam is the second-most practiced religion after Hinduism in India and the adherents of Islam are the world's largest Muslim-minority population in any country. Despite its minority status today, historically, Islam had remained as a strong binding factor of the Indian culture that spread beyond its shores, especially in Southeast Asia with which this paper is concerned.

The contacts between India, especially South India and the Southeast Asia go back far in history. For many years the terms Indianization, Brahmanization and Sanskritization have been dominant themes in academic scholarship in explaining the characteristics of early contacts. Furthermore, Southeast Asia was treated as an extension to an Indian based culture. Hence the recurrence of terms such terms as 'Farther India', and 'Further India' to denote early and medieval Southeast Asia as a whole. As researches on the Southeast Asian historiography developed with the input from largely local historians, these assumptions became subjects of controversy. The fact is that the Indian cultural influences did not flow in just one way direction only. Southeast Asia's response was to adopt and develop the traditions which then could be shared with the source regions. Since early periods, it cannot be denied that both regions remained culturally linked in what was known as trans-oceanic Brahmanic and Buddhist networks.

A study of Southeast Asian Islamic heritage follows almost the same pattern set during the previous centuries. Islam was introduced to the region as a corollary to trade while the propagation of the faith involved the incorporation of local traditions into Islamic practices. Thus the parallels in the economic, political and religious spheres deserve a closer analysis of direct contacts between the two regions forming part of mutual networks.

SOURCES OF SEA ISLAM

Since pre-Islamic times from as early as the seventh century, the Arabs had traded on the Ma'bar and Malabar coasts looking for spices and drugs. The travelers' tales of the Arabs, known as *Ajaib*, contained many references to Southeast Asia. Similarly Arab topographies and geographical dictionaries are replete with several place names in Southeast Asia. The references in the Arab sources increased in frequency especially after the advent of Islam. There had been an increase in the volume of trade due largely to changes in the political geography of the regions under study. This period synchronized with the rise of the Fatimids in Egypt, the Cholas in South India and the Sung dynasty in China as well as the expansion of the agricultural base and political growth of the Khmer and Burmese States.

The Islamic presence in maritime Southeast Asia from the time of Othman, the third caliph, is dated from at least the mid-seventh century. Envoys with Arabic names are known to have visited the Sumatran court of Sriwijaya between the tenth and twelfth centuries. An Islamic inscription on a tombstone has been found in East Java as early as 1092. This did not indicate that Islamic states began to appear early while incidences of conversions proceeded rather slowly. The first evidence of Indonesian Muslims comes from northern Sumatra, where gravestones demonstrate that from the late thirteenth century the area remained under Islamic rule and where both Marco Polo (in 1292) and Ibn Battuta (in 1345) noticed, while passing through, that local rulers were followers of Islam.

Islam spread slowly and steadily in the Western archipelago. Thus by the end of the thirteenth century Islam was established in north Sumatra followed by northeast Malaya in the fourteenth century. The great trading state of Malacca was founded around the beginning of the fifteenth century. It blossomed into an Islamic center for the archipelago until its capture by the Portuguese in 1511. Late fifteenth and sixteenth century graves document the establishment of additional Islamic states in North Sumatra and there is evidence that Islam was also spreading farther east than the Malay Peninsula and Java, all the way to the southern Philippines. Brunei's Islam was established in the Sultanate way back in the middle of the fourteenth century CE. In his sixteenth century account Tome Pires reports that the Sundanese of west Java remained outside the Islamic fold while the coastal areas of central and east Java were mostly Islamic while much of the interior remained untouched.

So who was responsible for the introduction Islam in Southeast Asia? Opinions differ on this issue. The scholars are divided depending on the nature of the source material they prefer to adopt to guide their intellectual orientation. Thus various theories have been forwarded citing Arabia, Bengal and Gujarat in India,[1] China and last but not the least South India as the possible sources of Islamization of Southeast Asia.[2] It is beyond the scope of this essay to examine in detail the pros and cons of arguments attributed to the source of Islam. This essay, however, seeks to focus on the role of South Indian Muslims, from the Ma'bar and Malabar regions region as an important source of the introduction of Islam in Southeast Asia, especially in the Malay world.

Indeed, Arabia is the home of Islam. As such there can be a tendency to argue that it was the Arabs who were primarily involved in the spread of Islam in Southeast Asia as well, just as they did in the continent surrounding Arabia in the Middle East region. On the other hand, the fact remains that Southeast Asia lies quite at a distance to be reached from the Arabian Seas in the olden times although the two regions were interlocked because of commerce and intra-ocean trade. The Arabs imported luxury goods from Southeast Asian port cities well known for its spices and camphor and other items much in demand abroad. Similarly Arabs plied the routes of Arabian Sea, Indian Ocean and the China Sea and sometimes acted as middlemen carrying goods from Persia and India in exchange for material they required from Southeast Asia. A main thrust of this essay, however, is to highlight the fact that the Arabs did not directly spread Islam all the way from Arabia, but it was their descendants, a mixed-population of Arabs and Tamil/Malayalam speaking Muslims from Ma'bar and Malabar regions respectively who acted as intermediaries in this Islamization process. Late Professor S. Arasaratnam, for instance, has identified at least one important group, the Muslim Chulias who did brisk trade from Ma'bar region in Southeast Asian ports.[3]

Why are Ma'bar and Malabar important for our study? Both regions were connected to the port cities in Southeast Asia in many ways. Both territories possessed suitable ports and facilities which acted as nodal points in the sea trading routes that linked the Indian Ocean with the China Sea. Using inter monsoonal winds, ships took off in both directions carrying goods demanded in both regions. As a result through commerce and resultant cultural exchanges the South Indian Islamic communities interacted continuously with Islamic communities from an early period and that went on even until recently. As Ronit Ricci rightly says that

> ...the coasts of Southeast India and Indonesia were part of the Indian Ocean's commercial network that was permeated – beginning in the fifteenth century – by an Islamic ethos, where goods and shared texts and values crossed the seas carried by Muslim merchants, pilgrims, soldiers and scholars, and where coastal towns, which functioned as important trade centers and ports, developed into major centers of Islamic learning and culture.[4]

Ma'bar is the name given by the Muslims to the Coromandel Coast and the region of Madura. Arabs knew it and it is their term Ma'bar, the crossing point, which was popularized later. The area consists of an area eastwards from either Quilon or Cape Comorin, that roughly corresponds to the present region of Tamil Nadu. Unlike the extensive studies on Malabar, Ma'bar has not received much attention from scholars. Its' Islamic traditions are much localized and are of less interest to a wider study on Islamic connections in the world. In this essay would like summarize and analyze some important recent studies relating to the role of South Indian Muslims in Southeast Asia.

THE MALABAR CONNECTIONS

The term Malabar was derived from the Malayalam word *mala* (hill) and a Semitic word *bar* meaning land. The term Malabar today refers roughly to the area formed by the districts of Malappuram, Kozhikode, Palghat, Wayanad, and parts of Trichur, Kannur and Kasaragod in Kerala.

Malabar is also synonymous with spices that had drawn foreign traders to its shores. At its zenith, Kozhikode was a prominent harbour, drawing traders from China, West Africa and Arabia. Following Vasco-da-Gama's visit in 1498, Syrians and Arabs followed in his wake, their trading vessels carrying Malabar products like pepper, coffee, rubber, coconut and coir to all parts of the Western world.

Very often bad weather disrupted the sailings and vessels, which were laid off for extended periods waiting for favourable winds to enable their return voyage. These long lay-offs created a special situation of marital needs for the visitors. For example, the Arabs began marrying native women – a kind of temporary marriages called *Muta* (pittance in Arabic) that required paying only a small *mehr* or bride price. This was in accordance with the Islamic teachings as well. When the weather cleared, they simply annulled the temporary alliance and departed. The medieval pilgrim Ibn Battuta delineated this particular aspect when he stayed as a Jurist in the Maldives as having practised the *Muta* marriage. Naturally, the local brides and their offsprings were admitted into Islam. Apparently many of the present day Moplah community and other Muslim Keralites can trace their origins to this practice to a smaller or larger extent.

Interestingly, the word Moplah is derived from the Tamil/Malayalam word Mappila or Mapillai, meaning newlywed groom or son-in-law of the house, a nod toward the sons-in-law of the original native population. Today the term refers to their descendents – the Malayalam-speaking Muslims of Kerala, making up the second largest community at 24.7 per cent of the population.

According to another theory the word *Mappila* is derived from ancient Tamil Language during the first century AD era. *Margapilla* (Margam mean 'the way') in Tamil/Malayalam which was the term used to call the Nasranis or early Christians of Kerala who followed Jesus who had shown the way to spiritual awakening among Jews. Later this was the term used to describe those who converted to Islam as well. This was shortened to Mappila. Later on whoever converted to other religions as opposed to the native or Hindu became known by this term. It also came to refer to those Muslims and Christians in Northern and Southern Kerala respectively.

According to another version, the Chera King Cheraman Perumal, who had embraced Islam was responsible for the spread of Islam here. In deference to his wishes, Arab religious leaders, notably Malik Ibn Dinar, sailed to Malabar and spread Islam among the locals. People from lower Hindu castes also began converting to Islam to gain social ascendancy and they brought with them their matriarchal system into the unfolding social milieu.

This essay avoids going into further details of Malabar Islam as many other scholars have dealt with this aspect more than the topic that is to follow, i.e. the role of Ma'abari Muslim in Southeast Asia.

ISLAM IN MA'BAR

The theories that highlight the contribution of Gujarati Muslims and Bengali Muslims tend to ignore the importance of the strategic locations of the Ma'bar community in the transmission of Islamic religion in Southeast Asia. Nonetheless, in some other quarters there had been some scholarly awareness regarding the significance of the transmission of Islam from Ma'bar and Malabar. For instance, based on the evidence from local legends and literary representations, Snouck Hurgronje, a Dutch scholar-administrator was one of the earliest to trace Southeast Asian Islam to South India. In his second volume of *De Atjehers* published in 1894, and in discussing the Achehnese literature, Snouck showed that by far the majority of Achehnese romances shared the same origins as the Malay. I shall return to this again later in this essay.

Many Achehnese romances are based on Malay models, and as a cradle of the bulk of romances in both languages one may certainly consider the same part of South India to which the popular mysticism and the popular religious legends of the Muslim peoples of the Indonesian Archipelago belong to. Hurgronje's inaugural lecture at Leiden 1907 entitled *Arabia and the East Indies,* further elaborated the relations of Indonesian Islam with South India. When Islam had once gained a firm hold in the port cities of South India, the inhabitants of the Deccan, who resided in great numbers in the port cities of this island-world as middlemen in the trade between the Muslim states (i.e. the states of western Asia) and the East Indies, were, as if in the nature of things, destined to scatter the first seeds of the new religion. However, Snouck Hurgronje did not define the exact location from which such influences emanated from South India. Once the base was established the Arab Sayyid or Sharif, the presumed descendants of the Prophet easily found opportunities later to demonstrate their organizational ability. As priests, priest-princes and as sultans they often put the finishing touches to the formation of the new realms.

The former keeper of the British Museum, G.E. Marrison directly suggested the Tamil speaking territory in South India as having played a significant role in the process of Islamization in Southeast Asia.[5] The Muslims had already been established for centuries in South India, without having gained political power, before the expansion of the Delhi Sultanate at the beginning of the fourteenth century. Here he points to the Moors of Ceylon, the Moplahs of Malabar and the Maracayars of the Coromandel Coast (Ma'bar), which are ethnic groups of mixed blood whose members are still traders and seamen. Marrison argues that the Shaf'i School of Law was not the dominant one in Gujarat, but was in South India; that the whole *Hikayat Raja-Raja Pasai* has a background strongly coloured by South India (Tamils are mentioned in it repeatedly; Tamil merchants and Tamil jugglers and wrestlers appear on its stage), and that the spiritual influence of Gujarat is not evident before the first half of the seventeenth century, when Nuruddin al-Raniri came to Acheh.

The Dutch scholar G.W.J. Drewes later shed more light about Tamil Islam. He pointed out that an investigation into the literature of the Muslim population of South India would be required in order to obtain a greater degree of certainty on these questions. Drewes referred to the difficulty in working with the Tamil language sources in reaching tangible conclusions about the Tamil origins of Southeast Asian Islam. As Drewes opined, a resumption of the archaeological research in North Sumatra and painstaking study of Islam in South India required a thorough knowledge of Tamil. Lately there seems to be a revived interest in this field and a couple of Western scholars who are proficient in Tamil have highlighted the sources from Tamil and Arabu-Tamil (Tamil written in Arabic script).[6] Their researches shed light on the importance of the Ma'bar region in the dissemination of Islamic knowledge and practices in the East. Another scholar who showed much interest in the Tamil Muslims' role in Southeast Asia was the late Professor Cyril Skinner, the Head of the Department of Indonesian and Malay Department at the Monash University, Australia. He was particularly concerned with the influence of Tamil Muslims who lived in Singapore, Malacca and Penang, and in the Straits Settlements. He was investigating the Nagore ancestry of the great Abdul Kadir Munshi who is hailed as the father of modern Malay literature. Moreover, Professor William Roff, in his path breaking study of the origins of Malay nationalism' discusses in detail the role of Tamil Muslim in the late nineteenth century as pioneers who were also given the epithet of Jawi-Peranakan which referred to the descendants of Arab-Tamil fathers and Malay women.

THE EARLY ORIGINS OF MA'BARI ISLAM

It must be emphasized here that the archeological studies suggest an Islamic presence far earlier that was as mentioned above – rooted in Arab trade – in the Coromandel region since the eighth century CE. Scholarship on Indian Ocean trade points to a continuous and dynamic Islamic presence in the Malabar, Coromandel and Sri Lankan regions from around that time through the Portuguese colonial period, with Coromandel ports forming important trade centers. Such trade, especially in horses, gems, textiles and pearls has historically sustained the Muslim coastal communities.[7]

As in the case of the Indonesian-Malay archipelago, tombstones in the Tamil region provide evidence of, and approximate dating for, an early Islamic presence. Inscriptions on gravestones in the mosque on Kilakkarai's shore attest to the existence of Arab settlements from the seventh or eighth centuries. Arab traders received permission from local kings (the Cholas, and later the Pandyas) to settle in the area, and were sometimes granted land and the right to create their own community.

The numbers of such settlers increased as the region began to play a central role in the international textile trade which linked South India to the ports of West Asia and the Indonesian archipelago. One consequence of this process was the rise to prominence of foreign Muslim commercial men in the Tamil country's local courts. Further evidence on the spread of Islam and Muslim life in the region comes from traveler accounts, including those of Marco Polo and Ibn Battuta. Both famous travelers arrived in Tamil Nadu after visiting Sri Lanka and reported landing along the coast called Ma'bar by the Muslims, referring to the Coromandel Coast.

Besides trade, which clearly played a crucial role in the early introduction of Islam, other factors have been understood as central to the process. Intermarriage probably occurred early on, and even at present descent from early Arab migrants is considered a mark of high rank among Tamil Muslim families. The influence of sufis, with their focus on personal devotion, healing and the charismatic power of teachers and saints has provided a bridge between the beliefs of non-Muslims and Muslim worship, as it has in many other regions of South and Southeast Asia. Furthermore, tomb shrines (Tamil[8] *Dharga*)) have given rise to devotional cults which served as a critical force in the expansion of Islam.

The port towns along the Coromandel Coast, with their trade links to Arabia and the Indian Ocean, became South Indian Islamic centers with clearly identified Muslim populations by the twelfth or thirteenth century.[9] These towns (for example Kayalpattnam, Kilakkarai and Pulicat) were also crucially important places for the region's pre-colonial rulers, supplying as they did imported war horses and large revenues from the pearl and conch industries. The towns were dominated by the Maraikkayar, groups of elite Sunni, Tamil-speaking trading families. All other Tamil speaking Muslims in the south were known as Lebbais, a population which was probably introduced to Islam by the thirteenth or fourteenth century, was also Sunni and included fishermen, pearl divers and many hinterland cultivators, artisans and petty traders.[10]

Important events in somewhat later times were the founding of a short lived Muslim 'sultanate' in Madurai in AD 1334; the period of Portuguese rule (1501-75) which brought much hardship to the Muslim population; and a period of sustained Muslim rule in the far south in the eighteenth century which saw the rise of the Nawabs of Arcot as well as successive attempts by various military powers including Hyderabad, the Maratha confederacy, the French and the British to control the region.

Whereas in the case of the archipelago a major question remains as to how Islam became such a powerful and dominating force, the parallel question for the Tamil region (and South India more broadly) is why it never became as fully "Islamized" as Java or the North Indian regions of Bengal or the Punjab, with its Muslim population remaining a small minority?[11]

The Muslims of South India and the archipelago shared a variety of relationships: from at least as early as the seventeenth century they had a shared set of pilgrimage sites, some of which are still popular today. Well known in South India is the lineage of the seventeenth century sufi mystic Sheikh Sadaqatullah of Kayalpattnam, whose tomb continues to attract devotees from Malaysia and Indonesia. Muslims on both shores maintained mutual trade contacts, with the Nagore-Acheh route becoming one of the most profitable in the eighteenth century network. The Marakkaiyar trading groups of the Coromandel coast, claiming Arab seafarers and traders as their ancestors, had well established ties with the Muslim ports of the archipelago, exporting tobacco, cotton textiles, gems and pearls. Also, men of the Tamil coastal towns traveled to Southeast Asia, sometimes remaining there for months at a time;[12] members of the two communities even inter-married, the Marakkaiyars preferring intermarriage with the Muslims of the archipelago over marriage with the lower strata of Tamil Muslim society.[13]

The *madhab* (school of Islamic law) followed by Javanese and South Indian Muslims living along the coast is one and the same (*Shafi'i*); contacts in the sphere of Islamic education appear to have been strong, with similar institutions emerging in Tamil Nadu, Sumatra and Java.[14] Indonesian pilgrims on their way to Arabia used to stop in the Maldives,[15] in the eighteenth century a Coromandel mosque existed in Batavia,[16] while in the early nineteenth century an approximate 2 per cent of Batavia's population were "Moormen", natives of the Coromandel and Malabar coasts.[17] Under colonial auspices contacts – whether through trade or the deployment, employment or exile of subjects – continued.[18]

ROLE OF ISLAMIC AND ARABU-TAMIL LITERATURE

One area in which the influence of Tamilian Islam, if we can coin this term, is the way the literary history in the Malay World had received impetus and inspiration from the Islamic literary works that were much in vogue among the Ma'abari Muslims. Apparently, works of Arabic and Persian origins were either adapted and/or translated into South Indian languages, especially Tamil. Some well known Islamic works, epics such as *Hikayat Muhammad Hanafiyyah*,

Hikayat Amir Hamza, *Seribu Masalah* and other stories of Prophet (*Sal*) are common to Tamil and Malay literature. The Islamic Tamil texts were written in Arabu-Tamil script, popularly known as Ariwi while the Malay works were written in Jawi. Both scripts were adaptations of Arabic and Persian script added with some special notation alphabets to suit the sounds in both the languages. Presumably, the Tamil-Muslim traders, also known as Chulias who traded and settled in the Southeast Asian cities, for example, Melaka, Acheh and Batavia, etc, must have brought the texts for their own reading for edification and entertainment. As the subject matter were Islamic and fascinating, there must have been interest among the Malay literati which resulted in the translations of these texts from Tamil to Malay. The large number of Tamil loan words in Malay is perhaps an indication of these activities.

Scholars like R.O. Winstedt who wrote a *History of the Malay Literature* and the Dutch scholar Snouk Hurgronje have referred to the possibilities of Tamilian origins of many Malay literary texts and some religious works. As in the case of literature, much of the Tamil speaking Islamic population became absorbed into the Malay population so as not to be distinguished easily in their ethnic mixtures.

ISLAM IN SRI LANKA

In this final part of this essay, I would like to point towards two Malay manuscripts that surfaced in Sri Lanka in late 1974 during my field research to prepare a *catalogue raissone* of Malay Mss in Sri Lanka towards my doctoral studies at the Indonesian and Malay Studies department at the Monash University, Australia. The manuscript I discovered included many well known epic tales such as *Hikayat Amir Hamza*, and *Hikayat Muhammad Hanafiyyah*, religious treatises in prose such as Syaikh Nural din al Raniri's *Sirat al Mustaqim*, and others in Syair poetry.[19] Among the Mss were a couple of interesting literary pieces which I have not found in any other collections of similar manuscripts preserved in the Malay World archives or libraries. I can briefly describe here their contents which are important in the context of this essay.

The first one is titled *Hikayat Raden Bagus Gusti* (*The Epic Tale of Raden Bagus Gusti*) and the second work is titled *Syair Syaikh Fadlun* (*The Rhymed Chronicle of Syaikh Fadlun*). The first text is a prose tale describing the exploits of one of the nine *Walis*, or saints who spread Islam in the island of Java. The main protagonist in this tale is Raden Sunan Giri aka Raden Bagus Gusti is quite popular in Java as one of the important persons responsible for Islamization of the coastal regions of Indonesia, especially around the present day Gresik. But the tale spreads into the Surakarta history which embraced Islam around thirteenth century. A most important element in the story is how the Raja of Surakarta was converted to Islam by a saint from South India, possibly from the Tamil Nadu.

Unfortunately this *Hikayat* remain unstudied. When the *Hikayat* is edited and analysed it would certainly supplement similar tales well documented in such famous Malay works as *Hikayat Raja Pasai* as well as *Sejarah Melayu.* Both texts attribute conversion of the Malay royals in Sumatra to a South Indian or Ma'bari Sultan turned Faqir. The tales refer to a person called Ismail prompted by a Prophetic command reaches Sumatra from Mecca. On his way he befriends the Sultan at Ma'bar who was said to be a descendant of Caliph Abu Bakar. The Sultan who adopts the life style of a Faqir (Mendicant) accompanies Ismail on his tour of Sumatra. The significant part of this event was that it was actually the Ma'bari Sultan, not Ismail who was responsible for the conversion of the King of Pasai to Islam. Doubts have been cast on the truth of these tales, but one cannot escape the fact that the legends of Ma'bari Sultan's role in the Islamization of the Malay Sultans is an important pointer to the direction in which serious research is needed. Thus in this regard the hitherto unknown Sri Lankan manuscript of the above *Hikayat Raden Bagus Gusti* has special significance.

Apparently the early Indonesian population that settled in Sri Lanka carried back the kernel of the Sunan Giri story which was either rendered into a fully fledged epic tale in Malay or it had been copied from a similar Ms. found in the Nusantara area. In either case it remains clear that the South Indian dignitary was remembered as the person behind the conversion of the Surakarta king. I have tried to dig into various catalogues of Malay manuscripts preserved in the libraries elsewhere, but I am yet to come across a similar story or a manuscript in Malay as the Sri Lankan one.

The second Ms. *Syair Syaikh Fadlun*, was copied, translated or compiled in Sri Lanka in the mid-nineteenth century. There were three extant manuscripts of the text, two come from the Malay settlements in the hill country town of Kandy where the Ceylon Rifle Regiment soldiers were based. According to the colophon of one of the text, the work was originally an Arabic story which was later translated into Koci (Malayalam) i.e., language spoken in the Malabar region. The story deals with an episode during Caliph Omar's period, but it remains to be seen if the text had been popular in the Malay world proper. So far this text remains unique to Sri Lanka. At any rate, the fact that Arabic and Malayalam are named as the sources to the text translated into Malay indicate the influence of Malabari Islamic textual traditions permeating into the Malaly speaking territories including Sri Lanka. Sri Lanka may be an isolated case in the transmission and retention of Malay textual traditions but a leading contemporary Malayologist do not dismiss it so easily. As explained by Ronit Ricci, it a historically significant example which certainly deserves further, in-depth research and exemplifies the potential for studying contacts between Tamil and Indonesian Muslims of a community known as the "Malays" of Sri Lanka.

> This community, which has its origins in exiles from the Dutch East Indies sent to Sri Lanka beginning in the seventeenth century, was in fact in large part Javanese. Retaining much of their original language and culture in exile, this group also interacted and mixed with local Muslims, many of whom were Tamils. That the Muslim communities of Sri Lanka and Tamil Nadu were closely related by ties of trade, learning and family is well known. Therefore, there is a very high probability that literary works popular among these communities – the Malays, Sri Lankan and Indian Muslim-Tamils – were exchanged, shared and locally transformed.[20]

The connections between Ma'bar, Malabar, Sri Lanka, and the Nusantara need further exploration in pursuance of the ideas presented in this paper. I am raising this to start off future endeavours in that direction. This is not a place to discuss, however, the detailed literary history of the Sri Lankan Malays dealt elsewhere. It will suffice to conclude that a study of Sri Lankan Malay Mss. that deal with common textual traditions must be considered important also to prove the Ma'bar and Malabar connections with the Southeast Asian Islam.

NOTES

1. For Bengal origins of SEA Islam see S.Q. Fatimi, *Islam Comes to Malaysia,* Singapore: the Malaysian Sociological Research Inst. Ltd., 1963.
2. See G.W.J. Drewes, 'New Light on the Coming of Islam to Indonesia?' *Bijdragen tot de taal-, land- en volkenkunde van Nederlandsch-Indie,* 1968, p. 124.
3. Sinnapah Arasartnam, 'Chulia Muslim Merchants in Southeast Asia, 1650-1800', *Moyent-Orient et Ocean Indian, 4,* 1987, pp. 126-43.
4. On the relationship between trade and Islam in these regions see, for example, Andre Wink, '"*Al-Hind*". India and Indonesia in the Islamic World Economy, *c.* 700-1800 A.D.' in India *and Indonesia during the Ancien Regime* (Leiden: Brill, 1989): 48-9.
5. G.E. Marrison "The Coming of Islam to the East Indies", *JMBRAS* (pt. 1), 1951, pp. 28-37
6. See Torsten Tischacher, 'Circulating Islam: Understanding Convergence and Divergence in the Islamic Traditions of Ma'bar and Nusantara', in R. Michel Feener and Terenjit Sevea, eds, *Islamic Connections: Muslim Societies in South and Southeast Asia,* ISEAS Series on Islam, Singapore: ISEAS, 2009, pp. 48-67 and Ronit Ricci, "From Jewish Disciple to Muslim Guru: On Literary and Religious Transformation in Late Nineteenth Century Java' (ibid., pp. 68-85).
7. Schomburg, *Reviving Religion,* 19-20.
8. Susan Bayly, *Saints* 74-75. Bayly notes some similarities between sufi saints in Tamil Nadu and the nine saints who are said to have converted Java to Islam (J. *walisongo*). For a study of the ways in which Sufism influenced the acceptance of Islam in a neighboring region see Richard Eaton, *Sufis of Bijapur 1300-1700. Social Roles of Sufis in Medieval India.* Princeton: Princeton University Press, 1978.
9. The following section is based on Bayly, *Saints* 78-100.

10. A third group of Muslims residing in the Tamil region sees itself as distinct from the Tamil-speaking Muslims, claiming Dakhni (a southern variant of Urdu) as their mother tongue. Most claim descent from soldiers, officials and literary men in service of the Muslim ruling houses of the Deccan (Bayly, *Saints* 96-101).This population is outside the scope of this study.
11. For some speculations on this topic see Bayly, *Saints* 101-3. It is not my intention to try and answer this question but its juxtaposition with a central question for Islamic history of the archipelago is important.
12. Vasudha Narayan. 'The Ramayana and its Muslim Interpreters', in Paula Richman, ed., *Questioning Ramayanas.* New Delhi: Oxford University Press, 2000: 265-81.
13. C. Bayly: 'Islam and State Power in Pre-colonial South India', in P.J. Marshall and R. van Niel, eds., *India and Indonesia During the Ancien Regime.* Leiden: Brill, 1989: 145.
14. For example Umar Wali, an eighteenth century Tamil scholar of Arabic and Islamic law who had a large following, went to Sumatra in 1763 and spent fourteen years there. According to Tamil sources he established a number of *madrasah* schools called *pasenthiran* in the region. Shu'ayb notes that a system of providing food and lodging to madrasah students was initiated in Tamil Nadu in the early nineteenth century, a system which sounds similar to the one on Java. Further research is needed on possible links but the similarities between educational institutions are intriguing.
15. Shu'ayb, 26.
16. Karel A. Steenbrink, *Dutch Colonialism and Indonesian Islam: Contacts and Conflicts 1596-1950.* Amsterdam: Rodopi, 1993: 72.
17. Thomas Stamford Raffles, *The History of Java.* 1817; Kuala Lumpur: Oxford University Press, 1965: 246.
18. Raffles notes that native soldiers often served first in India, then Java. He mentions the quarters of Javanese soldiers in Calcutta and the fact that such neighborhoods existed in several Indian cities.
19. For details see B.A. Hussainmiya, *Orang Rejimen: The Malays of the Ceylon Rifle Regiment,* Bangi: UKM Press, 1990.
20. Ronit Ricci, *Islam Translated: Literature, Conversion and the Arabic Cosmopolis of Sout and South East Asia.* Chicago: The University of Chicago Press, 2011: 10-11.

WORKS CITED

Arasartnam, Sinnapah. 'Chulia Muslim Merchants in Southeast Asia, 1650-1800', *Moyent-Orient et Ocean Indian, 4,* 1987.

Bayly, C.A. 'Islam and State Power in Pre-colonial South India', in P.J Marshall and R. van Niel, eds., *India and Indonesia During the AncientRegime.* Leiden: Brill, 1989.

Bayly, Susan. *Saints, Goddesses and Kings: Muslims and Christians in South Indian Society 1700-1900.* Cambridge: Cambridge University Press, 1990.

Day, Anthony. 'Islam and Literature in Southeast Asia: Some Pre-Modern, Mainly Javanese Perspectives.' *Islam in Southeast Asia,* ed. M.B Hooker. Leiden: E.J Brill, 1983.

Drewes, G.W.J. 'New Light on the Coming of Islam to Indonesia?' *Bijdragen tot de taal-, land- en volkenkunde van Nederlandsch-Indië,* pp. 124.4, 1968.

Eaton, Richard. *Sufis of Bijapur 1300-1700. Social Roles of Sufis in Medieval India.* Princeton: Princeton University Press, 1978.

Fatimi, S.Q. *Islam comes to Malaysia,* Singapore: The Malaysian Sociological Research Inst. Ltd, 1963.

Hussainmiya, B. A. *Orang Rejimen: The Malays of the Ceylon Rifle Regiment.* Bangi: UKM Press, 1990.

——. *Lost Cousins: The Malays of Sri Lanka.* Bangi: Universiti Kebangsaan Malaysia, 1987.

Marrison, G.E. 'The Coming of Islam to the East Indies', *JMBRAS,* pt. 1, 1951, pp. 28-37.

Narayan, Vasudha. 'The Ramayana and its Muslim Interpreters', in Paula Richman, ed. *Questioning Ramayanas.* New Delhi: Oxford University Press, 2007, 265-81.

Raffles, Thomas Stamford. *The History of Java.* Original print 1817; Kuala Lumpur: Oxford University Press, 1965 (rpt.).

Ricci, Ronit. *Islam Translated: Literature, Conversion and the Arabic Cosmopolis of Sout and South East Asia.* Chicago: The University of Chicago Press: Chicago, 2011.

Schomburg, Susan Elizabeth. '"Reviving Religion":The Qadiri Sufi Order, Popular Devotion to Sufi Saint Muhyiuddin 'Abdul Qadir Al-Gilani, and Processes of "Islamization" in Tamil.' Ph.D dissertation. Harvard, 2003.

Shu'ayb, Tayka 'Alim. *Arabic, Arwi and Persian in Sarandib and Tamil Nadu.* Madras: Imamul 'Arus Trust, 1993.

Steenbrink, Karel A. *Dutch Colonialism and Indonesian Islam. Contacts andConflicts 1596-1950.* Amsterdam: Rodopi, 1993.

Torsten Tischacher. 'Circulating Islam: Understanding Convergence and Divergence in the Islamic Traditions of Ma'bar and Nusantara', in R Michel Feener and Terenjit Sevea, eds. *Islamic Connections: Muslim Societies in South and Southeast Asia.* ISEAS Series on Islam. Singapore: ISEAS, 2009.

Wink, Andre. ' "*Al-Hind*". India and Indonesia in the Islamic World Economy, *c.* 700-1800 A.D.' *India and Indonesia During the Ancien Regime.* Leiden: Brill, 1989.

22

Impact of Indian Culture in Vietnam

GEETESH SHARMA

Dialogue between civilizations is not a new phenomenon. It existed in prehistoric times and still continues. Although trade has a special significance in this process but culture and literature play an even more important part in development of the social and cultural structure of human society. Today, the modern and quick means of communication and technology are available to mankind that help countries connect. Moreover, the development of trade has also made the international scenario mutually dependent.

However, the great role played earlier by culture and literature is presently shrinking; the warm relations that once existed are weakening now and the cordiality has diminished. An urge to establish one's ethnic superiority has led to a breach among the people and even India is no exception to it. It is an irony that we only remember our golden past and try to live in it ignoring the present realities and still claim that India would lead the world – the very idea seems to be self-deceptive.

India helped Vietnam during Vietnam's freedom struggle. After its liberation we extended both moral and material support to the devastated country for its national reconstruction. However, India should ponder over and analyse how Vietnam, that was underdeveloped compared to India till 1990, is now far ahead of it in several spheres like health, cleanliness, environmental awareness and education. Moreover, Vietnam has been able to shed off its age-old feudal character. Clearly, the Indian society that is still continuing with its age-old orthodox and inhuman social traditions may learn a lot from Vietnam's experiences. This sort of a dialogue between civilizations would bring the people closer to each other and help develop peace and progress world over.

Our relations with Vietnam date back to first century CE. The most important feature of these relations has been cordiality. Indian traders travelled to various Southeast Asia states either by land or sea route with their merchandise and started settling there. A large number of them travelled to China, Vietnam, Cambodia, Laos, even Brunei, from the Champa region (presently Bhagalpur area in Bihar and the contemporary Kalinga Desh in Orissa). They were accompanied by Brahmin priests and Buddhist monks for religious purposes and security guards for their protection. Later, apart from Banga Desh, Kalinga, people from other parts of India also migrated in large numbers to Southeast Asian countries, including Vietnam. As customary with every religious group in the world, they built their temples in the new locale. According to the historical accounts, construction of the Hindu temples in Vietnam started in fourth century CE.

As mentioned earlier, Brahmanical culture and Buddhism went to Vietnam in the first century CE. It is a common belief that Buddhism found its way to Vietnam through China, but excavations in the Mekong Delta of South Vietnam where Buddha statues and images of second-third centuries CE were recovered contradict this belief. The first convoy of Indian traders set off to Vietnam from Champa Puri (Bhagalpur) via Tamralipta (Bengal) and Gopalpur (Odisha) also during the first century. Subsequently, they established a Hindu Kingdom in central part of Vietnam during the second century CE and which lasted till the fifteenth century CE. According to recent discoveries, Hindu culture and religion had its deep influence in the Mekong Delta and the southern part of Vietnam under the Funan Empire.

It is an established historical fact that there was a Hindu/Champa Kingdom located on a narrow strip of land that runs for more than 1,000 km along the coast of Central Vietnam, spreading from Binh Thuan to Quang Nam. It was divided among three regions, viz., Amaravati, Kauthara and Vijaya, where the Hindu residents not only constructed thousands of temples but also installed the idols and images of myriad deities like Siva, Vishnu, Brahma, Ganesha, Mahishamardini, Indra, Skanda. Siva was predominant among the Hindu deities followed by Vishnu and Bhagwati. According to available historical documents MySon was the first temple city of Champa Kingdom that was established by Bhadravarman, who ruled from AD 349 to 361. It was during his regime that the construction of Hindu temples, which are called Cham Towers, began. It was he who established Amravati State and declared Simhapura as its capital. First, the temples used to be made from wood but when those got destroyed or burnt, new temples with bricks were built. Constructions of Cham Towers or Hindu temples continued till fifteenth-sixteenth centuries CE. The architecture of Hindu temples or Cham Towers shows a noticeable influence of the architecture of the temples in Odisha and South India. Indeed, most of the Hindu temples of Vietnam are to some extent replicas of the style of South Indian temples. The statues of Hindu gods and goddesses as well as the carvings on the stone, unearthed during excavations, are influenced by the sculptures of Mathura, Gandhar, Amravati (Andhra Pradesh), and Kalinga (Odisha). In view of these facts, it can be said that it must have been done on a large scale by the artisans and craftsmen who migrated from India, of course, with the assistance of local artisans and craftsmen.

According to a Thai inscription (discovered in Quang Nam Province) it is known that Bhadravarman II, father of Indravarman II (870-95) was the founder of the Indrapura Dynasty (Dong Duong Dynasty). It should be noted that steles of the Indrapura Dynasty only recognized Indravarman II as King of Champa country (Champa Adhip). Bhadravarman II was titled as nominal king rather than actual king of Champa. Dong Duong stele dated AD 875 provided more specific information about the founder of the Indrapura Dynasty and his ancestors. According to Stele I of Dong Duong, the genealogy of King Indravarman II started from Rudravarman (AD 860-70). Rudravarman was the father of Bhadravarman II and grandfather of Indravarman II. However, the stele of Dong Duong also certified that Indravarman II AD 870-95) took the throne, thanks to the power of God Maheshvara (God Shiva), to hard exercises and to his intelligence rather than his blood relations. Consequently, researchers believed that the father and grandfather of Indravarman II were kings of the satellite state of Champa Kingdom.

Hoa Que stele (discovered in the north of DaNang City) dated in AD 898, 908 and 909 provided much information about King Bhadravarman and his religious activities. Side B of this stele praised Bhadravarman II as a person belonging to "Bhgrurace" which ruled the urban area in the name of Champa (or Indrapura). This urban area was established under the order of Bhgru philosopher. After that the stele names seven religious structures were built by Bhadrvarman II, including: Prakabhdresvara, Rudrakotisvara, Bhadiramalagesvara, Bharmesvara and Bhadrapuresvara. These five were a combination between the god names and the king names – one of the typical characteristics of god-king religion in Champa. It was by no means a coincidence that Hoa Que stele compared Bhadravarman II with Yudhisthira, son of Pandu and key character of the *Mahabharata*. With the decline of the Hindu Kingdom, its rulers assimilated themselves with mainstream Vietnamese society, with a nominal distinction in their identity as Chams and their number is about 120,000 today.

The Vietnamese Hindu society did not have the 'Sudras' among them, nor were they rigid in their caste division, unlike India. They were liberal enough to have commensally and matrimonial ties among each other. Hindu religion flourished in the Hindu Kingdom but it is a fact worth mentioning that this Hindu Kingdom was not established through an invasion or by force but by common acceptance as there was never a religious or communal conflict between the natives and the Hindus of Vietnam. With the decline of the Hindu Kingdom, Hindu religion declined as both were interdependent.

The most astonishing part, however, is that the remarkable similarity between both Sanskrit and Champa language has escaped the attention of Indian historians and linguists. According to the facts available the mother tongue of the Cham belongs to the family of Sanskrit. In fact, in ancient times it was Sanskrit itself. However, in course of time, it underwent a change in script and dialect. It may not be just a coincidence that the vowels and consonants used in the Cham language and their pronunciation even today are almost identical to those of Sanskrit/Hindi.

The distinct influence of the Indian art, culture, tradition and refinement is still very much evident in Vietnamese society. The ruins of about two hundred Hindu temples built between seventh to thirteenth centuries in various regions of Vietnam are existent. Vietnamese society neither converted nor destroyed the Hindu temples. On the contrary, under the supervision of the government of Vietnam, the restoration work of the ruined temples is in progress with the assistance of local and foreign archaeologists. Through various excavations thousands of idols and images of myriad Hindu deities have been recovered and are displayed in various museums and temple complexes.

In addition, there are about three 150 to 200 years' old Hindu temples in Ho Chi Minh City that are in use. These were built in South Indian style by the Chettiyars, who had migrated to Vietnam from Tamil Nadu. Deities of these temples are worshipped in traditional Hindu style and these temples are the source of livelihood of some of the Vietnamese families of Indian origin, who look after the maintenance of these temples. It is interesting to note that the 99 percent of the visitors to these temples are devout Vietnamese, who are least aware of the basics of the Hindu religion and are drawn towards it for some miracles.

Though India has shared warm and cordial relations with Vietnam in the past but in the last 65 years there has not been a serious effort to further explore the new findings and discoveries. Intellectuals, activists and the archaeologists from India should have risen to the occasion to undertake the restoration work of the Hindu temples in MySon area when those were declared World Cultural Heritage Sites by the UNESCO. Unfortunately no heed was paid to the great cause. Any efforts in this direction would bring the people of the two countries closer and add to the knowledge base of the whole of Asian region.

It is regrettable that the restoration work is being carried out by the archeological specialists from Japan, Germany, Poland, and Italy under the supervision of UNESCO and the government of Vietnam. However, very recently the government of India sanctioned a fitting amount for the restoration of Hindu temples. The work is yet to be completed and much more is still to be done.

To know the history of Hindu Kingdoms in Vietnam, the spread of Hindu religion and its impact on the Vietnamese society, there are two main sources. The first source is the account of French historians and archeologists who discovered Champa Kingdom in the modern era. The second source is the ancient historical documents available through the Chinese sources.

China had, in fact, ruled over a vast area of North Vietnam from the first till the tenth century AD. They were never on cordial terms with the natives, who always clashed with them to evict them from their land. The Chinese rulers were also not on good terms with the Hindu states and most of the time, except for a small period, they were at war with each other. There are few instances when a Chinese king colluded with a Hindu king to fight against a Vietnamese king. Similarly, the Khmer Hindu King of Cambodia invaded a Hindu Kingdom in Vietnam. The reason for this lacunae in identifying Hindu traditions is that Chinese historians were prejudiced while writing their historical accounts. They named some of the Hindu kings with Chinese names and the Champa Kingdom as Lin Yi. Additionally, the French historians had established the proposition that Cham or Champa community had its origin in Austro-Asian countries and since Vietnam had been a colony of France, under the influence of the French historians, it accepted their theory by and large. Some of the Indian historians, though with a bit of reluctance, accepted their theory. However, pondering over the available discoveries and archaeological evidences that we observed and found, proved the said theory materially wrong. The Chams or Champa community, in fact, had its roots in India rather than Austro-Asia.

It is also essential to mention here that most of the historians, who present an account of Khmer and Java influence over Champa regions, ignore mentioning in their findings that Khmer and Java of that time were, in fact, under the governance of federal Hindu Kingdoms and that their Pauranic or Brahminic Hindu religion besides Buddhism and culture of that period obviously had its origin in India and therefore the so-called influence of Khmer and Java was, in fact, Indian influence.

It seems, the French historians were unaware of the Indian history or they rather chose to ignore the fact that around fifth-sixth centuries BCE. India had its place already in the world trade map as a thriving and prosperous country having bilateral cultural and trade relations with various distant nations including Vietnam.

Some Indian historians have termed the Hindu Kingdom in Vietnam as a Hindu Colony which does not fit in the definition of the term. Had the Hindu Kingdom been a Hindu Colony, there would have been colonial exploitation of the natives and export of the capital. There is, however, no such evidence in history.

In fact, the royalty, the security personnel, the maritime traders and all those who went to Vietnam from India not only settled there permanently but got assimilated in the mainstream society except a few who did try to maintain their original identity ritually and these are the people who call themselves Champa or the Chams (or the Hindus) ethnic group: they have preserved some of their ancient traditions. Besides worshipping their ancestors, some of the Cham families have idols of Hindu deities in their household and they worship them by offering incense, holy water and resin. This Cham ethnic group still follows the *Saka* calendar and celebrates its religious and domestic festivals according to it. The person who leads all these rituals is called 'Brahmin' by society. There are about 10 per cent Muslims among this Cham ethnic group, whose traditions and way of life are like the Hindus and they are not rigid in their approach towards religion.

The present day globalization signifies that one should benefit from each other's experiences and it can be possible only when we come closer to each other and provide a people-orientation to the process of development on national and international scales. India and Vietnam may present a role model through their initiatives in this direction. The people of both India and Vietnam need to be impressed upon and made aware of the strong historical relations that existed between the two countries since centuries. If properly highlighted, these relations may develop into further stronger ties in the greater interests of both the peoples.

WORKS CITED

Guillon, Emmanuel. *Cham Art.* Np.: Thames and Hudson, 2001.

Lien, Le The. *Nghe Thuat Phat Giao Va Hindu Giao.* Hanoi. Nha Xuat Ban The Gioi, 2006.

Majumdar, R.C. *Champa: History & Culture of An Indian Colonial Kingdom in the Far East, 2nd-16th Century.* Delhi: Gyan Publishing House, 1985.

Nag, Kalidas. *Discovery of Asia.* Np. Institute of Asian African Relations, 1957.

Nehru, J.L. *Discovery of India.* Delhi: Oxford University Press, 1946.

23

A Review of Indian Cultural Representation in the Philippine Urban Setting: Reconnecting and Realigning with an Earlier Value System

JOSE J. VALENCIANO

For the Philippine people, it is only recent history that impacts most on their sphere of collective awareness. Thus, for the Philippine, it is the American and Spanish colonial rules that consciously influence the lives of the Philippine people. Spanish colonial activities lasted for nearly 400 years, from 1521 to 1898. The American experience of the Philippines started from where the Spanish left off and continued on until the end of World War II. And of course, considering the close ties the two countries had after the war, American influence continues to the present.

However, before the Spaniards arrived on Philippine shores, an earlier and less remembered influence was that of India. The Indo-Malayan Empires of Sriwijaya of Palembang, Sumatra (seventh-thirteenth centuries CE) and Majapahit of Java (1293-1527) both carried with them the stamp of Indian culture, the former more Buddhist and Hindu and the latter more Hindu in identity. Although faint in the collective memory of Filipinos, this cultural link with India helped enrich the cultural terrain on which communities thrived and led significant lives.

This review traces Indian cultural influence in the Philippines. It also describes how my notion of Indian culture developed, as a student of Indian classical music and sitar in particular, and how this notion further developed as I lived in India to further my studies in music. I then describe how, during my later interaction with urban culture in Manila, I discovered the manner in which Indian cultural iconography is represented and misrepresented. It is my desire for the Philippines to reestablish strong links with Indian culture and reshape the cultural environment to accommodate Indian cultural iconography and values as valid options for the enrichment of cultural aesthetic sensibilities and existence as a whole.

INDIAN INFLUENCE IN THE PHILIPPINES

As mentioned previously, the Philippines was exposed to Indian culture from the seventh century to the 1500s via the influence of the Indo-Malayan Empires. Traces of this influence still exist today. As a young boy in school, I was taught that our word for teacher "guro", came from "guru". Also, I did not realize it at the time but my friends and I would play the outdoor game "siyatong": it is a game involving a short stick and a long stick. Later on, I discover that the game has its roots in India where it is called "gilli-danda", "chinni-dandu" among other names. As a college student studying musicology, I learnt of a Philippine chordophone, a two-stringed lute known as the "kudyapi", and due to my growing interest in Indian music, I discover that there existed in India, a now extinct chordophone known as "kachchapi".

There are several other links between India and the Philippines' Pre-Hispanic past. In the field of literature, for instance, the epic *Ramayana* is represented in the "Maharadia Lawana" (Mahārāja Rāvaṇa) of the Maranao ethno-linguistic group from the Southern Philippines. The ancient writing system called "Baybayin" is based on written Sanskrit. Textile manufacturing processes like the "tinalak", still practiced today in the South Philippine have their origins in India.

Below is a collection of words in two Philippine languages that are borrowings from Sanskrit:

Philippine Language		English	Sanskrit
	budhi	conscience	bodhi
Tagalog	dukha	sufferer	dukkha
	sampalataya	faith	sampratyaya
	laho	eclipse	rahu
	sutla	silk	sutra
	lasa	taste	rasa
	kalma	fate	karma
Kapampangan	damla	divine law	dharma
	mantala	magic formula	mantra
	upaya	power	upaya
	lawu	eclipse	rahu

A JOURNEY OF DISCOVERY INTO A CULTURE

As mentioned earlier my introduction to Indian culture started with learning the sitar as a college student. Little did I know that learning the instrument would be a doorway through which I would discover Indian Classical Music, and the cultural values imbedded within it. My learning of the instrument started in the Philippines with my first teacher, Veena Waidande, a Visiting Professor at the University of Philippines. She had to leave after a year but my interest in the instrument was such that I endeavored to continue studies in India, which I was able to arrange after a year. This was not a trip arranged formally between institutions. I strove to learn the music in the traditional manner of master and disciple, against the consideration that this was a methodology difficult to valuate and validate when I returned home as an academe. But, what I understood was that the way to learn about a culture is from the "inside", via immersion.

I was honoured to be accepted as student of Pandit Debu Chaudhuri under who's mentorship I learned about sitar, music, and Indian culture and values as well. The Guru-Shishya system operates within the framework of several core values. The fact that the Guru accepts someone as "student for life" dictates that the teacher accepts the student as his "son" and is able to monitor and understand the student intimately. Thus, as is true with children in a family, each of the guru's students, receives tutelage based on their individual differences. The guru strives for complete knowledge transfer to his disciple. He teaches the student all he knows, in the proper time, and at the proper pace. The student, on the other hand, submits himself to the absolute control of the guru. Every student thus, shows great humility to his guru. Even the guru is a disciple to his own guru, in whose presence his humility is exhibited.

Indian classical music is improvisatory. Each musician must be a combination of performer and composer. His proficiency on his instrument must be equally matched with his intellectual knowledge of music theory and judgment of the application of aesthetic concepts. The musician is a package of holistic development manifesting physical, intellectual, and emotional soundness. Furthermore, the focus on music improvisation is illustrative of a culture that recognizes the value of each individual. Artists are valued for their respective creativity and their individual differences are recognized and appreciated.

During my stay in India, I learned a facet of spirituality I had not been exposed to before. It became very clear to me, very quickly, that for musicians, music in fact was their reason for being. They exhibited great passion, respect and love for their music and the music of others. I was taught that musical sound is a manifestation of God and that the more sophisticated the performance of a musician was, or even the more sensitive the level of listening on the part of the audience, the clearer the realization of the self.

"I do, therefore I am. I experience, therefore I am." During my stay in India, I came to know many people from other disciplines who lived out this statement through the passion they had for their vocation.

INDIA IN THE PHILIPPINE MIND

At the present time, my interaction in the Metro Manila urban scene, as a cultural worker for music and a university professor has led me to observe Indian iconographic representation in this urban setting.

My activities as *sitarist* bring me to commercial and cultural sites. These would range from performances at private parties, commercial establishments such as malls and restaurants, concert halls, and television. These events and the general site at which they take place are prime examples of the urban experience in Manila. This gives me the opportunity to monitor what representations of Indian culture there are and the manner in which they are framed.

Since I have an interest in music, I make Indian musical representation my starting point. Bhangra, the music genre that originates from Punjab and its many hybrid forms, is "the Indian Music", as far as the Philippine urban public is concerned. Its festive nature lends itself to the party scene. Through my research on this genre, I discovered that much modern day Bhangra was developed by Indian immigrants who employed it to express their ethnicity in a foreign land by fusing this folk genre with Western musical rhythms and sound samples. A fitting import then, coming from one urban environment and transferring to another. This festive music has a series of dance moves associated with it. The Philippine urban public is not familiar with these dance steps. The Bhangra presence in the Philippines in fact, is not a strong one; it could be noticed as a sound byte employed in a DJ's mix of fusion music, or as part of a commercial jingle as a means of suggesting an idea of World Culture or Globalism.

I also find it interesting that Indian Classical music in the Philippine urbania may be noticed by its absence. There used to be a time, decades ago, when Ravi Shankar left his mark on the world music scene primarily via the Beatles. Through his work, many have been led to discover the path to this music genre. It is unfortunate that the presence of this music, together with the cultural values it contains, has faded.

An interesting addition to Indian iconography in the Philippine urban setting would be belly dancing. It is surprising for this dance genre to be considered Indian for it originates from West Asia or the Arab world. But this dance has gained some popularity, and dancers are invited to perform in Indian restaurants and cultural events that provide a feature on Indian culture. It has come to a point where even the local Indian community, though aware of this misrepresentation of their culture, have become familiar with the dance being featured at Indian events.

Yoga would be another Indian cultural icon that manifests its presence in the Philippine urban scene. And here yet again, it takes on a hybridical form as it can be found practiced in a spa as an exercise class. The local notion of yoga is that it is primarily a body strengthening activity akin to aerobics. Or, for others, it is a way to counteract the effects of a stress laden lifestyle. Sadly, the more complex idea of yoga as a path to the holistic development of the mind, body, and spirit is not given primary focus.

As a Professor of music, I teach a course in Music cultures of the world.

In this class, I have the opportunity to survey my students for baseline information on their knowledge of Indian culture. Again here, a better awareness of Indian culture would be ideal. The students do know that Bollywood films are films made in India and that they feature singing and dancing, that is about all most everyone in a class would know. Do not query them on who Aamir Khan is or the story line of *Sholay* for they would not have an answer. The average student would know what a kimono or sushi is, but not what a kurta or samosa is. This is despite the fact that there is a sizeable Indian community of thirty to fifty thousand in Manila interacting with the rest of the population.

Interestingly, this lack of information on Indian culture exists at a time when data access is at a peak. The internet is there to provide answers to all who query. But the balance of information on the net is tipped towards the West, and Western hegemony prevails, especially when the one considers that the bulk of information Filipinos would access on the internet would be in English. Thus, much of the data on Indian culture on the internet would be on India, as seen through the filters of the West.

RESTORING LINKS AND STRENGTHENING TIES

It is my view that a facilitation of cultural exchange between the Philippines and India would be most beneficial. Understanding the cultural reality of a global neighbour is always a good thing. It enriches our perspective of our neighbour, giving us the opportunity to review other culture and values systems and when deemed beneficial, to incorporate these values into our daily lives to provide richer, more meaningful life experiences.

WORKS CITED

Arcilla, Jose S. *An Introduction to Philippine History,* 3rd edn., Quezon City: Ateneo de Manila University Press, 1984.

Fajardo, Libertad V. & Mary Joan V. Fajardo. *See the World in Dances.* Metro Manila: National Book Store, 1992.

Majumdar, Sachindra Kumar. *Introduction to Yoga Principles and Practices.* New Hyde Park, N.Y.: University Books, 1964.

Nettl, Bruno. *The Western Impact on World Music: Change, Adaptation, and Survival.* New York: Schirmer Books, 1985.

Satchidananda, Swami. *Living Yoga: The Value of Yoga in Today's Life.* New York: Gordon and Breach, 1977.

Shankar, Ravi. *My Music, My Life.* Delhi: Vikas Publishing House, 1968.

Titon, Jeff Todd ed. *Worlds of Music: An Introduction to the Music of the World's Peoples* Belmont, Calif: Thomson Schirmer, 2005.

Contributors

SUNG-DOO AHN teaches Philosophy at Seoul National University. Her major was in Indian Yogacara Buddhism. She is proficient in Sanskrit, Pali, Classical Tibetan, Classical Chinese, English and German.

TAMALIA ALISJAHBANA, a lawyer by training and profession, specializes in the History of Law. She has interest in discourses on human and political rights and the preservation of cultural heritage. She is currently working on a book on the history of Indonesian Heritage law.

WANG BANGWEI is a Professor and Director of the Institute of Oriental Studies and Oriental Literature Research Centre in Peking University. His academic works cover a vast range of cultures and countries. His wide publications include the areas of cultural exchange history between India and China.

SUGATA BOSE is the Gardiner Professor of History at Harvard University. He has served as Director of Graduate Studies in History at Harvard and as the Founding Director of Harvard's South Asia Initiative. A specialist in modern South Asian and Indian Ocean History, he crosses area studies and disciplinary frontiers as he bridges the domains of political economy and culture.

M.R. CHAKRAROT CHITRABONGS is a retired Permanent Secretary in the Ministry of Culture, Thailand. He is currently engaged as a Deputy Chairman of Rajini Foundation, Secretary General of the Naris Foundation and Patron of the National Museum Volunteers of Bangkok.

MEGHNAD DESAI, Peer of the British Parliament, is Professor Emeritus at the London School of Economics where he taught Econometrics, Macroeconomics, Marxian Economics and Development Economics over the years. His range of publications includes *Rethinking Islamism: Ideology of the New Terror* (2006), *The Route to All Evil: The Political Economy of Ezra Pound* (2007), a novel *Dead on Time* (2009) and *The Rediscovery of India* (2009).

SUDHIR T. DEVARE was a member of the Indian Foreign Service from 1964 to 2001 and has served on many Indian missions. He has been associated with the evolution of India's 'Look East' Policy. He has authored *India and Southeast Asia: Towards Security Convergence* (2006), *A New Energy Frontier:*

The Bay of Bengal Region (2009) and also co-edited *Emerging China: Prospects for Partnership in Asia* (2011) and *Delhi Dialogue III* (2012).

B.A. HUSSAINMIYA is Associate Professor with the Department of History in the University of Brunei Darussalam. His research interests range from Malay Manuscripts Studies, Classical Malay Literature and Malay Diaspora to the study of History and Comparative Education within South and Southeast Asia.

RAZALI ISMAIL is a retired Malaysian diplomat who was involved in articulating and developing positions in various bodies on issues such as development and sustainability, poverty and maginalization, political reforms in the United Nations and issues of human rights and the environment. He has authored *Environmental Challenges and Responsibilities on National and Global Levels* (1998).

K. KESAVAPANY is a career diplomat. Currently he is the Non-Resident Ambassador to the Hashemite Kingdom of Jordan. Prior to this, he was Singapore's High Commissioner to Malaysia from 1997 to 2002 and served in several projects of strategic international importance. He is a member of the Singapore Mediation Centre's International Panel of Mediators. He was also the Director of the Institute of Southeast Asian Studies, Singapore, which houses the Nalanda-Sriwijaya Centre.

VINOD C. KHANNA is a retired Indian Foreign Service officer who is currently Emeritus Fellow at the Institute of Chinese Studies. He is also engaged in the field of education for the underprivileged and related development work.

KHIN MAUNG NYUNT is Emeritus Professor at Departments of History, Archaeology, International Relations, and Buddhist History and Art at the International Theravada Buddhist Missionary University, Yangon. He has been recognized for his outstanding performance in public and state welfare.

CHIRAPAT PRAPANDVIDYA is an Advisor to the Sanskrit Studies Centre at Silpakorn University, Bangkok. Formerly he has taught at the Faculty of Archaeology. He has been awarded an Honorary Doctorate degree from Mahachulalongkornrajavidyalaya.

NGUYEN NGOC QUYNH works at the Centre for Vietnamese Studies and Inter-culture and at the Institute of Religious Studies, Vietnam Academy of Social Sciences.

JOEFE B. SANTARITA is an Assistant Professor at the Asian Center, University of the Philippines. His research interests and publications focus on India's 'Look East' Policy, diaspora and history of South Asia.

MALINI SARAN is an Art Historian who has been extensively working on Southeast Asia. She has co-authored *Ramayana in Indonesia* (2004) alongwith Vinod C. Khanna. One of her latest essays is 'Preliminary Notes on Shared Peculiarities of the *Ramayana* in 9th Century Java and Tibet" (2011).

K.T.S. SARAO has been teaching Indian Buddhism, History and Pali at the University of Delhi for the past three decades and currently heads the Department of Buddhist Studies at University of Delhi. Professor Sarao has published many books and research papers.

VO VAN SEN is Deputy Director of the Centre for Continuous Education, and Deputy Director of the Centre for South Asian Studies at University of Social Sciences and Humanities, Hanoi. He is a member of International Cooperation and Scientific Management Office and the People's Council (Provincial Legislative Assembly). He helped ICCR establish a 'Tagore Chair' on Contemporary Studies at USSH.

GEETESH SHARMA is a journalist and humanist and strives to develop relations between various communities in India and also outside India. He is involved in the solidarity movement with Vietnam for more than three decades.

ANJANA SHARMA is Dean, Academic Planning, Nalanda University. She is on deputation from the Department of English, University of Delhi, where she teaches English Literature. Among her publications are: *The Autobiography of Desire: English Jacobin Women Novelists of the 1790s* (2004); *Frankenstein: Interrogating Gender, Culture and Identity* (2004) and *Agamemnon's Mask: Greek Tragedy and Beyond* (2007). Her current work is on the critical year in Indian history, 1947, and the figure of M.K. Gandhi in the print media.

NIRMALA SHARMA is an Art Historian and associated with Buddhist Studies at the International Academy of Indian Culture, New Delhi. She is currently working on the project of Indira Gandhi National Centre for the Arts on 'Iconography of the Mandalas of the Dukhang of Alchi'.

SATYA VRAT SHASTRI is a scholar and Professor in Sanskrit. He is the first recipient of the Jnanpitha Award in Sanskrit. He has written travelogues in Sanskrit, the *Sarmanyadesah Sutaram Vibhati* on Germany and the *Thaidesavilasam* on Thailand. His forthcoming autobiography is titled *Bhavitavyanam Dvarani Bhavanti Sarvatra.*

JOSE J. VALENCIANO teaches at the Department of Musicology, College of Music, University of the Philippines, Diliman. His avid interest in the creative potential of impoverished music keeps his performance activities centered on Classical Indian Music and Jazz. He is the founder and musical director of the Majam Chamber Jazz ensemble.

MARIKA VICZIANY teaches Political Economy in the Monash Asia Institute (Faculty of Arts) at Monash University, and is Chair of the Monash Asia Series, President of the South Asian Studies Association of Australia and Honorary Professor at the Institute of Development Studies Kolkata in India. She is an advisor to various universities and business councils.

Index